Biography
as
Theology

How Life Stories Can
Remake Today's Theology

Biography
as
Theology

How Life Stories Can
Remake Today's Theology

James Wm. McClendon, Jr.

Nashville ■ ABINGDON PRESS ■ New York

BIOGRAPHY AS THEOLOGY

Copyright © 1974 by Abingdon Press

Library of Congress Cataloging in Publication Data

MCCLENDON, JAMES WILLIAM. Biography as theology. Includes
bibliographical references. 1. Theology—Methodology. 2.
Christian biography. 3. Christian ethics. I. Title.
BR118.M28   209′.2′2[B]   74-9715

ISBN 0-687-03540-6

Scripture quotations noted RSV are from the Revised Standard
Version of the Bible, copyrighted 1946, 1952, 1971 by the
Division of Christian Education, National Council of Churches,
and are used by permission.

Scripture quotations noted NEB are from the New English
Bible, copyright © the Delegates of the Oxford University
Press and the Syndics of the Cambridge University Press, 1961,
1970.

Quotations from *Markings*, by Dag Hammarskjöld, translated
by Leif Sjoberg and W. H. Auden, Copyright © 1964 by Alfred
A. Knopf, Inc., and Faber & Faber Ltd., reprinted by permission
of Alfred A. Knopf, Inc., and Faber and Faber Ltd.

Material from *Theological Dictionary* by Karl Rahner and
Herbert Vorgrimler, Copyright © 1965 by Herder KG. Used by
permission of the publisher, Seabury Press, and Search Press
Limited, the publishers in the United Kingdom.

Quotations reprinted from *ESSAYS BEFORE A SONATA, and
Other Writings*, by Charles Ives, Selected & Edited by Howard
Boatwright. By permission of W. W. Norton & Company, Inc.
Copyright © 1961, 1962 by W. W. Norton & Company, Inc. Also
by permission of Calder and Boyars Ltd.

MANUFACTURED BY THE PARTHENON PRESS AT
NASHVILLE, TENNESSEE, UNITED STATES OF AMERICA

to marie with love

Preface

There is currently a stir among students of religion about 'narrative theology'—the way or ways in which the ideas of religion may be expressed in story form. It seems likely that this book will be regarded as one aspect of that flurry of interest, and it will probably do no harm for it to be so regarded, unless it is therefore seen as an abandonment of serious inquiry into the *truth* of religious stories, or their adequacy to facts. What I have done here, however, is not in any sense a bundling up of the several sorts of 'story theology.' For that sort of survey one must look elsewhere.

The book has grown, instead, out of my own teaching of theology over several years' time. In the decade 1960–1970 I dealt with the life of Martin Luther King, Jr., in courses at the University of San Francisco, Stanford, Temple, and the University of Pennsylvania. I was appointed Jeffery Lecturer at Goucher College for 1970–71, and decided that in the public lectures that job required, I would set alongside King's another, contrasting modern life, that of Dag Hammarskjöld, and in a third lecture would consider the theological harvest that might be gathered from these two studies. The Jeffery Lectures thus written and delivered in 1971 became Chapters 2, 3, and 4 of this book. From 1971 through 1973, teaching at the Church Divinity School of the Pacific, a constituent member of the Graduate Theological Union in Berkeley, I continued classroom work on these lives, adding those of

Clarence Jordan and Charles Ives. Meanwhile the duty of teaching theological ethics helped me form the ideas of the first chapter. And so the book became possible. I am grateful to my students at each of these places, and to my teaching assistants Axel Steuer at Pennsylvania, June O'Connor at Temple, and Terrence Tilley at the Church Divinity School for the advice and encouragement they generously gave. And I am especially grateful to the trustees, administration, and faculty of Goucher College for the opportunity and incentive that the Jeffery Lectureship provided.

Versions of Chapters 2 and 4 have appeared in scholarly journals, the former in *Review and Expositor,* Louisville (spring, 1973), and the latter in *Cross Currents* (fall, 1971), and I am grateful to their respective editors, Glenn Hinson and Joseph Cunneen, for advance permission to publish them in a slightly changed form.

I have talked with so many helpful friends about the work that a list of my creditors would doubtless be marred by shameful omissions, so I will only attempt to list those who have read part of the typescript and written criticisms. They will see how much or how little I have obeyed their (always helpful) advice: Robert Cunningham, James M. Smith, Stanley Hauerwas, Margaret Duerr, Rhoda Dorsey, Leo Malania, the late Walter Morris, LeRoy Moore, the late Cornelius Berry, Robert Handy, Timothy Smith, Richard Lawless, Edward Hobbs, John Chamberlain, Florence Jordan, Diane and John McEntyre, Norman Mealy, Joseph Powers, Massey Shepherd, Thomas Drain, Michael Novak. To all of them, heartfelt thanks.

In a quite different class are the criticism and encouragement I have had at home from my wife Marie and my sons Will and Thom. They know, or at least no preface can say, how much I valued their loyal but independent judgment and aid at every stage of the work.

I am grateful, too, to the typists who have turned my own shoddy drafts into readable copy, and especially to Sr.

Esther Davis, who served without pay, and to Sonja Ridenour, who often went beyond the bounds of duty to make everything right. And even as I write this, Esther is again busy helping to read proof, as is Tom Drain, while Maureen and Terrence Tilley are preparing the index.

My thanks to the trustees and to Dean Frederick Borsch of C.D.S.P. for providing circumstances in which the work could be done, and to my colleagues at this and each place where I have taught, for their stimulus and encouragement.

I hope that you, my reader, will accept here a salute, which in the nature of the case cannot be personally tendered, and will regard yourself as invited not only to read these chapters, but also to enter critically yet happily into the investigation of which they are only a part. And I *hope* you will consequently be inclined to join me in saying, insofar as it is right, *soli deo gratias*.

Larkspur, California JAMES WM. McCLENDON, JR.
May 8, 1974

Note to reader: In this book, double quotes (" ") are used for all quotations except for quotes within quotes (" ' ' ") and 'scare' quotes.

Contents

I.	In Search of an Ethics of Character	13
II.	Dag Hammarskjöld—Twice-Born Servant	39
III.	The Religion of Martin Luther King, Jr.	65
IV.	Biography as Theology	87
V.	The Theory Tested: Clarence Leonard Jordan —Radical in Community	112
VI.	Expanding the Theory: Charles Edward Ives —Theologian in Music	140
VII.	Toward a Theology of Life	170
	Appendix: Christian Worship and the Saints	204
	Index	217

Chapter One

In Search
of an Ethics of Character

Where are we now in theology? A shift is in progress. The old landmarks set by Barth and Rahner, by Tillich and Congar, are slipping away, or perhaps the changing countryside makes the old features unrecognizable. What seemed so durable when the present generation was in school may seem quaint or incredible. These changes are not equally clear to all, and what may be taking the place of the old positions is even less clear. For the changes in theology are a part of a shift in the general mood, a shift which is neither religious nor political nor aesthetic nor moral but which so pervades all these realms as to make some sorts of thinking in each of them unlikely or even impossible and other sorts possible or even inevitable.

The role of this book is to explore a way now possible (and I believe, desirable) in theology. Because of the changed landscape of our times, this way may seem altogether new.

The shift is pervasive, and its religious aspect may not be most conspicuous. Therefore I will first turn not to religion or theology but to another indicator, the new mode in ethics or morality. I will suggest that utilitarianism, which in practice has dominated the secular age now dying, is dying with it, even though the moral features of the age to come have not clearly appeared. I will claim that with the passing of utilitarianism the present sorts of religious ethics—Niebuhr's 'Christian realism' and the so-called 'new morality' of decisionism—are moribund as well. And I will argue that the hope of ethics, both secular and religious, lies in the recovery of what may be called an ethics of character. I must of course say what I mean by an ethics of character, and saying it will make plain the need for a *theology* of character: the problems of ethics lead to the problems of theology and back again. So in this chapter we will enter, via the door of the ethics of the present age, into a way in theology which incorporates the study of character—biography as theology.

I

Utilitarianism as a special theory is chiefly associated with Jeremy Bentham and John Stuart Mill, but as a style, a *Zeitgeist*, it became already in the nineteenth century the possession of thinking men everywhere. Christians accommodated themselves to it, and (as always) some declared it to be the very marrow of Christian divinity. Politicians adopted its style, and set out in this style to attack the difficult social problems of the late nineteenth and early twentieth centuries. Utilitarianism in its purest form taught that 'right' and 'wrong' were nothing but means to pleasure and pain, respectively. Some actions or policies produced what could broadly be called pain, were therefore called 'wrong,' and to be avoided; others produced what could broadly be called pleasure, were therefore 'right,' and to be

14

encouraged. Most, of course, produced some of both, or produced pain for some but pleasure for others. Hence a calculus was required—what will produce the greatest good, i.e., the greatest pleasure, for the greatest number?

The doctrine of utilitarianism was not altogether pernicious. After all, pain is bad, other considerations aside, and pleasure good; to acknowledge this and act accordingly may therefore be indeed beneficial. What is to the point here is that, for better or worse, the utilitarian calculus became the model of the way in which governments determined and legislated the welfare of their citizens, and ordinary enlightened men shaped their lives. Government experts present a proposed policy by weighing up all the expected benefits and liabilities of its adoption; in the process they set side by side apparently incommensurable interests: the loss of liberty by this group against the loss of commercial income by that one; the death of these men, women, children, babes in arms, against the expected benefits to (others') posterity—all are weighed in one government scale. The private procedures are similar.

These procedures are familiar enough, and no modern person altogether avoids such calculations. What a noted contemporary moral philosopher, Stuart Hampshire, has pointed out, however, is that the era of utilitarianism now shows strong signs of coming to an end. The utilitarians caught the spirit of the age, but that age is judged and found wanting.

Persecutions, massacres, and wars have been coolly justified by calculations of long-range benefits to mankind; and political pragmatists in the advanced countries, using cost benefit analyses prepared for them by gifted professors, continue to burn and destroy. The utilitarian habit of mind has brought with it a new abstract cruelty in politics, a dull, destructive political righteousness: mechanical, quantitative thinking, leaden academic minds setting out their moral calculations in leaden, abstract prose, and more civilized and more superstitious people destroyed because of enlightened calculations that have proved wrong.[1]

Now, however, Hampshire declares, many and especially younger persons are no longer willing to accept the "large-scale computations" by which our experts are guided. The former feel that the calculus of death, the calculus of "protective reactions," the calculus of poverty, require a price in brutalization of feeling and dehumanization of life among the survivors which they are simply unwilling to pay. This revolt of the young (and of many of their elders), accompanied though it may be by many a moral inconsistency of their own, thus becomes itself part of the evidence that modern morality has failed.

So far this may sound like a call to turn from the 'modern' utilitarians back to a traditional ethic supporting classical conservative politics and in turn supported by supernatural religion. The latter, at least, is by no means what Hampshire intends. He believes that ethics concerned with character, attentive to traditional moralities, and more interested in valued "ways of life" than in the calculus of pleasure or usefulness, must nowadays be based not on supernatural but on purely natural premises. He fears, however, that his words will be mistaken as a call for a return to religious or Christian ethics. But I would suggest that Hampshire's fear is misplaced.

II

For there is no danger that religious ethics, at least as it has been conceived in the recent past, will provide any rival to the aging doctrines of utilitarianism. Rather, modern religious ethics shares so fully in the presuppositions of

[1] Stuart Hampshire, "Morality and Pessimism," *The New York Review of Books,* January 25, 1973, p. 26. Also see correspondence, *N.Y.R.,* September 20, 1973.

modern secular ethics which may have brought the latter into disrepute that the former must sink or swim with the latter. There have, of course, been a wide variety of ethical views put forward by recent Christian thinkers, but the only two which have commanded rank-and-file (American) support are the views represented by the situation ethics debate, and epitomized by the writings of Professor Joseph Fletcher, and the view represented by the thought of the late Reinhold Niebuhr.[2] Bernard Häring, H. R. Niebuhr, Emil Brunner, Karl Barth, Paul Ramsey, Paul Lehmann, Dietrich Bonhoeffer, James Gustafson, Helmut Thielicke, John Bennett, Otto Piper, Joseph Fuchs, and many others have written at length on ethical questions from various theological viewpoints, many of which are of great intrinsic interest, but each has attracted at most only a coterie of followers in this field. Fletcher and Reinhold Niebuhr between them, however, have not only taught the religious community in this country, but have in large measure spoken assumptions that educated church people were already believing, or at least all ready to believe. Thus they have epitomized the Christian ethics of the times. Indeed, it is somewhat unfair to say "Christian," or "church," or "religious," for both these outlooks have been widely shared by persons outside, as well as within, these communities. For many, Christian realism (sc. Niebuhr) has provided a social ethic, while contextual decisionism (sc. Fletcher) has provided a personal ethic, and in this way all bases are covered. My present claim is that the prevailing religious morality symbolized by these two differs in no very important way from the prevailing secular morality of

[2] A significant exception may be the widely used texts of Paul Ramsey (*Basic Christian Ethics* [New York: Scribner's, 1950]; *Deeds and Rules in Christian Ethics* [New York: Scribner's, 1967]), but for all his distinctive emphases, Ramsey shares enough, in ways I hope to indicate in the following paragraphs, of the popular mood typified by R. Niebuhr and J. Fletcher to relieve me of the need for a separate treatment in this brief sketch.

our time, a morality (and a time) which is now being weighed in the balances. . . .[3]

Consider first contextual ethics, or situation ethics, or (as I shall somewhat derisively call it) one sort of *decisionism*. In thus singling out Fletcher's situation ethics, I may seem to be conceding the claim made by its advocates that it is a unique and distinctive method of moral thinking, to be sharply distinguished from the methods of its vocal opponents, whom the situationists dub legalists or antinomians.[4] In truth, what interests me about situationism is exactly the feature which it shares in common with these 'rivals'—the central importance which all of them give to moral *decisions* as the very stuff of morality. Situationists hold that the situation or context of an ethical choice provides the most important input for the decision, while 'legalists' regard rules or laws of morality as more important, yet each concedes the necessary role of both inputs. 'Antinomians' such as the existentialist philosopher Jean-Paul Sartre deny that in crucial situations either rules *or* norms can afford guidance for right decisions; the decider

[3] Since this seems an empirical claim, it might be interesting to compare it with the opinion of two widely read sociologists of religion, Rodney Stark and Charles Y. Glock. In a 1968 article, "Will Ethics Be the Death of Christianity?" *Trans-action,* June, 1968, pp. 7-14, they point out statistics which show that the more thoroughly church members adhere to the view they call "ethicalism," which seems to me to be indistinguishable from utilitarianism ("the creation of a humane society"), the *less* likely they are to be "orthodox" in faith and practice—to attend and support the church, believe in God, etc. While Stark and Glock regard this bifurcation as potentially the "death of Christianity," I regard it as a strong hint that "ethicalism" may not be the ethics of true Christianity, after all.

[4] See Joseph F. Fletcher, *Situation Ethics, the New Morality* (Philadelphia: Westminster Press, 1966), *Moral Responsibility, Situation Ethics at Work* (Westminster Press, 1967). For a handy summary of the attacks on this form of decisionism, see Harvey G. Cox, ed., *The Situation Ethics Debate* (Westminster Press, 1968). A helpful and fairminded introduction to decisionism introduced and edited by a philosopher is Robert L. Cunningham, ed., *Situationism and the New Morality* (New York: Appleton-Century-Crofts, 1970). The first selection, by Fletcher, is a good, brief summary of decisionism.

must merely and autonomously—decide. Yet what this illustrates is that for antinomians, all the more, it is the decision which is all-important in ethics. Hence we can group all these debating participants, together with the emotivist ethics of British-American analytical moral philosophy, under the general term "decisionism." As such, they are merely in line with the popular utilitarianism of the age just gone by; thus it is decisionism itself, rather than its separate and warring schools, which is also now in question.[5]

If ethics is not concerned with problematic decisions, then what is it concerned with? Is it not just self-evident that the decisionists are occupying the only possible ground? It is not.[6] For one thing, their main concern—though widespread, as we have noted, in modern thought—was not similarly central for ancient and other pre-modern thinkers—not for Aristotle, nor for Aquinas, nor for Spinoza. Jesus, according to Matthew's judgment-parable of the sheep and the goats, tells his hearers that the actions by which their final destiny is judged are not the result of their deliberate choices, but are instead ones in which they acted unknowingly, and yet showed themselves for what they truly were: it is 'unconscious' acts of charity and mercy (or their absence) which are the true harbingers of our last estate, these and not our informed 'decisions' (Matt. 25:31-46).

What decisionism lacks, and previous ethical systems so regularly display, is concern with the qualities of human character in the individual and the community. This difference is pointed up by the stories often used by Fletcher

[5] It is important to note that Jeremy Bentham was not a pure decisionist. His life work was concerned with legislation, not mere moral choice as such. Nevertheless, in that work lay the seed of popular modern decisionism. See D. H. Monro, "Jeremy Bentham," in Paul Edwards, ed., *The Encyclopedia of Philosophy* (New York: Macmillan and the Free Press, 1967).

[6] For the critique of decisionism, I am especially indebted to Edmund Pincoffs, "Quandary Ethics," *Mind,* October, 1971, pp. 552-71.

to illustrate his ethical views. In a typical story, a briefly described 'situation' is set forth, and the reader is then asked to infer the obvious conclusion. Take this paragraph:

Ponder this: Along the Wilderness Road, or Boone's Trail, in the eighteenth century, westward through Cumberland Gap to Kentucky, many families and trail parties lost their lives in border and Indian warfare. Compare two episodes in which pioneers were pursued by savages. (1) A Scottish woman saw that her suckling baby, ill and crying, was betraying her and her three other children, and the whole company, to the Indians. But she clung to her child, and they were caught and killed. (2) A Negro woman, seeing how her crying baby endangered another trail party, killed it with her own hands, to keep silence and reach the fort. Which woman made the right decision? [7]

But how *can* we know, when all we are given is these minimal facts? What was the community to which these mothers and infants belonged, and what were its commitments? Who was the father in each case? What did he have to say? Besides being Scottish and Negro (not an exhaustive characterization, to say the least), what were the mothers *like?* We can surmise Fletcher's own answer to his question—he seems to prefer the bold and shocking choice, and infant sacrifice seems to fit that category well enough. But will not other decisionists choose differently, opting, say, for every effort to spare the innocent? Surely the question whether either mother did right is answerable in Fletcher's way only if the real evidence is as stark as that he provides us. But is it ever really so stark? Is it really true, then, that from such simplistic accounts we can learn anything at all about Christian ethics—about loyalty, or temptation, or being harmless as doves yet wise as serpents, or even about sacrificial mother love?

The general charge against decisionism, or "Quandary Ethics," as Edmund Pincoffs names it, is that it sets out to

[7] Fletcher, *Situation Ethics,* pp. 124-25.

show how to make decisions, but never reckons with who it is who makes these decisions, never reckons with the *character* of the 'Scottish mother,' or the 'young lover,' or the 'French soldier' who is type-cast in these case histories. But in reality, we are not types; we have (or significantly fail to have) character of our own, belong to communities of our own, are not just "anyone in this situation," but ourselves.

Quandary ethics asks what a conscientious man would do in such a situation. But in doing this, it tends to reduce the valued traits of human character to just one: conscientiousness. Yet conscience alone cannot always be a sufficient guide to good or right decisions, or conscientious men would not make such diverse choices, and when we remember that life is made up of many acts and many relationships which involve no decisions (imagine the young mother who on seeing her baby awaken 'decides' to love the baby!) we may recognize that decisionism has failed to tell us of many other equally vital elements in character: of loyalty, for example, or generosity, or courage, or tenderness. "Very well," the decisionist may reply. "I can enlarge my descriptions of situations to take account of qualities of character, as you suggest. They are just part of the situation." But to concede that is to concede that such enlargement is indeed needed, and that an ethics of character cannot be content with mere conscientiousness applied to set situations.

Pincoffs argues that quandary ethics (a term which he applies not only to situation-based, but also to principle-based decisionism) constricts morality into a kind of case law, in which typical or novel situations can be handled by appeal to one or more moral principles, but quite without recourse to the moral qualities of the persons involved in the cases, just as law courts resolve their cases (and there properly) without recourse to the special qualities of character of the plaintiff or the defendant.[8] ("Negro mother

[8] Pincoffs, "Quandary Ethics," pp. 560-65.

acquitted in strangling case.") My own corresponding doubt is whether this is an adequate method for the ethics of the Christian or any other human community.

For example, does decisionism teach the community how to educate its children? The decisionist may reply that we must teach children to make decisions. "Indeed, it is hard to see what else would be likely to bring about a change of moral outlook other than the having to make a difficult moral decision," writes a British decisionist.[9] Is it so hard? What about the growing influence of a friend whose life impinges on one's own? Or the acquisition of a new respon- sibility, say the arrival of a baby in a formerly childless family? Or the sense of God's presence and his care newly acquired? Should we not rather ask whether decision-mak- ing is ever of value unless another kind of moral education has first been accomplished—unless at least *some* qualities of character have been attained? The Christian, for exam- ple, might regard forgiveness and truthfulness, loyalty and sensitivity to suffering as qualities he would wish to bring not only to his decisions, but also to that everyday conduct which according to Matthew 25 reveals our characters, even when it occasions few or no decisions. But to say this is to say that there is necessarily an ethic—another ethic—which lies behind decisionism. For want of a better term, we can call this an ethic of character, and we may wish to add that such an ethic can best be learned within a community which displays and evokes that very character.

Aristotle did not give open lectures; St. Paul did not write open letters. When they used the word "we," they spoke from within a community of expectations and ideals: a community within which character was cultivated.[10]

Still another count against decisionism is that it seems so

[9] John Lemmon, "Moral Dilemmas" in Ian T. Ramsey, ed., *Chris- tian Ethics and Contemporary Philosophy* (New York: Macmillan, 1966), p. 276. Originally in the *Philosophical Review*, 1962.
[10] Pincoffs, "Quandary Ethics," p. 570.

ill equipped to understand and shed light upon those dark struggles of our selves in which, confronted with imponderables, we do flounder about, sometimes conscientiously, sometimes self-deceived, sometimes locked in the struggle which classical Christian theology calls temptation. In the classic view, man's life is a journey, a pilgrimage, in which one's self is not mere datum, nor an electronic calculator reading 'decisions' off new 'situations,' but a soul in the making, a self which can become itself only as the weight of sin is fully recognized and the self recognizes a center of meaning and source of power beyond itself, forgiving and remaking that self. In this regard, there is far more to be said for the Christian realism ethics of Reinhold Niebuhr than for situationism.

Fletcher regards Niebuhr as an ally, "closer to situationism than to any other ethical method," [11] and as we shall see there is a measure of truth in that claim, but it seems more instructive to treat Niebuhr's contribution to modern religious ethics separately.[12] Nor will we quickly be able to dismiss the Niebuhrian view. It is important to see Niebuhr's ethics as a rebellion against both the social gospel liberalism in which he was schooled and the Marxian perfectionism in which he subsequently schooled himself. Like so many rebellions (not excepting the one reflected by the

[11] Fletcher, *Situation Ethics*, p. 61.

[12] Reinhold Niebuhr's ethical writings are extensive, and in no one place did he draw together concisely his complex views. At a minimum, mention must be made of *Moral Man and Immoral Society* (New York: Scribner's, 1932); *An Interpretation of Christian Ethics* (New York: Harper, 1935); *The Nature and Destiny of Man*, 2 vols. (Scribner's, 1941, 1943); *Man's Nature and His Communities* (Scribner's, 1963); and the shorter occasional writings, many of which first appeared in the journal Niebuhr founded, *Christianity and Crisis*. Some of these shorter pieces are gathered up in D. B. Robertson, ed., *Love and Justice* (Philadelphia: Westminster Press, 1957). A most useful summary of Niebuhr's ethical thought can be found by comparing John Bennett's contribution to Charles W. Kegley and Robert W. Bretall, eds., *Reinhold Niebuhr: His Religious, Social, and Political Thought* (New York: Macmillan, 1956), with Bennett's more recent "Realism and Hope after Niebuhr," *Worldview*, May, 1972, pp. 4-14.

present chapter), Niebuhr's owed much to that against which he rebelled. As he came to see the matter, however, the social gospel had erred in a too simple expectation that a love ethic could be applied without exception to the complex and sinful nature of man and to the power-ridden and sinful structures of society, demanding simple conformity of the one and simple reformation of the other. This, said Niebuhr, was not "realistic." Instead, the most that could be hoped for in either case was an awareness of the "impossible" demand of love, and the approximate fulfillment of that demand via the struggle for justice (in the case of society), and via a complex set of ethical tensions generated by Christian faith (in the case of the individual).

Assuming this general framework, Niebuhr mounted a massive and largely effective critique of American life. He especially attended to the relation of competing interest-groups, capital and labor, rich and poor, and to American world interests, notably America's role in World War II and the Cold War of the forties and fifties. So widely accepted was this critique, and so devastating was Niebuhr in counterattacking his critics, that the literature is largely lacking in any full-scale critical rejection of Niebuhr's ethics as such. Attacks focused instead on his neo-orthodox theology, or on some other failure to appreciate the critic's theological position properly.[13] Only recently (but this is significant) some critical rejections of Niebuhrian ethics as such have begun to appear in theologically oriented journals.

A striking instance of this is the rejection of Niebuhr's ethics by Black theologian Herbert Edwards on the ground that Niebuhr's is ineradicably a racist ethic.[14] Niebuhr's commitment to "realism," says Edwards, was exactly a

[13] See for example the critical reviews of Niebuhr's work in Kegley and Bretall. The only essay directly treating Niebuhr's ethics there is John Bennett's "Reinhold Niebuhr's Social Ethics," and it is an appreciative summary.

[14] Herbert O. Edwards, "Racism and Christian Ethics in America," *Katallagete*, Winter, 1971, pp. 15-24.

commitment to the racist status quo. This made it impossible, on Niebuhr's own terms, for him to escape the ingrained system of American life of which conscious and unconscious racism was and is so much a part. Although Niebuhr spoke out more than any other theologian against "racial pride," he was able to write during the Cold War a book (*The Structure of Nations and Empires*) [15] which contains the strongest celebration of Anglo-Saxon superiority since Josiah Strong, says Edwards. While Niebuhr's arguments there "seem to provide justification for continued Anglo-Saxon domination of the darker peoples" [16] abroad, meanwhile at home Niebuhr was teaching that the "culturally backward" Blacks provided Whites, by the very "cultural backwardness" (a concept Niebuhr does not ever clearly define) of the former, with an understandable justification of their reluctance to send their children to school with Black children, as required by the Supreme Court. By praising "separate but equal" as "a very good concept for its day" which had avoided a popular revolt against the ideal of racial justice,[17] Niebuhr illustrates the classic shift of Christian realism: the "desirable" state of affairs is first exalted to the "ideal"; this tends to equate the merely desirable state of affairs with love, which is a regulative principle, *"but which must not, cannot, be determinative in the give and take of decision making."* [18] Christian realism in effect becomes racism.

If Edwards' view thus baldly presented seems itself biased (though to me it does not), consider instead the exploration of the connections between Niebuhr's ethics, his theodicy, and interest-group liberalism by my former colleague

[15] (New York: Scribner's, 1959.)

[16] Edwards, "Racism and Christian Ethics in America," p. 17.

[17] Reinhold Niebuhr writing on *Plessy* v. *Ferguson,* cited by Edwards, p. 19, from Harry R. Davis and Robert C. Good, eds., *Reinhold Niebuhr on Politics,* p. 228.

[18] Edwards, "Racism and Christian Ethics" pp. 19-20. My emphasis.

John C. Raines. Raines remarks that sociologists have pointed to a close link between the ethics of a given culture and the theodicy by which that culture handles the problem of the evil it finds in its world. Reinhold Niebuhr, says Raines, became the justifier of God's ways to Americans by starting from a picture of the world already accepted by interest-group liberalism, that is, by what I have here called the utilitarian *Zeitgeist*. In that picture

society is interpreted primarily as a scene of competing individual and group vitalities (as distinguished, for example, from St. Thomas Aquinas, who looked upon society as the cradle of human language and thus of human rationality). It is a market-place of prides, powers and interests in various modes of conflict, negotiation and temporary accomodation, where to be unorganized is to guarantee that one's interests will not enter the arena of serious political debate and trade-offs.[19]

Niebuhr's theology can give a 'realistic' rendering of this familiar modern picture, for it fully acknowledges the sins and illusions which taint each group and each individual.

Only God is good. But Niebuhr's God, says Raines, remains ever behind the scenes, unidentified with any single group. Pure love is impossible to those who wield power; the moral task is merely to increase relative justice by increasing the power of weaker groups in the social "marketplace." Meanwhile the promise of fulfillment "beyond history" nerves the competing individuals to carry on this endless twilight struggle; thus by this transhistorical promise God underwrites interest-group liberalism with its struggles.

In Raines's view, Christian realism, which at its best certainly possessed prophetic power and insight, thus too easily slips into a bland justification of the given world and its evil. This happens whenever "acceptance of the 'tragic limitations' of political life" turns into routine acceptance of "self-assured 'moral ambiguity.'"[20] Raines concludes

[19] John C. Raines, "Theodicy and Politics," *Worldview*, April, 1973, p. 45. A longer version of his article is to appear in a book titled *Conspiracy*, on the implications of the Harrisburg trial of 1971.

[20] Raines, "Theodicy and Politics," p. 46.

that (1) Christian realism in its absorption with rivalries has no ethic of the common good, that which people share as opposed to that which divides them; (2) Christian realism is insufficiently realistic because it has no theory of common life and the common virtues of everyday life; and (3) given the sense of fragility and aloneness which the human species now experiences in the vast galaxies, Christian realism's distant God (beyond history) brings no true comfort to men.

Of course, to list objections to Christian realism, or to decisionism, is by no stretch of imagination a refutation of those widely adopted theories of religious ethics. To attempt such a refutation in the confines of the present chapter would be pretentious. Indeed, it is doubtful if pervasive styles of thought, such as that represented by popular utilitarianism in secular ethics and by the two religious schemes just referred to, are ever refuted by argument. The most that this chapter can attempt is to call attention to a possible shift in ethical focus. It would be especially unfortunate if the force of the preceding remarks were taken to be an attack on the Christian morality of Fletcher and Niebuhr themselves. Rather, the point has been that on these themes, these two spoke for all of us, insofar as we were literate, twentieth-century Christians. This is as true of 'conservative' as it is of 'liberal' Christian groupings. It is not our brother Joseph nor our brother Reinhold who needs to repent, to think again, but we.

> Not the preacher nor the deacon but it's me,
> O Lord,
> Standin' in the need of prayer.

All of us are Niebuhrians; all of us are decisionists, and it is this which gives us pause.

For, alongside the widespread acceptance of these two compatible ethical styles, there is the fact of our recent national moral harvest, symbolized by the Watergate scandals and the Vietnamese war. The betrayals, burglaries, lies, bribes, subornations, hypocrisies which the scandals represent in American history can be helpfully seen as a direct product of decisionism; the Watergate principals were well schooled in the art of useful decisions. And behind that, and intimately connected with it, lies the tragic American involvement in Indochina—Vietnam—which in turn sprang from the policies of 'war against tyranny' and the implacable 'cold war' of a generation schooled in the Christian realism of Reinhold Niebuhr. The point here is not to blame Watergate on Fletcher, and Vietnam on Niebuhr. It is rather to suggest that Christian realism as we embraced it offered no adequate prophylactic against Vietnam, nor could the methods of decisionism, as high and low we employed them, forestall Watergate. Certainly it is no adequate reply to point out that Niebuhr in his retirement deplored our Vietnam policy, or that Fletcher would not have consented to the Watergate burglaries or the ransacking of Daniel Ellsberg's psychiatrist's files, for what stands condemned is not one or two thinkers, but a way of thinking in which men of our times have been largely involved, whatever the particular acts of particular individuals have been.

Nor am I claiming that Christian realism and decisionism made no valuable contribution, for they did; realism at least in reaction to the excesses of late-liberal optimism, and decisionism at least in freeing some from censorious legalism, or from service (or lip-service) to ethical constraints little valued in truth. But the shape of our times suggests that neither the one nor the other, nor both together, adequately express either the truly human or the truly Christian ethical demand of the age waiting to be born.

III

What will be the Christians ethics of the days ahead? What is said now must be even more tentative than the preceding suggestions. More than once I have referred to "character ethics" as a proposed replacement for the decisionism and realism of the recent past. Obviously, this is not so much shrewd prediction as it is straightforward promotion; my own judgment is that character ethics, or what I would prefer, were it not so awkward, to call the ethics of character-in-community, is a more truly Christian style of thought and life for the days now ahead. This judgment is itself risky, however, because character ethics has not been worked out by present-day thinkers with even the clarity and critical attention given the other two. Perhaps the nearest approach to a modern Christian character ethic is in one strand of the work done by the school of H. Richard Niebuhr.[21] His somewhat obscure, posthumously published book, *The Responsible Self*,[22] has been interpreted by some of his students mainly in terms of "responsibility."[23] Perhaps they would have done better to have attended instead to H. R. Niebuhr's notion of the "self." In any case, it is the self in its community with which character ethics is principally concerned.

The word "character" may call to mind someone of fixed or easily typified nature. Thus we speak of character actors (those who are regularly cast in stock roles—the dizzy blonde, the rural doctor), and we say "He's quite a character" of someone of pronounced habits or dispositions (garrulity, for example, or stinginess, or a pronounced ten-

[21] I have in mind here especially some of the work of James Gustafson; see his *Christ and the Moral Life* (New York: Harper, 1968), and *Christian Ethics and the Community* (Philadelphia: Pilgrim Press, 1971); and the work of a third-generation member of the school, Stanley Hauerwas; see his forthcoming books, *Vision and Virtue* (Notre Dame, Ind.: Fides Publishers, 1974); and *Character and the Christian Life: A Study in Theological Ethics* (San Antonio: Trinity University Press, 1974).

[22] H. Richard Niebuhr, *The Responsible Self; an Essay in Christian Moral Philosophy,* introd. James Gustafson (New York: Harper, 1963).

[23] Cf. Albert Jonsen, *Responsibility in Modern Religious Ethics* (Washington, D.C.: Corpus Books, 1968).

dency to buy loud and flashy cars and clothes). The association with fixity or tenacity can be misleading, but it is an important clue to the role of character in ethics; however, merely 'being a character' is not as close to the mark as is the notion of 'having character.'

Even having character is not itself deserving of praise or blame, for character can be good or bad. Perhaps, though, that is just the fact which must be attended to. The suggestion is that having character, being a person of *some* character, is one precondition of making responsible choices. Having character is a part of what we have in mind when we distinguish the moral or immoral acts of persons from the merely mechanical or biological activity of things or animals. A person with no (or very little) character may, to be sure, engage in deliberate activities, now playing a game of bridge, next helping a blind man across the street, now cheating in love, next paying a debt. To some of these single acts we may ascribe moral praise or blame. Yet this ascription is somewhat questionable until we know the motive of the doer—why did he pay, why cheat, why help or play? If we assume good motives in any of these cases, we may be assuming too much, for character is just that connection of purpose and policy and individual actions which makes possible motivation of any sort (as opposed to conditioned reflexes). The characterless rubber-ball person may bounce until he kills, and that killing may be for a fleeting 'motive'—anger, or envy, or bloodlust. And that *act* may be truly bad. Yet we may be inclined to say of the rubber ball himself that he has not yet risen to the level of badness. We would say this, for example, of a child whose characteristic ways were not yet shaped, but also of a pitiable social psychopath.

To have character, then, is to enter at a new level the realm of morality, the level at which one's person, with its continuities, its interconnections, its integrity, is intimately involved in one's deeds. By being the persons we are, we are able to do what we do, and conversely, by those very deeds we form or re-form our own characters. Only a man of (some) generosity will act generously, as a general rule; but also as a general rule the man who acts generously on this occasion is shaping himself along generous lines. Thus, character is paradoxically both the cause and consequence of what we do.[24]

It is most important here to recognize that character, though by definition deep-seated, is not necessarily rigid or unchangeable. A man's character is formed by the way he sees things, by his vision, we say. It is shaped by the way he does things, by his style. It is coincident with his deepest and most dearly held beliefs, his convictions. But we know that our convictions, though tenacious, *do* sometimes change, that style can be both acquired and modified, that the total vision by which one lives can sometimes be made over again.[25] It is just these possibilities of change which make the teacher's task worthwhile, and which give hope

[24] For the tenor of the preceding two paragraphs, I am indebted both to my friend and sometime writing partner James M. Smith, and to Stanley Hauerwas, who allowed me to read his unpublished paper, "Towards an Ethics of Character" (to appear in Hauerwas, *Vision and Virtue*). Concerning the paradox expressed by "cause *and* consequence," see Jonathan Edwards, *Freedom of the Will* (New Haven: Yale University Press, 1957 [1st ed., 1754]) .

[25] It is interesting that John Lemmon alludes to this puzzling possibility toward the end of the essay referred to above. Mentioning Sartre and others, he writes: "There may come a point in the development of a painter, say, or a composer, where he is no longer able to go on producing work that conforms to the canons of composition which he has hitherto accepted, where he is compelled by his authenticity as a creator to develop new procedures and new forms. It is difficult to describe what will guide him in the selection of new canons, but one consideration will often be the desire to be (whatever this means) *true to himself*. It may well be that an appropriate consideration in the development of a moral outlook is the desire to be, in the relevant sense whatever that is, true to oneself and to one's own character. But I will not pursue this topic here, because I confess myself to be quite in the dark as to what the sense of these words is." ("Moral Dilemmas," p. 278.) I take it that the last sentence refers in particular to the words "true to oneself and to one's own character," and that it is to these that Lemmon, whom I characterized above as a decisionist, can assign no meaning whatsoever. Decisionists cannot.

to the evangelist. Children grow up; old people change their ways (you can teach an old dog new tricks); conversions take place. Thus an ethics of character, far from being anti-thetical to education and evangelism, is exactly suited to them: character exists, so these activities are desirable; character need never be permanently fixed, so they are possible.

Nor does character ethics foster a whimsical and priva-tistic approach to morality. As already mentioned, we might do better to refer to the ethics of character-in-community, thus acknowledging the reference of character to the human setting which fosters and recognizes it. This can be seen clearly if we note that communities have their own distinc-tive characters, and that signs of this distinctive character are the community's holding certain convictions—the same convictions which inform and give shape to many individ-ual members of the community. We recognize the 'charac-teristic' laws of English-speaking communities, or the 'char-acteristic' ethos of a Spanish village, in part because we sense in each case the presence of deep-seated communal be-liefs about what is right, what is fitting, what makes for the common good. Such normative beliefs are the convictions of these communities. Individuals, while they may dissent from this or that common conviction (not all Englishmen believe that a man's home is his castle, nor every Spaniard that his family's honor is sacred), nevertheless are shaped by the need to agree or to dissent, and so their own con-victions are formed in interaction with the community's. The current flows the other way too, of course; individuals affect by their own beliefs the common store. All this is even more true of a religious community than of a linguistic or national one, especially if the religious community delib-erately seeks to nurture convictional faith in its members, as does Christianity. Men who belong to more than one type of convictional community (e.g., one who is both a socialist and a Christian) form themselves and are formed by each such community, though not without resultant conflicts in practice.

There can be little doubt that if 'character ethics' is understood in the terms now roughly indicated, it has many features which are compatible with Christian morality as widely understood by Christians of any age. Christians from New Testament times have been deeply interested in character,[26] though more correctly in character as redeemed by Christ, rather than in character as a natural or personal achievement.[27] Whatever difficulties scholars may find in the re-creation of the chronological biography of Jesus, his character is a touchstone of Christian life (Phil. 2:5 ff.). The Christian movement itself, varied though it may be in time and in historic circumstance, displays in particular communities definite enough moral character, now in confusion and disorder, now in some strength, now taking one formal appearance, now another, but continuing to guide its members into ordered ways of life regarding the taking of life and the regulation of sexual relations, the rights of others regarding property and privilege, the place of family duties, the claims of friendship and the claims of the stranger and the helpless. Those who would deny this continuity in the interests of some special ethical theory may do so, but there remain the solid social facts of Christian morality.[28]

The puzzling thing, then, is why Christian character ethics has seen so little development and exploration in our times. It may be answered that ours are unsettled or chaotic times, in which rapid change makes any settled ethics un-

[26] See the New Testament catalogues of virtues and vices, e.g. Gal. 5:19-24; Rom. 1:28-31; Eph. 5:3-5; 6:14-20; Phil. 4:8; Col. 3:5-15; I Tim. 3:2-13; James 3:13-18; I Pet. 3:8-13; etc. See Victor P. Furnish, *Theology and Ethics in Paul* (Nashville: Abingdon Press, 1968), and William G. Doty, *Letters in Primitive Christianity* (Philadelphia: Fortress Press, 1973).

[27] Rom. 12:1-2 and parallels; cf. also Augustine *versus* Pelagius.

[28] The classic account here remains Ernst Troeltsch, *The Social Teaching of the Christian Churches* (German ed., 1911), 2 vols. (Torchbooks; New York: Harper, 1960).

tenable, but this argument would apply equally well to Stoic ethics or early Christian ethics, for both attended earnestly to character, and yet endured for hundreds of years during which cataclysmic social changes occurred. Rather than speculate upon still other possible causes, I will suggest one factor the absence of which surely hinders the development of a contemporary ethics of Christian character, for this factor is one which will lead us directly to the connection between Christian ethics, Christian theology, and the biographical study which is to occupy us in the pages ahead.

Consider, then, the suggestion already made, that convictions, as well as traits, are integral to character, and to the existence of (Christian) community. Is this the necessary missing element? We may roughly define convictions as those tenacious beliefs which when held give definiteness to the character of a person or of a community, so that if they were surrendered, the person or community would be significantly changed.[29] Convictions may be distinguished from principles, in that the latter are the product of reflective thinking, have often a rather academic flavor, and are perhaps more often weapons for attacking others than guides for ourselves (most of us have at some time served on committees with men of principle); while convictions are very often particular and immediate in form, and may not be consciously formulated by their holders at all, yet when we do find our convictions, we find the best clue to ourselves. Convictions may be distinguished from opinions: men stake money on opinions, whether of lawyers or of handicappers, but they have been known to stake their lives on their convictions; opinions are argued, but con-

[29] For this understanding of convictions, and its relation to theology, see my "Theology," in William M. Pinson, Jr., and Clyde E. Fant, Jr., eds., *Contemporary Christian Trends* (Waco, Tex.: Word Books, 1972). See also my forthcoming *Religious Convictions and the Problem of Pluralism* (probable title) with James M. Smith, which explores more fully the relations of convictions, persons, communities, and the nature of theology.

victions are the hidden agenda in every argument, the unseen weight on even the most honest set of moral scales.

Now it must be that an ethics of character will be concerned with convictions, for to have convictions is to have at least that much character; moreover, convictions, unlike traits of character such as justice or mercy, may, if known, be expressed in propositional form, so they may evince the particularity of a man's character as the more general 'traits' cannot. To say that Pietro is just, or Salvador honest; is merely to praise them (though in a specific way); to say, however, that Pietro is convinced no man should go without food and shelter for lack of a job, or that Salvador is convinced that the truth is a more valuable commodity than money can buy, is to come much nearer to saying where Pietro and Salvador stand, and to open the way for appraisal of their respective characters. For as men are convinced so will they live. And similarly with convinced communities.

What is noteworthy, however, is that the realm of convictions is just the realm with which theology, too, is concerned. The best way to understand theology is to see it, not as the study about God (for there are godless theologies as well as godly ones), but as the investigation of the convictions of a convictional community, discovering its convictions, interpreting them, criticizing them in the light of all that we can know, and creatively transforming them into better ones if possible. By "convictional communities" I refer at least to Christianity or to its sub-communities (hence "Catholic theology," or "Reformed theology"), or to Judaism, or to Islam, or to Buddhism. Evidently there are nonreligious convictional communities as well, so that if we like we can discover a Marxian 'theology' and a libertarian 'theology,' but these are farther from my present interests. Theologians, then, are concerned with convictions, not merely in themselves, but in relation to the persons and communities which embrace these convictions, and they are interested in what those convictions are about. The Christian theologian cares not only to know that there is a belief in God, not only to know that that belief is the conviction of the Christian community, but also to know whether there be such a God and what difference God's being (as well as the belief in it) makes to those who believe or disbelieve.

Some convictions are ethical ones; all convictions are at bottom theological, i.e., of theological concern. This follows from the preceding. Only artificially can the ethical convictions be segregated from the rest. Theology and the ethics of character, then, are roommates, sharing the same space and obliged to come to terms with each other's concerns. It has often been hard for ethics and theology to live together: 'theological' ethics has seemed to many ethicists a bastard discipline, while 'ethical' theology has seemed to some theologians a moralistic debasement of true Christian theology. Nevertheless, both these risks may be required of us if an adequate ethic is to appear in our time, and if theology is to do its proper work. Ethics may have to acknowledge that the only truly universal ethical judgments are purely formal, providing little guidance for the formation of moral character, and may have to learn to attend afresh to the way of life of particular communities and particular men, though without sacrificing its yearning for universalizability. Theology may have to acknowledge that a theology of revelation or of reason, or a theology of secularity or of religiosity, if it does not enter into the actual shape of the lives of the people in its community of concern, is after all irrelevant to these lives. Does the meeting place of the two, then, lie in the investigation of actual character, with consequences for each partner in the investigation?

It must be clear that in this investigation there can be no *a priori* segregation of ethics from theology proper. This can hardly be attempted once we think of Christian morality as involving the shared ethical convictions of the community. For our several sorts of convictions do not exist in hermetic isolation from one another. My convictions about how to treat my neighbors cannot be segregated from the question, Who is my neighbor? and that is a question of my vision, of how I see the world and its inhabitants. And that in turn may be inseparable from my convictions about God-whose-world-this-is.

Now consider this fact. In or near the community there appear from time to time singular or striking lives, the lives of persons who embody the convictions of the community, but in a new way; who share the vision of the community, but with new scope or power; who exhibit the style of the community, but with significant differences. It is patent that the example of these lives may serve to disclose and perhaps to correct or enlarge the community's moral vision, at the same time arousing impotent wills within the community to a better fulfillment of the vision already acquired. But the same example may serve also to stir up other convictions of the community—its understanding of God, its doctrine of man, its appreciation of the earth and all that is in it. These convictions, too, may be negated or enlarged, altered or reinforced, by the lives of such significant persons. Such lives, by their very attractiveness or beauty, may serve as data for the Christian thinker, enabling him more truly to reflect upon the tension between what is and what ought to be believed and lived by all. To engage in such reflection, however, is the proper task of Christian theology. That the task can be fulfilled in this way is the theme of the present book.

By recognizing that Christian beliefs are not so many 'propositions' to be catalogued or juggled like truth-functions in a computer, but are living convictions which give shape to actual lives and actual communities, we open ourselves to the possibility that the only relevant critical examination of Christian beliefs may be one which begins by attending to lived lives. Theology must be at least biography. If by attending to those lives, we find ways of reforming our own theologies, making them more true, more faithful to our ancient vision, more adequate to the age now being born, then we will be justified in that arduous inquiry. Biography at its best will be theology.

Perhaps the ethics of character (for all its worthy precedents, and all our need) has done so little to this point in our day because it cannot become itself until there is also a 'theology of character.' Perhaps, that is, ethical concern with character necessarily implies questions which in some way must receive theological answers, answers which are best found through a fresh investigation of lives which again incarnate the life Christian faith continually celebrates.

Christianity turns upon the character of Christ. But that character must continually find fresh exemplars if it is not to be consigned to the realm of mere antiquarian lore. That is one good reason—there have been other reasons as well—why in Christianity there have been 'the saints,' not merely in the original, biblical sense of all members of the Spirit-filled community (cf. I Cor. 1:2), but in the historic sense of striking and exemplary members of that same community. I propose now, not to consult any official list of saints in the latter sense, but to attend to two men, Hammarskjöld and King, whose lives are widely recognized in our times as having this exemplary quality. Certain features of the work in these two chapters will make it possible in the following one to say more exactly how biography is or becomes theology. Then I will turn to two lesser-known lives, those of Clarence Jordan and Charles Ives, and show the method at work in these less familiar cases. A final chapter will gather up the conclusions to that point, and suggest ways in which this work can be carried still further. The lives I have chosen here have no exclusive claim upon any reader: they have in common just the fact of their intrinsic interest, their connection with twentieth-century Christianity, and (a negative criterion) that not a one of them is a professor of theology! Others can choose other lives and reap an equal or better harvest. I have chosen these because, with all their flaws, I like them very much.

Chapter Two

Dag Hammarskjöld—
Twice-Born Servant

This book advances the thesis that theology may be undertaken via biography. While the best argument for the thesis is the book taken as a whole, some preliminary reasons for making this approach have been set forth in the preceding chapter. Consider now one additional reason, of a pastoral nature, and one which may serve to make clear the point of view (or interest, or bias) with which I approach the life of Dag Hammarskjöld and every other life studied here. Suppose someone asks, "Why choose Dag Hammarskjöld and not someone else?" I can point to the somewhat arbitrary criteria of selection which were actually employed in making the choice: Hammarskjöld, and the others here, are of our own century, though they are not still living today. All are men whose lives have attracted a certain amount of interest among religious people, and each was in some way or other himself 'religious'. None, however, was a professional theologian by occupation—that is, none earned his living by teaching theology, writing it, going to professional academic meetings, guiding student research, and the like. Clearly, though, these criteria would permit almost limitless substitutions for my own list of subjects. Then why these? Why Dag? A first answer must be that I like him, and I will have more to say about that answer at the end of the book. Certainly, though, my intention cannot be to discover what Dag Hammarskjöld believed religiously, and then argue that we should believe the same. *That* is not what biography as theology means.

A partial explanation of the choices made is that theology is intended *for* someone: it has an assumed audience, a presupposed set of hearers. In some degree, I regard my subjects as representative of the audience for which present-day American theology must be undertaken. To dramatize this, suppose yourself a pastor who knows that his congregation includes the likes of a Dag Hammarskjöld, or the likes of a Martin King. Given such a fact, what form must your own theologizing take? It is not that you must think as they think, or say what they say. It is rather that your theology *must be adequate to lives such as these lives.* So far as it has attended to the modern world, theology has too often grown dilute because it has attended mainly to the thinnest strains in modern life (for example, to the most boring secularism). Let us rather seek to shape in our times a faith adequate to the intensity and the spiritual seriousness of men such as these. If that is a fair theological goal, then what is first required is to attend carefully to these representative (though certainly not average) parishioners. To that extent, but only to that extent, biography as theology employs what Tillich called a method of correlation.

I

When Dag Hammarskjöld died, in a somewhat sinister plane crash while on a United Nations mission in the Congo and Katanga in 1961, a diplomat friend and a lawyer flew from Sweden to dispose of the personal effects in the Manhattan apartment of the Secretary-General.[1] Beside his bed, they found a document whose content no living person knew. In form, it was a stack of typed pages, perhaps 200, held in a clipboard, with a note addressed to another Swedish friend, and marked "personal." When the whole was in due course examined, it turned out to consist of a diary of about 600 entries, ranging in length from a line or so to two pages, with dates from 1925, when he had just finished his undergraduate university work, until the final entry dated three weeks before the 1961 plane crash—a period of 36 years. A title page had been added—it read simply *Vägmärken;* that is, markings, blazes, trail marks. The subsequent publication, first in Swedish then in English, of *Markings* had a stunning effect. The entries were literary jewels, ranging from sharp-etched sketches of men and countryside and merciless psychological self-probings, to long stretches, at the end, of haiku verse. Even more remarkable was the discovery that these 'trail marks' constituted a private spiritual diary, recording the groping but finally successful journey into faith of one of the great men of our century. It was a side of Hammarskjöld the public had not known—some jolly good friends, themselves antireligious, were startled, as were many in the general public, to discover that they had had in their midst a secret believer. The effect of this upon the understanding of Hammarskjöld's life could not have been less than the effect upon geographers of the discovery, beneath the Mississippi River, of another, underground river, running its entire length, connected to the surface river by various ducts, and affecting the surface flow in unsuspected ways. It is symptomatic of the biographic problem created by this document

[1] The remainder of this chapter as well as chapters 3 and 4 originated as part of the 1970–71 Jeffery Lectures at Goucher College, Baltimore. The Hammarskjöld material appeared in slightly different form as an article in *Review and Expositor,* Spring, 1973, titled "The Twice-Born Religion of Dag Hammarskjold."

that twelve years after Dag's death, though there had been studies of his diplomatic career and studies of the content of *Markings,* no full-scale biography had appeared. Some reactions to the discovery of *Markings* are quite amusing. One Danish writer concluded that Hammarskjöld thought of himself as "a new Messiah," and a Swedish critic said it was a happy thing that he died before going completely berserk. Others said there was no connection between *Markings* and the public life of Hammarskjöld. It was the achievement of Henry P. Van Dusen, in a series of articles and a book [2] published in the sixties, to show that there was indeed a connection between the public events of Dag's life and the cryptic entries in the spiritual diary.

It may be helpful here to note the salient biographical outline.[3] Dag Hammarskjöld was born July 29, 1905, in

[2] Henry P. Van Dusen, "Dag Hammarskjöld's Spiritual Pilgrimage," *Theology Today,* January, 1965; *Dag Hammarskjöld, The Statesman and His Faith* (New York: Harper, 1967; rev. ed. 1969), retitled *Dag Hammarskjöld, The Man and His Faith.* See also the Van Dusen contribution to Cordier and Maxwell (cited below, footnote 3).

[3] The principal primary published sources for a study of Dag Hammarskjöld's life available to me are Dag Hammarskjöld, *Markings,* translated from the Swedish by Leif Sjöberg and W. H. Auden with a Foreword by W. H. Auden (New York: Alfred A. Knopf, 1965); Wilder Foote, ed., *Servant of Peace, a Selection of the Speeches and Statements of Dag Hammarskjöld* (New York: Harper, 1963). To these should be added Bo Beskow, *Dag Hammarskjöld, Strictly Personal. A Portrait* (Garden City, N.Y.: Doubleday, 1969), which contains personal letters from Hammarskjöld to the author as well as reminiscences. The secondary sources I have used in addition to Van Dusen are: Brian Urquhart, *Hammarskjold* (New York: Alfred A. Knopf, 1972); Joseph P. Lash, *Dag Hammarskjöld: Custodian of the Brushfire Peace* (Garden City, N.Y.: Doubleday, 1961); Gustaf Aulén, *Dag Hammarskjöld's White Book: An Analysis of Markings* (Philadelphia: Fortress Press, 1969) (Van Dusen and Aulén concentrate particularly upon Hammarskjöld's religious faith); Andrew W. Cordier and Kenneth Maxwell, eds., *Paths to World Order,* the Dag Hammarskjöld Memorial Lectures for 1965 (New York: Columbia University Press, 1967); Richard I. Miller, *Dag Hammarskjöld and Crisis Diplomacy* (New York: Oceana Publications, 1961); Emery Kelen, *Hammarskjöld* (New York: Putnam's, 1960); Sten Söderberg, *Hammarskjöld, A Pictorial Biography* (New York: Viking Press, 1962); and Sven Stolpe, *Dag Hammarskjöld: A Spiritual Portrait* (New York: Scribner's, 1966). (Urquhart, Lash, and Miller concentrate upon

Jönköping, Sweden, second of four sons of a distinguished Swedish family of statesmen and soldiers and on his mother's side, of clergymen. His father, a strict conservative, had been Sweden's prime minister, but during Dag's later boyhood, was Governor of Uppland, and the family then lived in the castle in Uppsala. Their nearest neighbor was the world-famous Archbishop of Uppsala, Nathan Söderblom, theologian and ecumenist. Dag's father was a stern disciplinarian; his mother a woman of unusual warmth and charm; she lived a deep, practical Christianity of worship and good works. The boy was a brilliant student, a vigorous outdoorsman. He progressed from the University of Uppsala, to a Ph.D. in economics at Lund, to a position in the civil service. He worked hard, rose rapidly, engineered Sweden's transition to a Keynesian planned economy in the thirties, became a top civil service official. Never married, he seemed married to his work, interrupting it only with intense periods of mountain climbing, sailing, and hiking, or with hours in the theaters, art galleries, and libraries. After World War II, he helped plan the economic reconstruction of Europe, and when in 1953 Trygve Lie was to be replaced as Secretary-General of the United Nations, that organization turned to Dag Hammarskjöld of Sweden.

The United Nations was at a critical juncture. Lie had been forced out because he played a bold hand in implementing the Charter's authority to make the Secretary's role more than that of a mere administrator. Hammarskjöld was chosen partly because he was a dedicated civil servant who, some expected, would be a mere passive Secretary-General. Nothing could have been more mistaken. Hammarskjöld gained attention when in 1955 he flew to Peking and obtained from communist China, though it was

the Secretary-Generalship.) I have not consulted some articles and one book, Hjalmar Sundén, *Kristusmeditationer i Dag Hammarskjölds Vägmärken* (Stockholm: Verbum, 1966), cited by Aulén; these are in Swedish. Where I depend upon the sources mentioned above I will hereafter not cite them individually, except for direct quotations, or in order to substantiate disputed points.

outside the U.N., the release of twelve U.S. airmen held captive there since the Korean War. The Secretary was hardly passive! In 1956 the Suez crisis erupted, and Hammarskjöld stretched the understanding of the Charter to develop a U.N. peace-keeping presence in the Middle East, thereby averting for the time a still-smoldering general war. In 1958 it was Lebanon, and in 1959 Cambodia, and again he devised means to keep "the brush-fire peace." In 1960 the Congo crisis threatened to turn Africa into a Cold War battle continent. Krushchev turned savagely upon Hammarskjöld and banged his shoe on the table to demand that he resign. But the Secretary-General acted with steadfast purpose to maintain African independence and the United Nations' international integrity, and was achieving those goals when his life was extinguished the night of September 17-18, 1961, near Ndola, Northern Rhodesia. These eight years at the U.N. were ones in which hard-headed diplomats and common men alike, around this world, began to dream a new dream of peace among the nations and of justice within. More than any one man, it was Dag Hammarskjöld, a reserved, seemingly colorless economist and diplomat, who evoked that vision. What then of the vision of the man behind the vision? What was the true faith of this man?

II

Let us begin to answer by examining the remarkable reticence of the man concerning his deepest convictions. It was not, we should note, that Dag totally concealed his faith. In the first year of his U.N. career, 1953, he was asked to contribute one of a series of radio talks arranged by Edward R. Murrow, and subsequently published under the title *This I Believe*.[4] In seven brief paragraphs, as today's reader can see, Hammarskjöld touched upon almost every

[4] Reprinted as "Old Creeds in a New World," in Foote, *Servant of Peace*, pp. 23-24.

theme which was central to his spiritual life. But until *Markings* appeared the 1953 credo was little noticed.

The fact is that Hammarskjöld regarded his job as one which called for a sharp separation between "the public man" and "the private man"; the former was the servant of many nations of diverse religious creeds, the latter must therefore remain in privacy. When work permitted, he liked to slip quietly into some Manhattan church for worship; *Markings*, as Van Dusen has shown us, reveals a man increasingly conscious of the Christian seasons of celebration —Good Friday, Easter, Pentecost. But he did not wish to appear an official church visitant; his job, he felt, precluded that.

Why, though, had he been so reticent about his faith during the earlier years in Sweden, when the special conditions at the U.N. did not prevail? Why were some friends at work and at play startled to learn of *Markings*? Perhaps the clearest answer, besides the personal reserve already mentioned, is that Hammarskjöld lived through a long period of doubt bordering on despair, a period in which, if faith survived at all, it was latent not dominant. In the 1953 radio talk, he said that "a never abandoned effort frankly and squarely to build up a personal belief in the light of experience and honest thinking has led me in a circle; I *now* recognize and endorse, unreservedly, those very beliefs which were once handed down to me." [5] So there was a time when he did not recognize them—a time, *Markings* shows, which stretched from his college days in the 1920s to the very threshold of the 1953 appointment— *a generation of despair*. Thus a characteristic trailmark from 1945–1949 reads:

What is one to do on a bleak day but drift for a while through the streets—drift with the stream? . . .

Slow and gray—He searches every face. But the people aimlessly streaming along the gray ditches of the streets are all like

[5] *Ibid.*, p. 23, emphasis added.

himself—atoms in whom the radioactivity is extinct, and force has tied its endless chain around nothing. (24) [6]

The characteristics of this period, Gustaf Aulén points out in his very important study of *Markings*, were a problem of loneliness, a torment of self-centeredness, and the apparent meaninglessness of life.[7] The irony of this, as Hammarskjöld saw, was that this inner pain accompanied an external career of unblemished success and prosperity. He rose rapidly in the ranks of the Swedish civil service, was given the hardest assignments, fulfilled them with flair, held cabinet rank in the government, was a man of "devastating charm," worked incredibly long hours, raced from work to revel in the natural glory of Sweden's mountains and coastline, was a good friend, a loyal member of his family, and withal a man of unassuming modesty. Yet this very paragon of achievement was a man possessed with thoughts of death and sometimes suicide. Dag expresses this paradox in a 1951 entry in *Markings* addressed to himself:

It occurs to you in a flash: *I might just as well never have existed.* Other people, however, seeing you with a guaranteed salary, a bank account, and a briefcase under your arm, assume that you take your existence for granted. *What* you are can be of interest to them, not *that* you are. (73)

"Loneliness" and "self-centeredness" are shorthand for the perplexing problems of human relations. Little stirred by sexual drives, or (in his own words) "incapable of being blinded by desire" (85), he never married.[8] Human relations at work were often marred by the savageries of the struggle for success, accomplishment, adulation. Some of the

[6] The number in parentheses in this and subsequent quotations refers to the page of *Markings*.

[7] Aulén, *Dag Hammarskjöld's White Book*, p. 16.

[8] The reader interested in pursuing the charge of homosexuality brought against Hammarskjöld should read the careful discussion of this charge, and its reasoned rejection, in Urquhart, *Hammarskjold*, pp. 25-27.

most brilliant markings of this period are those in which Dag turns off a thumbnail sketch of some co-worker. In one marking, his fellow men are compared with the screaming gulls which Hammarskjöld watched fighting over human- ity's garbage—or rather the gull reminds him of his fellow man— "a well-nourished carrion bird who feels so much at home among us all" (34).

This acidulous view of his fellows was matched, however, by profound sympathy. He never wavered from the in- grained ideal of service to all men. There was, however, less charity in his view of himself. "Do you really have 'feelings' any longer," he asks in a 1950 marking, "for anybody or anything except yourself—or even that? With- out the strength of a personal commitment, your experience of others is at most aesthetic" (48). He is ever ready to probe his motives with a zeal that would have done Freud credit: "Praise nauseates you—but woe betide him who does not recognize your worth" (14).

Of course, one level at which we can read such private self-probings is as monitors of the moral life, the alarm sys- tem and internal sprinkler valves by which superego main- tains control. To stop there, however, would be to ignore much of the evidence. For Hammarskjöld, the crises of self- knowledge and self-love were a *distraction* which had somehow to be overcome if he were ever to make his way up the pass to the unknown goal of his life. He makes this clear in one of the most crucial passages of *Markings:*

> These wretched attempts to make an experience apprehensi- ble (for my sake? for others?) —the tasks of the morrow—Y's friendship or X's appreciation of what I have done: paper screens which I place between myself and the void to prevent my gaze from losing itself in the infinity of time and space. (51)

The "wretched attempts" are the self-examination recorded in *Markings,* and the parenthetical questions are a way of asking himself about the real addressee of these diary entries—"Whom am I trying to fool?" The entry continues:

Small paper screens. Blown to shreds by the first puff of wind, catching fire from the tiniest spark. Lovingly looked after—but frequently changed.

So the three projects of Hammarskjöld's psyche, his diary ("these wretched attempts"), his work ("the tasks of to-morrow"), and his friends' goodwill ("X" and "Y") are subterfuges of escape—in an oriental metaphor, paper screens, screening . . . what?

This dizziness in the face of *les espaces infinis*—only overcome if we dare to gaze into them without any protection. And accept them as the reality before which we must justify our existence. For this is the truth we must reach to live, that everything *is* and we just in it.

In these sentences we are brought, I believe, into the center of the predicament of modern man. It has been suggested by many recent writers that the spiritual distinctive of modernity is man's nakedness to the cosmos, the absence of the "sacred canopy" [9] which medieval man and primitive man took to enclose them from the unknown. With Luther (who also asked how man could "justify" his existence) and Pascal (who spoke of the dizziness before *les espaces infinis*) Hammarskjöld experiences man's existence in the world unmediated. If there is salvation for modern man, he is saying, it will come, not by invoking a mediator, but by the naked discovery that the awefulness of infinitude can be borne, that in Luther's terms the God of wrath is none other than the God of grace, and that it is God alone with whom we have to do. Or as Dag Hammarskjöld put it, by gazing into the infinite spaces without any protection, to see that everything *is*.

[9] See Peter Berger, *The Sacred Canopy, Elements of a Sociological Theory of Religion* (Garden City, N.Y.: Doubleday, 1967) ; and John S. Dunne, C.S.C., *A Search for God in Time and Memory* (New York: Macmillan, 1969) .

The striking fact (or is this the usual case with such sagas of the human spirit?) is that Dag knew what he knew here, and yet remained in despair. Knew not only this, but, as an examination of *Markings* will show, knew everything else which was elemental to his later faith. Every such element—God, the God of the mystics and of Scripture, Jesus, the "hero of the gospels," faith as something other than assent to doctrines, sacrifice as the model for life and the answer to death—all are present in clear form in the parts of *Markings* written before the great conversion crisis of 1951–53. Conversions are not so much the introduction of new elements into the self, as they are the rearrangement of elements already present, the shifting of the center of gravity; for the 'new' elements were present before the conversion, and the 'old' elements are still present after.

I have spoken now of conversion, and I must justify my use of that term here. It is not one which Dag Hammarskjöld would naturally have applied to himself, or readily found in the religious tradition in which he was reared. Gustaf Aulén, the chief Swedish interpreter of Hammarskjöld's faith, says that "there was no sudden 'conversion.' He does not belong to those who have been called the 'twiceborn.' " [10] At least the first of these assertions is literally true—the conversion is not "sudden," but well prepared, and it extends over a period of months. The second, however, is mistaken.

We owe the term "twice-born" in modern theology to William James, who said he found it in Francis Newman. In this classification, the "once-born" are those congenitally happy souls who worry little about morality and less about evil, and who, therefore, require little if any help toward spiritual happiness. These look on all things and see that they are good. The best illustrations of this type are found, says James, in the Mind-cure movement, notably in Christian Science. James speaks with genial approbation of the

[10] Aulén, *Dag Hammarskjöld's White Book*, p. 13.

once-born type—more often than not feminine, and young, he remarks.[11] Now in contrast with this type is another, which takes the world's evil to heart, and thereby confronts difficulties of which the former do not dream. These are the twice-born, whose spiritual pain threshold is much lower, whose exemplars are Tolstoy and Bunyan, and who, as their name suggests, may require a conversion more profound than the once-born can attain, if they are to achieve happiness. And James holds that compared to the former, the twice-born range "over the wider scale of experience," [12] and that this type most fully illustrates the theoretic of such religions as Buddhism and Christianity—religions of deliverance.[13]

Given this distinction, the facts require us to classify Dag Hammarskjöld among the twice-born. Let us note some of these facts. The entries in *Markings* for 1951 include the somber self-criticism we have seen. They also include a remarkable reflection on Jesus at the Last Supper. As Hammarskjöld understands him from his reading of Albert Schweitzer and from his own study of the Gospels, Jesus was "an adamant young man," committed to "a possibility in his being" which, he has come to realize, "might lead to the Cross." Significantly like Dag, Jesus, despite the presence of friends, was "alone as he confronted his final destiny" (68). Concluding the reflection, Dag asks, "Is the hero of this immortal, brutally simple drama in truth 'the Lamb of God that taketh away the sins of the world'? Absolutely faithful to a divined possibility—in that sense the Son of God, in that sense the sacrificial Lamb, in that sense the Redeemer. . ." (69). Further, there is at the very beginning of *Markings* a poem, one which might have been composed upon Dag's graduation from the university in 1925. Its first lines are

[11] William James, *The Varieties of Religious Experience, A Study in Human Nature* (New York: Modern Library, n.d. [1st ed., 1902]), pp. 77-124.
[12] *Ibid.*, p. 160.
[13] *Ibid.*, p. 125-62.

I am being driven forward
Into an unknown land. (5)

A quarter-century later, in 1951, the entries begin to speak
of "frontiers." The frontiers of the familiar were closed to
Hammarskjöld, his life was full of despair, but there might
be another frontier. To Americans, "the frontier" has meant
recently a brand of politics, and earlier a sparsely settled
region to the west. To Europeans, however, it meant in
the first place the *border* between two countries. To cross
such a frontier is to enter a new land. It is at about this
time that Dag begins also to write of choice between two
alternatives; and again to speak of that "adamant young
man," Jesus, who saw a new possibility and who therefore
walked the road to the end. Finally he speaks of "the frontier of the unheard-of":

> Now. When I have overcome my fears—of
> others, of myself, of the underlying darkness:
>   at the frontier of the unheard-of.
> Here ends the known. But, from a source
>   beyond it, something fills my being with its
>   possibilities.
> Here desire is purified and made lucid: each
>   action is a preparation for, each choice an
>   assent [a yes[14]] to the unknown. (76)

When did he cross this frontier of the unheard-of?
Writing ten years later, he himself could not draw the line.

> I don't know Who—or what—put the question, I don't know
> when it was put. I don't even remember answering. But at
> some moment [so Hammarskjöld thinks there *was* such a moment]
> I did answer *Yes* to Someone—or Something—and from that
> hour I was certain that existence is meaningful and that, there-
> fore, my life, in self-surrender, had a goal.
> From that moment I have known what it means "not to look
> back," and "to take no thought for the morrow." (205)

[14] For the alternative translation, important for its correlation with
the great "yes" of the New Year's entry for 1953, see Aulén, *Dag
Hammarskjöld's White Book*, p. 25.

We may note next that the 1952 entries seem again predominantly somber, and self-critical, and loneliness is again the theme: "I dare not believe, I do not see how I shall ever be able to believe: that I am not alone" (86) reads a marking from the end of that year's entries. And yet, five entries later, everything is changed. Of the passage to which I next refer, Aulén says, "Here begins a new melody in *Markings*." [15] Dag preferred to spend New Year's, not at parties, which he hated, but alone or with a congenial friend or two in a Swedish mountain cabin, talking, reading, thinking. It had been his custom for several years to make the first entry in his journal for that year by quoting a line from a solemn hymn which his mother had customarily read to her family on New Year's Eve:

> How vain the worldling's pomp and show . . .
> The night approaches now . . .[16]

He would then add a journal meditation of his own. These meditations had been characteristically melancholy—1951: " ['The night approaches now—'] . . . And if this day should be your last . . ." (61). 1952: "['The night approaches now—'] How long the road is" (81). The 1953 New Year's entry again quotes the hymn, but what follows is different.

> ["The night approaches now—"]
> For all that has been—Thanks!
> To all that shall be—Yes! (89)

The frontier is crossed, the gates have been opened, and life can begin to yield its possibilities.

---

[15] *Ibid.*, p. 58.

[16] *Ibid.* W. H. Auden translates the line of this Swedish hymn, which appears in *Markings,* with the familiar English hymn line, "Night is drawing nigh," but the tone of the two hymns, Aulén points out, is quite different. The Swedish hymn Hammarskjöld quoted is somber and foreboding.

What is the meaning of this crossing? Aulén remarks that the Yes is the equivalent of faith. Certainly it is true that the common biblical operative word for faith exercising itself as faith is "amen"—and that the simplest translation of Hebrew *amen* is "Yes." The crossing is the discovery of faith. It is, as well, the reversal of the inward negations which had been the curse of Hammarskjöld's life, negations we summarized earlier as loneliness, self-centeredness, meaninglessness. For his *loneliness,* now, there was to be neither oblivion, nor indifference to others, but awareness of a deeper resource than any human friend: " 'For man shall commune with all creatures to his profit, but enjoy God alone.' That is why no human being can be a permanent source of happiness to another" (101) says a 1954 trail mark. For his *self-centeredness,* there was the realization that the goal of "the longest journey . . . the journey inwards" (58) is more real than the traveler himself. What he finds in that journey is "not I, but God in me" (90). And opposed to the earlier sense of *meaninglessness* was the stirring intuition, in the early entries of 1953, that "God has a use for you" (89) —an intuition borne out by the unforeseen invitation, from the Security Council, on March 31, 1953, to consider appointment as the Secretary-General of the United Nations.

III

Religion, in our quarter-millenium, has been treated sometimes as a kind of feeling, sometimes as a kind of knowing, sometimes as a kind of doing, depending on whether the speaker regards it as primarily a matter of heart or mind or will. Occasionally an audacious voice has been heard to suggest that it cannot be less than the three taken together. So far we have examined Dag Hammarskjöld's religion, as might a William James, primarily on its affective side; now, however, we must ask about the intellectual content of his faith, and about its consequences in his life.

We know even from the few passages in *Markings* which I have quoted, certainly from the remaining evidence, that Dag Hammarskjöld was a man of strongly skeptical mind.[17] This was no doubt a most useful characteristic in a diplomat, who must never be gullible. And skepticism has its uses in the realm of faith as well. The question we must now ask is this: given this skepticism, which persisted after the great Yes as well as before it, did Hammarskjöld believe in a spiritual reality, in a God who was something more than, other than, his own spirit and affects? And if he did, what was the nature of that other?

That "God" might be nothing more than an exalted or presumptuous misdesignation was certainly a possibility with which Hammarskjöld reckoned. For one thing, his university training in philosophy had been guided by the thought of Axel Hägerström, a philosopher whose work was closely akin to the Vienna logical positivism which is better known in the English-speaking world. Hägerström held that knowledge and meaningful utterance were limited to the material world of sensory experience, so that metaphysics, or a transcendent God, were logically nonsensical.[18] This helps to explain the reserve which Hammarskjöld always exercised in mentioning God. The language of religion, he believed, registers "a basic spiritual experience"; it must not be regarded as describing either the world of the senses or some magic-metaphysical otherworld.[19]

On the other hand, the discovery signaled by the great Yes was that life did have a meaning, a larger context, and that the role of religious language was to express that context appropriately. Hammarskjöld discovered a most

[17] See for example "Old Creeds in a New World," in Foote, *Servant of Peace*, pp. 23-24.
[18] On Axel Hägerström, see the entry under his name in Paul Edwards, editor-in-chief, *The Encyclopedia of Philosophy* (New York: Macmillan and the Free Press, 1967).
[19] Cf. *Markings*, p. 106, "metaphysical magic."

helpful resource in the language of the mystics. One of the mystics, John of the Cross, had given Hammarskjöld his definition of faith: "Faith is the union of God with the soul." [20] From "the great medieval mystics," he said, he had gained further help. It appears that this help consisted in an enlarged vocabulary for talking about God.[21] God is "Someone or Something." He is "the Other," "the Oneness," "the Unity." One must love God, says Hammarskjöld, quoting Eckhart, "as if He were a non-God, a non-Spirit, a non-Person, a Non-Substance: love Him simply as the One, the pure and absolute Unity in which is no trace of Duality. And into this One, we must let ourselves fall continually from being into non-being. . ." (110). These are what Aulén calls Hammarskjöld's "anonymous appellations" for God. We can connect them with Dag's nature-mysticism, his talk of merging, of losing himself in nature's being, as all flows together "like the rings made by raindrops falling upon wide expanses of calm dark waters" (118).

Regarding the help provided by the language of the mystics we must make two remarks, if we are to understand Hammarskjöld's faith aright. The first is that he would not use the mystical mode in a way which would confuse himself with God or God with himself. If I seek God on paths of inwardness, it is natural to wonder whether what I have found is indeed an Other, and not a projection of the self. But in a relatively early marking (1950) Dag explores the ethical dilemma entailed in *that* interpretation of religion.

> Treat others as ends, never as means. (57)

That is the familiar Kantian doctrine with which he begins. How, though, shall I treat *myself?* Also as an end, a valued object? Yes, but that must be qualified:

> And myself as an end only in my capacity as a means.

[20] "Old Creeds in a New World," in Foote, *Servant of Peace,* p. 23.
[21] See for the following Aulén, *Dag Hammarskjöld's White Book,* pp. 69-70.

"Only in my capacity as a means" is the guardian against self-centeredness. But in practice, how can this come about? One must learn

> to shift the dividing line in my being between the subject and object to a position where the subject, even if it is in me, is outside and above me . . . .

That is, if God (the "subject") is in me, he must also be beyond me, transcendent, for this doctrine of the transcendence of God can alone guarantee that religion be ethical, not selfish

> —so that my *whole* being may become an instrument for that which is greater than I.

Thus by an ethical (not a metaphysical) inference, Hammarskjöld discovers that the object of mystical religious awareness may not be treated as a mere aspect of the self!

A second remark: alongside the language of mysticism, Dag sets another set of terms or names for God—the word "God" itself, but also God as "the Lord, the Father, the creative will," in whom is righteousness and love, power and glory, mercy and awesome might.[22] Most frequently, Dag uses the intimate personal pronoun "Thou," a term which he found most used in the Psalms, in his address to God.

> Thou
> Whom I do not know
> But Whose I am.
>
> Thou   ·
> Whom I do not comprehend
> But Who hast dedicated me
> To my fate.
> Thou—
>
> (214-15)

[22] Cf. *ibid.*

reads a 1961 marking. The language of the personal God did not, however, obliterate the language of the impersonal God; instead one finds these two modes of speech side by side throughout *Markings*.

Hammarskjöld was not insensitive to the paradox produced by these two ways of speaking. Indeed, at the end of the Eckhart passage referred to earlier, which commands us to refer to God as "a non-God, a non-Spirit, a non-Person, a non-Substance" comes the paradoxical closing assurance: "God helps us to do this"! (110). We may conclude that Hammarskjöld, though he had been helped to transcend his early skepticism by the words of the mystics and their *via negativa*, had found in his own experience a reality which required both ways of talking. In this way he could maintain the mystery as well as the reality of the Thou, the One, whom he found.

Toward the end of his life, Hammarskjöld found himself strongly drawn toward the insights of Martin Buber, the Jewish theologian-philosopher, and left as an uncompleted task a Swedish translation of *I and Thou*. It is natural to suppose that one thing which drew Hammarskjöld to Buber was the latter's relational mysticism, which made the mystical union a matter of intimacy but not absorption. However, Maurice Friedman noted that he found no direct influence of Buber upon *Markings*,[23] so the relation between the two seems more nearly one of parallel than of dependency.

Most certain is it that Hammarskjöld's faith, though in continuity with the past, was uniquely his. He used the language of the mystics and the language of Scripture, but what he had experienced did not exactly fit those molds, or any other. This makes it the more remarkable that, in a series of markings in 1956, he adopts a trinitarian form of prayer.

[23] Van Dusen, "Dag Hammarskjöld's Spiritual Pilgrimage," p. 187; see also pp. 219 ff., Note: Dag Hammarskjöld and Martin Buber.

Before Thee, Father,
In righteousness and humility,

With Thee, Brother,
In faith and courage,

In Thee, Spirit,
In stillness.

Thine—for Thy will is my destiny,
Dedicated—for my destiny is to be used and used
up according to Thy will.

(123)

If one may venture to interpret this prayer, it reveals anew that Hammarskjöld's vision of God was shaped to his own life experience. The three 'persons' of the Trinity disclose three ways in which, as earlier markings show, he was related to God and God to him. "Before" bears the sense "in the presence of" as in the line "Before Jehovah's awful throne." The Father God is righteous, the author of goodness, the stern sovereign who sees the secrets of every heart, the sovereign and the judge. In his presence, before him, humility alone is appropriate.

The second 'person' of Godhead is the Brother—Hammarskjöld's term for Jesus viewed in his moral authority as the pioneer of faith. Here the relation is companionship, a not inconsiderable matter for a man whose great trial was loneliness—"with thee, Brother." As we shall see, the lonely Dag viewed *his* life also as moving toward the way of the cross, the way of self-sacrifice, where courage and faith would be all that mattered.

The third 'person' is the Spirit. Van Dusen complains, even after quoting this passage, that Hammarskjöld's faith was really deficient on the doctrine of the Holy Spirit. His "faith lacked the enrichment and reassurance, the sense of Divine intimacy and potency which are unfailing gifts of the Holy Spirit." [24] It seems a curious complaint. To be

[24] *Ibid.*, p. 204.

sure, *Markings* seldom uses the term "Spirit." But Hammarskjöld, who wrote in the first place for himself and who
had no need to build terminological bridges to Christian
tradition, had entered upon a spiritual experience, the
crossing of the frontier of the unheard-of, which had given
him a sense of presence, "a faith which required no con-
firmation—a contact with reality, light and intense like
the touch of a loved hand: a union in self-surrender without self-destruction, where his heart was lucid and his mind
loving" (110). Such a life hardly seems deficient in the
reality for which "Holy Spirit" is the traditional term. And
that Dag saw this himself is indicated, in the prayer just
quoted, by the change of prepositions—*"In* Thee, Spirit"
—and by the use of that term of art, "stillness," the term of
the mystics from whom he had learned this intimacy.

Having said something of the affective and something
of the cognitive aspects of Hammarskjöld's religion, I now
must say something of its role in the life of action which
he lived. W. H. Auden, in the Foreword to his translation
of *Markings,* remarks that he cannot think of another
"attempt by a professional man of action to unite in one
life the *via activa* and the *via contemplativa"* (xx). One
thinks of Bonhoeffer, but Bonhoeffer was a professional
man of reflection, a theologian, who turned to action in a
time of profound national crisis. Hammarskjöld was a man
of action who turned to faith *without abandoning action,*
who indeed wrote: "In our era, the road to holiness necessarily passes through the world of action" (122). Maybe
Hammarskjöld knew something we who live in the convergent, crisis-packed, horror-strewn, and nevertheless boring late twentieth century cannot fail to know, if there are
to be other centuries. How does the road to holiness, in
his experience, pass through the world of action?

Remember that Dag Hammarskjöld was from boyhood
dedicated to the ideal of service. One way in which he experienced the religious or central problem of his life was
to ask, How can I fulfill this service? Work was absorbing,

but to leave work was to return to "only ourselves, ourselves, ourselves" (63). His fear of faith had been twofold: that it might be dishonest, and that it might be another, monumental form of egocentricity, the very opposite of a life of unselfish service. "Your cravings as a human animal," he wrote to himself in 1941-42, "do not become a prayer just because it is God whom you ask to attend to them" (11). Could there be for him a faith which was free from self-idolatry, which was intellectually honest, and which came to expression in the service to humanity which he so much wanted to give?

His discovery, aided, he said, by Albert Schweitzer and the mystics, was that that was the very faith which was his heritage from his earliest years, so that in it he had been led in a circle. What Hammarskjöld learned from Schweitzer, we remember, was that the Gospels can be read as the story of a man fully and truly human, an "adamant young man" who set out to live, without benefit of superhuman knowledge or aid, the role which life had assigned to him. This task, Jesus came to realize, was a risky venture, but he was not deterred, either by his ignorance or even by the threat of death on a cross, from fulfilling the "possibility" which he sensed for his life. In the words of that crucial 1951 roadmark, Jesus was "a young man, adamant in his commitment, who walks the road of possibility to the end without self-pity or demand for sympathy, fulfilling the destiny he had chosen . . ." (69). What Dag learned from the mystics was that in interiority there can be a 'self-surrender' which is the way to self-realization, an inner place in which one can be strengthened "to say 'yes' to every demand . . ." .[25]

These discoveries were no sooner made than Hammarskjöld found them put to a critical test. The *Markings* entries of 1953 begin to bear dates, so that it is possible to correlate them with events in Dag's public life. It is evident

[25] "Old Creeds in a New World," in Foote, *Servant of Peace*, p. 24.

from these entries that he was quick to realize the inner connection between his great Yes and the summons to service from the U.N. One of the entries from the period when he was leaving Sweden and taking up the new task reads: "To be free, to be able to stand up and leave *everything* behind—without looking back. To say *Yes*—" (91). And another, joyous one from about that time

To say Yes to life is at one and the same time to say Yes to oneself.

Yes—even to that element in one which is most unwilling to let itself be transformed from a temptation into a strength. (92)

The inner journey of this (ever-so-moral) 'prodigal son' had come full circle, and when he arrived at home, at duty, he found there acceptance, even acceptance of these wayward elements of his psyche, the loneliness, self-centeredness, and despair which had tried him so sorely.

We have seen that Dag interpreted his great reconciliation with himself, his Yes to life, upon the model of Jesus found within the Gospels. Central to that story is the place of the cross, and it was central, too, to Dag's self-understanding. Jesus' Yes to destiny entailed a Yes to a possible, even probable, crucifixion; must not Dag's Yes entail the same? It did, and we must seek to understand him here. Some critics have supposed that Hammarskjöld had a Messiah complex, that he thought he was a new Christ come to save the world. This reflects a serious misunderstanding of *Markings*, of Christianity, and of Jesus as Dag understood him.

Taking the last first, it is true that in one haiku late in his life, Dag speaks in traditional language of Jesus as "the victim who chose to be sacrificed" (190). But in many other places, he makes it plain that this was the humble acceptance of his fate, not a thirst for a martyr's death. He writes: "Would the Crucifixion have had any sublimity or meaning if Jesus had seen Himself crowned with the halo of martyrdom? What we have later added was not there for Him. And we must forget all about it if we are to hear His commands" (151). The only sense in which Jesus "goes to" the cross is that he does not rebel against his grim fate: "Nevertheless, not as I will, but as Thou wilt," quotes Dag (154).

Second, we must note that it is the regular teaching of Christianity that *every* disciple take up his cross. The age-long problem is to find disciples who will take the summons seriously, but it is the irony of *our* times that when one man did so, he was accused of psychic derangement! In any case, Dag took the summons to walk the way of the cross to apply to him; that is, he believed he was called to a hearty and unselfish fulfillment of duty to his neighbors in the world community, even though that meant being misunderstood (as he was), even though it meant much suffering (as it did), even though he should suffer tragic death in that service (as, in the event, he has done). But it did not mean that he regarded his case as peculiar or unique: meditating on Good Friday, 1956, Dag writes, "Jesus dies in someone who has followed the trail marks of the inner road to the end . . ." (126) ; and what are those trail marks? Not a martyr complex, but

> love and patience,
> > righteousness and humility,
> faith and courage,
> stillness.

It was then the choice of full commitment to his destiny, treated not arrogantly as *his* destiny but humbly as the destiny which God assigned to him, which Dag accepted when he saw submission to his lifework as submission to the cross. It would be the way of the cross only if it were purified of arrogance, only if to take up the cross meant not only self-affirmation, but also self-denial. And Dag had always known that that was the Way. That was the point of the 1950 marking in which, in language which suggests a close familiarity with the Gospels, he wrote: "O Caesarea

Philippi: to accept condemnation of the Way as its fulfillment, its definition, to accept this both when it is chosen and when it is realized" (36). In one of the most severe of paradoxes, then, only failure can ever be success.

How did it work out, this ethic of the cross, in the rough-and-tumble world of international negotiations, played on a field without an umpire, and with the stakes the lives of governments and the survival of humanity in the age of the Bomb? It is far beyond the scope of this chapter to assess the historic significance of the United Nations in the years of Hammarskjöld. He set out, on foundations laid by Trygve Lie, to develop the Organization into a service truly international, always responsive to the needs of all the member nations, never merely responsive to the wishes of any one, grounded upon the Charter, but active in such a way as to enlarge the precedents for international interest over the interest of private nations. The degree to which he succeeded, in the Peking mission, in the Suez and Arab-Israeli crises, in Lebanon, in Cambodia (there was a Cambodian crisis then, too!), in the Congo, in laying a groundwork for a future world peace under world law, is for history to decide.

What should be clear by now is that in the degree to which he did succeed, that success was intimately linked with an interiority, a discipline, a vision which was formed by the gospel of the cross, a vision which found in Jesus, and in the way of sacrifice, and in the mystical apprehension beyond the frontiers of the unheard-of, models for self-knowledge, images for action, which made *that* life possible.

Dag Hammarskjöld wrote on New Year's Day the sober "the night approaches now . . .".[26] It is not unusually melancholy to apply this grim line not only to modern *lives* which know, in the midst of affluence and success, the torture of existential despair, but also to a time like our own, in which the virtues of past ages seem to have vanished,

[26] Aulén, *Dag Hammarskjöld's White Book*, p. 58.

leaving only savagery, while a new age, if it struggles to be born, cannot guarantee us either live birth or length of days. In such a time, we may look at one life which, fully aware of the savagery without and the nameless terrors within modernity, can not only quote the solemn line, "the night approaches now," but can (with full knowledge of the times in which we live) write

> For all that has been—Thanks!
> To all that shall be—Yes! (89)

Chapter Three

The Religion of
Martin Luther King, Jr.

In the early months of 1960, Ralph Bunche, a high official in the United Nations Secretariat, brought a visitor to the New York office of the Secretary-General. The visitor was Bunche's friend Martin Luther King, Jr., a young Black upon whose shoulders was falling the heavy burden of leadership in the minority freedom struggle in America. What did these two, Hammarskjöld and King, talk about in their visit that day? We are not told by those who recorded the meeting, nor do we know with what clarity the two, so similar in spite of their vast dissimilarities, perceived their likeness. Yet it may be instructive to note patterns which link them together.

Each was born to a heritage of service; each found a unique way to transcend his heritage—Hammarskjöld through the United Nations, King through the freedom movement. Each, by that transcendence, was cast upon the stage of world history, with its pitiless glare of publicity and incessant demand for further achievement. Each was strengthened by a faith (and I would call it the same faith) ; and each was able, by means of that faith, to discover the point of his own life, the point of living and not dying. And each, in mid-career, while struggling to overcome man's violence against man, died a violent death.

In this chapter, we will attempt to uncover the central threads which give the fabric of Martin King's life its unique significance. In doing so, we will once again, as in the Hammarskjöld study, encounter pervasive patterns of meaning which others have laid upon King, and we must find our own way through these. Neglecting the view that his own native religious vision, the religion he had drunk in almost with his mother's milk, could possibly provide the organizing principle by which to understand his life, many interpreters have come up with a variety of alternative explanations of his life. By doing so, I believe they have given us flawed portraits of King, and have created a man with different goals, different standards, and therefore different achievements. I cannot here assess, incident by incident, the biographical consequences of this neglect of Martin King's faith. I do hope to call attention to that central faith, show what it was and how it worked, and suggest that it offers organizing principles for the understanding of his life clearer and more comprehensive than the political and racial motifs which have fascinated some.

The December, 1970, program of NBC television's documentary, "First Tuesday," told that Martin Luther King's funeral in Atlanta was thickly attended by agents of the FBI. With their customary resourcefulness, some agents were inside the church, relaying reports by walkie-talkie to others outside. Mrs. King, an agent inside the church reported, still expected the dream of her husband to be fulfilled. Back came the rather worried radio instruction from the command post outside: "Find out what that dream was."[1] From a different perspective, this is the question

[1] For a preview of this program, see the *New York Times*, December 1, 1970, p. 40.

with which we are concerned. What was the dream? I claim
that we will not understand his dream or his achievement
if we neglect the role of Martin King's religion, which happened to be the religion of a Black Baptist from the South.

I

Martin Luther King, Jr., was born in Atlanta, Georgia,
January 15, 1929, the second of three children of Martin
Luther King, Sr., pastor of Ebenezer Baptist Church, and
Alberta Williams King, daughter of the founding pastor of
that church.[2] It was a ministerial family. Martin, Jr., was
educated in the segregated public and private schools of
Atlanta, and entered Morehouse College, Atlanta, at the
precocious age of fifteen. During college, young Martin responded to the call and was ordained as assistant pastor
of Ebenezer Church. He attended Crozer Theological Seminary, completing his work at age twenty-two, and Boston
University, where he took a Ph.D. in philosophical theology
under Edgar S. Brightman and L. Harold DeWolf. Married
to Coretta Scott, he became pastor of the Dexter Avenue
Baptist Church in Montgomery, Alabama, in 1954. In
1959 he returned to the Ebenezer Baptist Church in Atlanta as associate pastor, an office he held until the time of his

[2] I have found the most useful single biographical source to be
David L. Lewis, *King, A Critical Biography* (New York: Praeger,
1970), which is furnished with a useful "selected bibliography" and
notes, and is based upon extensive interviews as well as written
sources. Equally substantial is William Robert Miller, *Martin Luther
King, Jr.: His Life, Martyrdom, and Meaning for the World* (New
York: Weybright and Talley, 1968). Also useful are Lawrence Reddick,
Crusader without Violence (New York: Harper, 1959), which takes
the King story through the Montgomery events; Lerone Bennett,
What Manner of Man (Chicago: Johnson Publishing Co., 3rd rev. ed.,
1969); and Coretta Scott King, *My Life with Martin Luther King,
Jr.* (New York: Holt, Rinehart, and Winston, 1969). Where these
are my sources, I will make no further citations except to acknowledge
direct quotation or indicate support on controverted issues. These
substantial books are so recent that they gather up the work reported
in periodicals so that few references to these are necessary, except
as noted below.

death. In 1955–57 he helped to organize and led as president the Montgomery Improvement Association, which conducted a successful boycott and legal battle against discrimination on Montgomery's public transit buses. In 1957 he helped to found and became president of the Southern Christian Leadership Conference, which subsequently conducted or aided in campaigns for racial justice and decency in Albany, Birmingham, St. Augustine, Selma, Chicago, Memphis, and other places. King traveled to Ghana in 1957, to India in 1959, and to Stockholm to receive the Nobel Peace Prize in 1964. In 1965, almost alone among Black civil rights leaders, he made public his opposition to the Vietnam war. He was the father of four children, wrote during his thirteen years of fame five books[3] as well as numerous articles, delivered several notable speeches before national audiences, and was regarded during his lifetime as the Black leader most admired as leader by other Blacks. He died of an assassin's bullet on April 4, 1968, in Memphis, Tennessee, and was buried in Atlanta, Georgia. This is, in outline, the set of facts among which we must find those which disclose the springs of King's character and conduct.

One interpretation of King, widely held though perhaps more often spoken than written, is that he was simply a failure. He was too stupid to see that he was causing the riots he deplored, or in a slightly more ingenious version of the 'failure' thesis, he became disillusioned about the

---

[3] *Stride Toward Freedom: The Montgomery Story* (New York: Harper, 1958) ; *Why We Can't Wait* (New York: Harper, 1964; Signet Books, 1964) ; *Strength to Love* (New York: Harper, 1963 [I will quote from the Pocket Book edition of 1964]) ; *Where Do We Go from Here: Chaos or Community?* (New York: Harper, 1967) ; and *The Trumpet of Conscience* (New York: Harper, 1968). King wrote also a large number of articles and occasional pieces, a useful list of which is to be found in Lewis's bibliography, mentioned above. There are also about 83,000 items in the King collection in the library of Boston University, and additional unpublished material in Atlanta.

possibilities of nonviolence, and turned away from reliance upon it to achieve his goals. Even so sensitive a historian and King interpreter as James Smylie seems to lend support to the latter view.[4] It is even widely believed that King abandoned nonviolence at the end. There is not, as far as I know, a scintilla of evidence for this claim. The truth is, as the most scholarly and careful King biographer, David L. Lewis, points out, that "Martin became even more opposed to violent social action after the July [1967] riots."[5] That is, in the months just prior to his death, the man who had for years staked his own life on nonviolence became even more opposed to the escalating violence around him. What is true is that King recognized that his commitment to nonviolence was not equally shared by the younger Black radicals.[6]

Perhaps the confusion on this point is heightened by misunderstanding of the term "nonviolent." As it was used by King and others in the fifties and sixties, it is to be distinguished from two other terms, "nonresistant" and "unviolent." The King James version of the Gospel according to Matthew, if taken literally, commands Christians to "resist not evil" (5:39). Literal obedience would be nonresistance, and that is a way which has been taken by a few Christians in every age, especially by the helpless. On the other hand, most of us are unviolent most of the time, whether we are cops or robbers, ghetto dwellers or suburban householders. In contrast to both of these, the nonviolent man is one who, either as a tactic or as a way of life, is profoundly committed to avoiding the maiming or destruction of his enemy, but who has an enemy, and who does not leave that enemy alone, either. Instead he goes to him, and by various means—conversation, marching, standing, even sitting down or lying down—confronts the enemy with

[4] James H. Smylie, "On Jesus, Pharaohs, and the Chosen People," *Interpretation,* January, 1970, p. 91.

[5] Lewis, *King, A Critical Biography,* p. 365.

[6] *Ibid.*

himself as a person, forcing the other to deal with an actual human reality here and now.[7]

Obviously this is risky business, requiring training as well as dedication. It is perhaps remarkable enough that King made the method work so well so long for so many Black —and White—Americans. That he could not overnight enlist troops from Northern ghettos for his nonviolent army may say even more about the condition of those ghettos than it does about King's method. (Maybe, too, Northern racism was and is too slippery to yield promptly to a straightforward moral challenge such as nonviolent direct action.)

A more profound statement of the failure thesis makes King's story essentially tragedy.[8] David L. Lewis, in *King, A Critical Biography,* treats King as a gifted orator and populist politician, who (besides having the misfortune of being a Baptist preacher) was handicapped by lack of skill in organization and by ignorance of the political realities. King didn't understand that you couldn't trust those Southern 'rednecks,' and so he made peace with them too quickly and too trustingly. He didn't understand big city power politics, and so he was hopelessly outmaneuvered by Mayor Daley in Chicago. On this theory, the real meaning of the Vietnam war opposition, of King's sojourn in Chicago, and of the projected Poor People's Campaign of 1968, was that these represented progressive steps in the politicization of Martin Luther King. The luckless preacher was

[7] The classic presentation of the nonviolence theory by which King was influenced is Richard Bartlett Gregg, *The Power of Nonviolence* (New York: Fellowship of Reconciliation Publication, 1959; 1st ed., 1935). For a bibliography of nonviolence see William R. Miller, *Bibliography of Books on War, Pacifism, Non-Violence and Related Studies* (Nyack, N.Y.: Fellowship Publications, 1965).

[8] The "failure" thesis is worked out at book length in a Howard University dissertation by Hanes Walton, now published as *The Political Philosophy of Martin Luther King, Jr.* (Westport, Conn.: Greenwood Publishing Co., 1971). The following discussion of Lewis, Miller, and Williams represents further reflection upon views I express in "M. L. King, Politician or American Church Father?" in *Journal of Ecumenical Studies,* Winter, 1970.

about to be converted into a great politician when he was tragically gunned down in the Lorraine Motel in Memphis.

Now there is enough fact, and enough good judgment, in Lewis's interpretation to justify careful reading of his book. However, alongside it needs to be set a rather different interpretation of King's life: William R. Miller's biography, *Martin Luther King, Jr., His Life, Martyrdom, and Meaning for the World.* While Lewis's King is judged from the vantage point of SNCC militancy, Miller has the vantage of a man himself committed to Christian nonviolence. He sees King's 'weakness' in negotiations with the power structure as reflecting two facts: the fact that King was always looking for a reconciliation after the battle, in which the two races might live together in brotherhood; and the fact that though he was involved in local struggles in Birmingham, St. Augustine, or Selma, King's eye was always on the national political battle, on the legislation before the Congress, on the attitudes of the current occupant of the White House and of the nation at large.

However the relative failure or success of Martin King as political leader may be adjudged by further historical inquiry (and the evidence is not all in), one element of the success/failure theme is perhaps now incontrovertible— Martin Luther King was a crucial factor in the awakening toward freedom of Black America, because he gave his people *hope.* By providing a new idea, says Lerone Bennett, and by raising the level of expectation in Blacks, King produced "a deep groundswell of anticipation" during the late fifties. Thus filled with hope, men acted, whether in King's own way or in other ways, to end the long night of repression.[9]

This suggests another category of interpretation—that King is to be understood essentially as a race leader, another in the long series of notable sons of Africa who have led their people on the tortuous road out of slavery into their

[9] Bennett, *What Manner of Man,* p. 90.

birthright. David Lewis remarks that in his struggle for dignity the American Black leader has embraced one of four contradistinctive ideologies: the armed militancy of Denmark Vesey and Nat Turner; the Black nationalism of Martin Delany and Marcus Garvey; the accommodationism and economic boot-strapping of Booker T. Washington; or the psychological and intellectual competitive program of Frederick Douglass and W. E. B. DuBois. It was the genius of King, says Lewis, to combine three of these four ideologies, "militance, meekness, and merit," in a new creative syncretism.[10] Significantly, the one element King found no place for was "migration"—the separatist ideology of the Black nationalists. The one thing nonviolence cannot do is ignore the adversary; it cannot just leave him alone.

A somewhat less flattering form of the racial interpretation is provided by C. Eric Lincoln. On this view, "the enduring significance of Martin Luther King has far less to do with the life of an individual than with the times and the circumstances against which that life was played out." [11] Eric Lincoln's King was a symbol—and as such a reproach to (mostly White) America.

The most sensational of the race-leader accounts of King is John A. Williams' *King God Didn't Save*.[12] It is noteworthy for having accused J. Edgar Hoover's FBI, with the Catholic hierarchy, the "Jewish establishment," and other elements of the White power structure, of conspiring to destroy King. The FBI's tactic, Williams implies, was to use tape recordings, wiretaps, and 'bugs,' which if played for the appropriate listeners would discredit King and his staff. Williams, however, outdoes even the FBI. He publishes alleged interviews with anonymous persons which imply (no direct statements, no lawsuits) that King

[10] Lewis, *King, A Critical Biography*, pp. 86-88.

[11] C. Eric Lincoln, ed., *Martin Luther King, Jr., A Profile* (New York: Hill & Wang, 1970), p. vii.

[12] John A. Williams, *The King God Didn't Save, Reflections on the Life and Death of Martin Luther King, Jr.* (New York: Coward-McCann, 1970).

was personally as busy integrating the bedroom as he was the lunch counter.

What are we to make of this curious charge? We may do well to remember what Booth Tarkington said: "There are two things that will be believed of any man whatsoever, and one of them is that he has taken to drink." As far as evidence that would convince a judge or a historian is concerned, we had better say what the careful historian David Lewis says: these are only rumors.[13] However, there is another side to the matter. Williams clearly regards King's destruction as a tragedy for Blacks. Not so King's alleged sexual prodigality; one feels that the Black Williams admires rather than deplores this alleged virtuosity in his hero. Have we not here the making of a mythical figure? For it is a part of the power of mythic heroes to be sexually omnicompetent. And lest the reader merely smile at the myth-making propensities of *other* twentieth-century Americans, let him ask himself how ready he was to believe this tale in the absence of any real evidence. Is it not strangely important to Americans, Black and White, to make of the Black a figure of mythic sexual potency?

On the wider theme of Black racial leadership let me merely make two reflective notes. The first is this, that nothing said in this chapter should detract from Martin Luther King's role as the hero, the champion, the *nigrator* of Blackness in America. And the second is that that role cannot, for all its glory, be the whole story, for reasons I have now to make more plain. The trick will be to bring out the second without detracting from, without *de*nigrating, the first.

II

Perhaps the most satisfactory exploration of King's religion would take us, in the psycho-biographical fashion of

---

[13] Lewis, *King, A Critical Biography*, p. 258. But see further *The New York Times*, May 21, 1973, p. 25.

Erik Erikson, to explore King's boyhood, his upbringing in which church and home were virtually indistinguishable, his calling to the ministry and his decision for graduate studies in theology, his choice of the Black Baptist church in the South and his enduring commitment to that church after fame had opened other options. I cannot explore these matters here, but I will point to three episodes in King's working career which are certainly cruxes for the interpretation of his action. Fortunately, these were episodes on the stage of history, so that published records are available, including King's own records and some of his later reflections. Consider, first, *the Montgomery bus struggle of 1955–1957*. It has been well pointed out that the Montgomery movement marked a significant advance upon the classic American social gospel—an advance from mostly words to mostly deeds. Although the social gospel churches had sometimes become centers of social amelioration, providing counseling, fellowship, clothing, and work for the down-and-out, their direct attack upon oppressive institutions had been made by way of pulpit and press. By shifting from preacher's talk to nonviolent mass action, King's group introduced a new dimension into American social Christianity.

It has been less widely noted that the focus of the Montgomery movement and of subsequent King campaigns was the mass meeting, a meeting with all the trappings of a revival meeting: hortatory preaching, clapping and amens, singing (wonderful singing!), and earnest prayer. All this is faithfully reflected in King's history of the Montgomery campaign, *Stride Toward Freedom*. The leaders of the movement were for the most part clergymen, many of them Black Baptists like King and his neighboring pastor, Ralph Abernathy. The protesters were mostly Baptists or Methodists—if not enrolled members, at least familiar with the ways of a church meeting. Of course other models for the mass meetings of the Montgomery movement might have been found; the labor movement comes to mind. But that model was regrettably not familiar to Southern Blacks, while church was.

Social historians have noted that the church was the Afro-American's earliest institution, perhaps earlier than the gospel it embraced. And the Montgomery movement (and after it, the whole freedom movement King led) had this Black Southern church meeting, this revivalist, Spirit-filled, praying, singing church meeting at its very center.

Prayer was not only the public utterance, it was also the private cry of many a heart, including notably King's own. *Stride Toward Freedom* makes evident the crucial role of personal prayer in King's leadership and action in Montgomery. At the time of Rosa Parks's arrest, a mass protest meeting having been called, on whose outcome, it was realized, everything hinged, King was faced with the necessity to prepare, in twenty minutes, the opening speech, "the most decisive speech of my life." [14] Then Martin prayed. Driven to distraction by the telephoned threats of vicious Whites, he prayed. Gripped by a strong sense of guilt for having provoked the very violence which he and his fellows had suffered, he stood before the people and prayed.[15] Without ceasing to work, without diminishing his realism, in season and out, King prayed. These were no bits of window-dressing designed to placate pious followers. They were private or spontaneous cries of his soul, strong inward wrestlings in which the man of flesh knelt in weakness before the God of all flesh, and rose again in strength; they were the inner dialogues of a man whose last resource was not himself but God.

For a second crucial period, consider *1963, the year of the Birmingham campaign and the March on Washington.* Perhaps it was these events in which King's self-understanding came to clearest expression. During the Birmingham struggle came the jailing of King and his trusted partner Ralph Abernathy, and the writing of the Letter from Bir-

[14] *Stride Toward Freedom,* p. 45.
[15] *Ibid.,* pp. 114, 155.

mingham Jail, begun on newspaper margins and bits of toilet paper. In the letter, King recited the evils which had led to the campaign, and explained the tactics of nonviolent direct action, using Gandhian terminology. Even before that, however, he set out the prophetic-apostolic motivation of his work. Why was King, an 'outsider,' in Birmingham? He was there, like the prophet Amos preaching in Bethel, "because injustice is here." As Paul had been compelled before him, "so am I compelled to carry the gospel of freedom beyond my own home town." [16] Like John Calvin, King used the story of Shadrach, Meshach, and Abednego to justify civil disobedience against a wicked government.[17] He closed with lines which have few equals in the Christian church:

> Never before have I written so long a letter. I'm afraid it is much too long to take your precious time. I can assure you that it would have been much shorter if I had been writing from a comfortable desk, but what else can one do when he is alone in a narrow jail cell, other than write long letters, think long thoughts and pray long prayers?
>
> If I have said anything in this letter that overstates the truth and indicates an unreasonable impatience, I beg you to forgive me. If I have said anything that understates the truth and indicates my having a patience that allows me to settle for anything less than brotherhood, I beg God to forgive me.[18]

That same year, on the steps of the Lincoln Memorial in Washington, came the "I have a dream" speech. In spite of the difficulties, he told the audience,

> I still have a dream. . . . I have a dream that one day this nation will rise up, live out the true meaning of its creed: We hold these truths to be self-evident, that all men are created equal.

[16] *Why We Can't Wait*, p. 77.

[17] *Ibid.*, p. 84. The tradition of civil disobedience is strong in the Calvinism which was King's Baptist theological heritage. See Calvin's Commentary on Daniel. I do not know, however, whether King was conscious of the Calvinist and medieval roots of the argument he used here.

[18] *Why We Can't Wait*, pp. 94-95.

I have a dream that one day on the red hills of Georgia the sons of former slaves and the sons of former slaveowners will be able to sit down together at the table of brotherhood. I have a dream that one day even the state of Mississippi, a state sweltering with the heat of oppression, will be transformed into an oasis of freedom and justice.

I have a dream that my four little children one day will live in a nation where they will not be judged by the color of their skin, but by the content of their character.

I have a dream . . .[19]

Thus King moved on into his peroration, drawing upon the language of the prophet Isaiah, upon the national imagery of freedom ringing from every hill, and at the end upon the lines of the old Negro spiritual—"free at last." It would require a high order of cynicism to suppose that the man who so eloquently spoke and so profoundly moved his hearers was not speaking from the deep wells of his own being, was not then truly declaring his own dream, his own faith.

The third episode comes at the very end of his days, a time when reaction to his antiwar stand, factional strife among Black leaders, and White reaction to further racial progress North or South had cast its shadow over his life. In late March, 1968, he was in Memphis to give aid to a city-wide strike of Black garbage workers. Violence, that old enemy, gnawed at the heels of the movement. Out of the discouragement of the hour King evoked another testament of his own vision: "I've been to the mountaintop." In his speech, he was for the moment another Moses, who had seen from the mountaintop the promised land his people would reach, though he himself might not be permitted to enter.[20] A few hours later, April 4, 1968, his public ministry was ended by a gun fired by an assassin, perhaps hired, but in any case White.

[19] Cited in Coretta Scott King, *My Life with Martin Luther King, Jr.*, p. 239.

[20] Miller, *Martin Luther King, Jr.*, pp. 287-88.

77

These three episodes may be enough to suggest that for the man himself his religion was more than peripheral, more than a politician's tool, more than a reformer's stratagem. Yet to see how this was so, we must go beyond experience to interpretation, and especially to King's own interpretation of the history in which he was involved.

Herbert Richardson has pointed out that King's insight into the structure of evil made it possible for him to oppose the Vietnamese war and domestic oppression as manifestations of a system, not merely as the wickedness of wicked individuals or groups. But that is to say that King's was a theological interpretation.[21] Simplistically, there are in the world good men (and nations) and also evil ones. The good men must destroy the others or be destroyed. King's view, however, was more complex. It was concerned not only with relatively good and relatively evil men and groups, but also with structures of evil which hold all men in their grip. Here appears what Richardson calls the asymmetrical character of King's struggle against evil: there must be a retaliation against hate, not with more hate, but with love. In this view it was a profound theoretic, rather than cowardice or expediency, which led Martin King to call out to the angry Black crowd which gathered, muttering, before the steps of his bombed-out Montgomery home:

If you have weapons take them home; if you do not have them, please do not seek to get them. We cannot solve this problem through retaliatory violence. We must meet violence with nonviolence. . . . Jesus still cries out . . . "Love your enemies; bless them that curse you; pray for them that despitefully use you." This is what we must live by.

And they were voices as old as the Black church, perhaps as old as Blackness itself, which cried out from the passionate crowd in the night, "Amen." "We are with you all the way, Reverend." [22]

[21] Herbert Warren Richardson, "Martin Luther King—Unsung Theologian," Commonweal, May 3, 1968, pp. 201-3.
[22] Stride Toward Freedom, p. 117-18.

Moreover, this theoretic was grounded in the gospel of Christ. Writing about those days, King said: "It was the Sermon on the Mount, rather than a doctrine of passive resistance, that initially inspired the Negroes of Montgomery to dignified social action. It was Jesus of Nazareth that stirred the Negroes with the creative weapon of love." [23] King then goes on to pay tribute to the distinctive shaping of that love weapon by Gandhi. And we must pay ours to the reinterpretation provided by King himself. If we compare King with his American predecessors Rauschenbusch and Niebuhr, we may say that while Rauschenbusch regarded *agape* love as good will, to be expressed by the organized kindness of social amelioration,[24] and Reinhold Niebuhr saw it as powerless goodness which could be directly expressed only by nonresistance to evil, thus as an "impossible" ideal,[25] King saw *agape* love as aggressive nonviolent direct action, a powerful *force* reaching out toward the alienated enemy.

To King, it was at the heart of the gospel to recognize that such love could really change a particular human situation of enmity into something quite different. No doubt this faith made him appear softheaded to some among his fellow civil rights workers, as it does to some present-day biographers. It was not, however, a lack of appreciation of the persistence and power of evil that gave King his special point of view. It was rather his evangelist's faith that even the most hardened sinner runs the risk of being converted, and that, powerful as evil is, reconciling, aggressive *agape* love is more powerful still. Martin really believed those 'redneck' Southern sheriffs and politicians were human beings, sheep who had strayed from the fold,

[23] *Ibid.*, p. 66.
[24] For the views of Walter Rauschenbusch, see Robert Handy, ed., *The Social Gospel in America* (New York: Oxford University Press, 1966).
[25] See chapter 1, pp. 23-27. King, in an article which he turned into a chapter of *Stride Toward Freedom*, describes his relation to Rauschenbusch, Niebuhr, and Gandhi.

men who could be redeemed by love. It is not a faith to be corrected by those of us who have had less experience of the matter than had he. "Remember him," says Coretta Scott King, "as a man who refused to lose faith in the ultimate redemption of mankind." [26]

III

Whether we judge all that to be profound or foolish (and our saints have always looked both foolish and profound to the rest of us), where did Martin Luther King get such a faith? Where but from the church at whose breast he was suckled, from the Black church in the South? "Three things," says W. E. B. DuBois, "characterized [the] religion of the slave—the Preacher, the Music, and the Frenzy." [27] DuBois, writing seventy-five years ago, noted the survival of all three of these in the Black church of his own day: the preacher surviving as a combination of medicine man and idealist, "the most unique personality developed by the Negro on American soil";[28] the music yielding up supremely the spiritual, its roots in Africa, its heartthrob preserving the sorrow of a race enslaved but not destroyed, a people with a hope;[29] the frenzy as old as religion, "the weeping and laughing, the vision and the trance." [30]

And what did, what does it mean, this Black religion so expressed? Two suggestions have gained much assent: the

[26] Preface to *The Trumpet of Conscience*, p. xii.

[27] William E. B. DuBois, *The Souls of Black Folk* (first published 1903), republished in *Three Negro Classics* (New York: Avon Books, 1965), p. 338.

[28] *Ibid*. DuBois's view should be balanced with the equally lyrical Preface to James Weldon Johnson, *God's Trombones* (New York: Viking Press, 1927), and by the sober account in E. Franklin Frazier, *The Negro Church in America* (New York: Schocken Books, 1964), *passim*.

[29] DuBois, *The Souls of Black Folk*, pp. 377-87.

[30] *Ibid.*, p. 339.

religion was a code; the religion was an escape.[31] It was a code: when Blacks sang "Steal away to Jesus," it was not inner raptures but a furtive trip on the underground railroad of which they·secretly sang. It was no accident, in this view, that Nat Turner was a Baptist preacher. The meaning became overt in another song:

> O freedom, O freedom, O freedom over me!
> Before I'll be a slave
> I'll be buried in my grave,
> And go home to my Lord
> And be free.[32]

Martin King was to quote *that* song in his day to good effect.

Or the religion was an escape. If freedom and justice, rest and peace and joy, are denied in this world, never mind, they will be available in the next. Benjamin Mays, in two surveys of Negro religion published in the thirties, worried because Negro religion seemed all too escapist. He pointed to "compensatory" views of God, which seemed to him to say, never mind, don't struggle, it will all be better by and by.[33] James Cone, in *Black Theology and Black Power*, speaks in harshly condemnatory tones of this escapist motif in Negro religion. Is not such religion indeed an

[31] See especially LeRoy Moore, Jr., "The Spiritual: Soul of Black Religion," *American Quarterly*, December, 1971. A similar view was subsequently expressed by James H. Cone. See "Black Spirituals: A Theological Interpretation," *Theology Today*, April, 1972; and *The Spirituals and the Blues* (New York: The Seabury Press, 1972). For the escapist view, see especially Benjamin E. Mays, *The Negro's God as Reflected in His Literature*, first published 1938 (New York: Russell & Russell, 1968). For the 'code' view, see especially Vincent Harding, "Religion and Resistance Among Antebellum Negroes," in August Meier and Elliott Rudwick, eds., *The Making of Black America* (New York: Atheneum, 1969), pp. 179-97.

[32] Cited in DuBois, *The Souls of Black Folk*, p. 345.

[33] Benjamin Elijah Mays and Joseph William Nicholson, *The Negro's Church* (New York: Institute of Social and Religious Research, 1933), pp. 245-46.

opiate of the people? [34] At least the evidence seems clear that, deplorable or not, Black religion in America has sometimes taken this compensatory form.

However, one need not deny the escapist element or the secret code element in Black religion in order to detect the presence of still another element. My friend LeRoy Moore, in an examination of the Black spiritual, calls attention to this third element.

> As I see it the spiritual always has to do with freedom, with salvation and with escape. There is an escape, a freedom and a salvation which is neither other-worldly nor necessarily concretely realized in any immediate situation in this world, though its devotees may desire both and deny neither. I refer to a mystical escape, a mystical flight, not away somewhere but into the self, into the soul, to God in the soul. This is the religious experience which produced and is expressed in the spirituals. "My Soul's Been Anchored in de Lord." [35]

If the term "mystical" distracts anyone, we might rephrase the interpretation in this way. In his spirituals, the Black man did not merely cry out and conspire for justice, though he did that; he did not merely invoke another realm where justice *shall* prevail, though he did that, too. Rather, the Black man discovered that God was with him and he with God already, discovered God in himself and thereby his own humanity. It has been suggested that the dignity of man is an essential of Black religion.[36] This is profoundly true, not because such a doctrine is uniformly preached from the Negro pulpit (though it is preached), but because *a religious experience,* engraved in spiritual and sermon and frenzy alike, *lies at the heart of that religion, and that experience is* an experience *of God and self at one.* From this unity, all further unities can spring.

Benjamin Mays pointed out in the study just mentioned

---

[34] James Cone, *Black Theology and Black Power* (New York: The Seabury Press, 1969).

[35] Moore, "The Spiritual: Soul of Black Religion," p. 673.

[36] Cf. Cone, *Black Theology and Black Power,* chapter 2.

the surprisingly low level of racial prejudice in Negro pulpits and pews.[37] Whites were welcome to attend those churches and even to speak, although the same courtesy was not reciprocally extended by Whites to Blacks. Black sermons proclaimed the unity of mankind and the significant place of Blacks in that unity.[38] Such an ethic can be understood as the natural product of the religion which was at the center of Black experience in America. Perhaps the kind of church into which Martin King, Jr., was baptized was the only institution in America at that time which was free enough of race prejudice to enable him to become the man he did become.

If with due caution, and on the basis of the evidence submitted, we tentatively say that his Black religion is the clue to this life, we are presented with a problem. How, in this case, are we to account for the tremendous activism, the pragmatic drive, the special dynamism of King and of the movement he led? For may not God-and-soul mysticism lead only to quietist resignation of this world? What is it that gives Black religion marching power? To answer, let us note with James Smylie two "basic insights" into King and his life:

The first is that the biblical theme of exodus out of bondage has been an important influence upon the Negro's interpretation of his experience in America, while Moses has been a primary paradigm for black leadership. Secondly, if King is to be considered in the proper perspective, he must be treated within the context of the biblical witness, as an interpreter of the Bible and a Christian humanist.[39]

I think I should want to turn the second proposal around, with apologies to Professor Smylie, and say that King interpreted *the present situation* and his own role in it by means

[37] *The Negro's Church*, pp. 388-89.
[38] *Ibid.*, chapter 4.
[39] Smylie, "On Jesus, Pharaohs, and the Chosen People," p. 74. I heard a similar insight expressed by Vincent Harding in his address to the AAR meeting in October, 1971, in Atlanta.

of the Bible. King did this without arrogance or presumption; yet he enabled his followers to see that the lesson of the Old Testament, the lesson that God was doing things in history, was true of the Black man in America now. In the words of a junior high school Black student writing after Memphis, "He was our Moses. . . ." [40]

What this shows us is that we must press behind the New Testament to the Old in order to understand the religion of Martin King. King's use of the image of oppressive Pharaohs, Hebrews longing for freedom from Egypt, the threatening wilderness, and the Promised Land in his writing did not generally take the form of extended analogies between the Bible story and the American story (though in one published sermon it did [41]). Often it took the form of incisive *metaphors*. As 2,000 marchers gathered for the symbolic journey from Selma to Montgomery in 1965, King addressed them outside Brown Chapel A.M.E. Church: "Walk together, children; don't you get weary, and it will lead up to the Promised Land. And Alabama will be a new Alabama, and America will be a new America." [42] However, when God's people try to get free, King knew, Pharaohs always act the same way. The "Pharaohs of the South" would seem to yield to pressure, but at the end they would risk drowning their own armies rather than let God's people go free. "When the pressure is increased, pharaohs will say, 'Wait.' Then pharaohs will say, 'Go slower.' What the pharaohs mean . . . is 'Never.' Pharaohs may try tokenism, but this is only a way to end pressure, not to begin the process of liberation." [43] And at the end of King's own journey, again there appears the metaphor of Moses: "I've been on the mountaintop. . . . He's allowed

[40] Smylie, "On Jesus, Pharaohs, and the Chosen People," p. 74.
[41] Martin Luther King, Jr., "The Death of Evil upon the Seashore," *Strength to Love*, Sermon 8.
[42] Cited in Lewis, *King, A Critical Biography*, p. 287.
[43] Smylie, "On Jesus, Pharaohs, and the Chosen People," pp. 82-83.

me to go up to the mountain. And I've looked over, and I've seen the promised land." [44]

Nor was it only the exodus. Old Testament and New alike provided Martin with a rich panoply of images, some expressed, others hovering in the background of his thought, guiding, shaping the faith by which he walked. My present point is that it was especially in the Old Testament that he found two elements of his faith, man's own role and the role of the God of history, held together in productive tension. Had he emphasized only the humanistic ethic of freedom, King might have been one more Black militant determined to wring today's revenge from yesterday's injustices. Had he spoken only of God's purpose to redeem, he might have fallen prey to the compensatory religion against which Benjamin Mays had warned. But to this Baptist it was both: man who must act, and God who is acting. Man on his own loses his way, grows weary, discouraged, while passive dependence on God alone is disobedience to God. Either half of the paradox of God-with-man taken alone produces falsehood, but taken together they produce the true vision of the purpose of God and the significance of man's history.[45]

Does this not remind us of the spiritual's message of God and the soul together, of the essential Black religious experience, perhaps of the essential Christian experience? And does that in turn not support the thesis that the clue to Martin King's biography is to be found in the Black religion of the Southern church, that in that religion is to be found the key to the greatness we perceive in him?

What was the dream, whose content we were set to learn? It was a dream welling up from the secret springs of strength of the Black man in America, a secret perhaps best evoked from Martin's soul by the songs of his boyhood— "Precious Lord, take my hand," "Softly and tenderly Jesus

[44] King, cited in Miller, *Martin Luther King, Jr.*, pp. 287-88.
[45] Cf. *Strength to Love*, p. 152.

85

is calling," "There is a balm in Gilead." [46] It was a dream which overflowed into a mighty flood of concern for America and beyond America, for all to gain the strength to love. It was a dream which remembered old stories, told long ago, of a God who did not desert his people on this earthly journey, but who went before them night and day. It was a dream whose interpretation required a voice to cry out, and weary feet to march, and many a soul to pray. The dreamer is done, but the interpretation is not ended until we are also free.

[46] These hymns with others were King's favorites, chosen for his funeral services. See Coretta Scott King, *My Life with Martin Luther King, Jr.*, pp. 330, 350-51.

Chapter Four

Biography as Theology

I notice sometimes a certain reaction when I tell strangers that I do theology. I say my field is theology, and then there is a rather strained silence. Do I see behind the filmy eyes which confront me a bit of concealed merriment which says, "Ah, your interior is showing, and it is quite empty, old boy, quite empty"? Or do I see instead restrained boredom, which, were it not rude, would be expressed with a yawn, but which comes out as "How interesting" (to conceal the truth, say the opposite)? Alas, I never find out, for in the cases where the one behind those filmy eyes becomes my friend, he has in the process gotten to know me, and his notion of what I do is therefore irreversibly tainted with my own impressions of it. And in the other cases, we merely drift on, from the boredom of theology to the fogginess of San Francisco or other sorrows, and there is no light at all, not even the incandescence of disagreement. I suspect, however, that the thought behind those eyes is that theology is the most delusive of disciplines, causing men to believe that they are learning, understanding, even knowing something or other, when in fact they are being provided with a sop for their prejudices, a megaphone for subjectivity, a screen behind which intellectual fraud is committed. When, though the truth is not on their side, men want nevertheless to believe, they retreat to theology.

Now this scurrilous description is not, alas, all wrong or always wrong. Augustine would teach us, if Freud did not, how many and how "scientific" are the devices by which we protect ourselves from unwelcome reality. Surely theology may be such a device—such a vice. However, my own experience with theology has been so different from this caricature that I must report it to you in whose eyes I see no film, but a glint of curiosity, perhaps of hopeful puzzlement.

I came to theology because I wanted serious, theoretically engaged answers to life's most serious problems. I thought I knew some satisfying answers, but I wanted better ones, better grounded ones. The sciences (I had been in physics) did not seem to me to be engaged with the questions I cared about, questions I would have expressed as "Where have we come from? Why are we here? Where are we going?" Philosophy in my brief exposure did not seem adequately engaged with them, either. To theology, then, I came. Now perhaps luckily for me, my theological education was a very slow one. My seminary teachers, it now seems to me, did not teach very much theology (there were exceptions). So the greater part of my theological education was on-the-job training, gained as I set out to care for a church, and later as I taught my students.

My education was thus slow, but it was intense. The chief theological systems of modernity, i.e., of the last two hundred years, came to me as discoveries, as live options, proposals to answer the questions confronting my own existence. So, too, did the chief difficulties in theology, from the Enlightenment to the present, enter me as living difficulties. From the cheerful, winsome skepticism of David Hume, from the psychological antitheism of Ludwig Feuerbach and Sigmund Freud, from the loyal disloyalty of the alienated theologians of today, I have been a learner; I have felt their difficulties with religious belief as my own. Indeed, it would be accurate to say that I devoted more attention to the critics of faith than to its advocates, though I learned from these as well. In sum, my theological education was and is slow, and it has been an education which consisted in large part of confronting difficulties which I saw as my own.

Thus my secret, or perhaps unconcealed, amazement when men reveal that they think of theology as essentially a tranquilizer of the urge to know the truth, or a cold-storage locker for preserving dogmas. For me theology has been more often a trial by ordeal, the very arena of conscientiousness. Given that personal history, one may ask why I did not abandon the discouragement of theological inquiry for some sunnier task. To which the best answer is the plain one that it still seems to me that there is no more important inquiry than the one which sets out to answer those whence and why and whither questions (or slightly updated versions of them), and my slow theological upbringing had the further effect of giving me time to discover that philosophers, for example, had no better answers to those questions than did their theological counterparts. In a word, some problems *are* hard problems, and turning away from them if they are my problems is neither easy nor a solution.

The point of this book is to show one way in which theologians may do better work. That way is through a certain attention to compelling biographies. Now let us consider the suggestion that a key to these biographies is the dominant or controlling *images* which may be found in the lives of which they speak. Dag Hammarskjöld and Martin Luther King, Jr., it can be shown, were each possessed of certain characteristic images—for Hammarskjöld, servant,

Brother, the "One," the unheard-of; for King, the Egyptian bondage of segregation, the Pharaohs, the promised land; for both, the cross—by which each understood himself, faced the critical situations in his life, and chiseled out his own destiny. I take it that the convergence of such images in a particular person helps to form his characteristic vision or outlook. (Moreover, I believe that *the living out of life under the governance of such a vision* is the best way to conceive of "religious experience" insofar as the latter can be a datum for theology, but I do not intend here to press home this further claim.)

Before I attempt to enlarge and illustrate this claim, let me acknowledge that my own position on the theological map is of some relevance, for the reason that there is a bias in theological work, a subjective factor, though it is not the only factor. I have referred to my doubts. What of my doubting faith? How should you locate me? As an alienated, left-wing Southern Baptist? That is accurate, however comical it also is. As one who must speak a loving, gentle "no" to 'belief' *and* 'unbelief,' that is, to Catholicism and to secular atheism alike? That too is accurate, and not comical, but it is still negative. Say then that I am an *ecstatic Protestant.* "Protestant"—that pays tribute to Calvin, and Edwards, and Schleiermacher, and Barth. "Protestant" also says to challenge all pat solutions, all proximate loyalties, as idolatrous. "Ecstatic"—that affirms my continuity with experience-saturated believers: with Puritans so little known, with revivalists and pietists, with Pentecostalists and communal celebrants of many sorts. And *that* says (as the word "Protestant" alone does not) to appreciate the rich psychic depths available to men of biblical faith, their title to the full diapason of human feelings, wants, hopes, fears, fantasies, imaginings, longings, visions. (To appreciate does not, of course, mean to accept at face value—appreciation means evaluation, too.)

This stance entails the uncritical acceptance of no doctrines—not even those of ecstatic Protestantism, whatever

they are—nor does it exclude responsibility to those outside that camp. It is noteworthy that one of our two exemplars so far considered, King, stands within the tradition
I have just described, as a Black Baptist, while the other,
Hammarskjöld, a Swedish Lutheran, apparently stands outside it; yet both provide me with important data. Moreover,
theology is done not only from a perspective but to and for
a community, and the community which I want to address
is that which stands in the biblical line; that is, I take myself especially to be addressing those in whatever sect or
clan who have inherited the Bible as focal for tradition or
for life. Quite possibly this includes Jews and Muslims, as
well as Christians; certainly it means biblical doubters as
well as biblical believers.

But what can it mean to share the Bible as "focal" for
our understanding? May it not mean at least this (and now
I offer a theological proposal) : hearing the central deliverance of biblical religion, seeing the central vision of its
theology (theologies) as *God and man in meeting.* In the
opening narratives of Genesis, God confronts *Adam* (i.e.,
Everyman) ; in the closing vision of the Apocalypse, the
seer points his readers away from himself: "I am but a
fellow-servant. . . . It is God you must worship" (Rev. 22:9
NEB) ; and in the pages thus enclosed, prophet, priest, and
Son of Man share in, and summon their hearers to, this
meeting with the Holy One of Israel. (Even the exceptions
[Esther? Ruth?] can be understood only in terms of that
central concern from which they depart.) So it is with
the religion which springs from the Bible down the years.
The meeting between God and man may be sharpened into
transcendence and judgment, or it may be softened into
mutual interpenetration and indwelling; *God* may be
broadened into a world-soul or sublimated into the Holy
Nothingness of Jacob Boehme or abstracted into the *alter
ego* of Ludwig Feuerbach; *man* may be narrowed into the
solitary individual of Sören Kierkegaard, or he may be
broadened into the solidary human race of Jonathan Ed-

wards and Horace Bushnell; but, let these terms be adjusted as we may, the central theological canon remains a recognizable one: it is that we have business with the Eternal; he has made us for himself and all our alienation is estrangement from him; our chief end, the true glory of life, is to enjoy him forever.

The central affirmation, of course, comes down into others—affirmations which explore the nature of God, man's own nature, the modes of our intercourse with him and with one another, the nature of religion, etc., and I will soon say something of some of these. For my own business as theologian is to show how a theology on the basis of experience, and here as illustration the image-governed experience of King and Hammarskjöld, may shed light on the central affirmation, establish it more firmly against the twin threats of superstition and vacuity, and relate it more clearly to the pluralist present world in which together we live.

I

First, let us see what light the method may shed upon the question, *What is religion itself?* This is a subsidiary question, and we should not expect too great things to come of the correct answer. One of the curiosities of religious thought in the last two centuries has been that so much has been made to ride upon the answer to this question. Thus Schleiermacher in the *Speeches* addresses "despisers" of religion on the assumption that if they but knew what religion is, they would not despise it.[1] Sigmund Freud in a series of essays and monographs sets out a characterization of religion in the apparent belief that its delusive grip can be broken, if at all, only by analytic understanding of

[1] Friedrich Schleiermacher, *On Religion, Speeches to Its Cultured Despisers,* trans. John Oman (New York: Harper, 1968 [1st German ed., 1799]) , see pp. 17-18.

religion, or more exactly, of religious "illusions," [2] and one can distinguish liberal from neo-orthodox twentieth-century theologians by ascertaining whether they like the word "religion" or dislike it;[3] while for a contemporary theologian like Gerhard Ebeling, the nature of faith is still today the central, the all-encompassing theological question.[4] We are beginning, then, in sharply disputed waters, a useful way for any theory to be launched.

We have touched upon the central role, for Hammarskjöld and King, of certain momentous images. Hammarskjöld understands himself as Christ's brother, as brother to the Brother; he sees the point of his life as a sacrifice to be offered; life is lived in the confidence that the unheard-of *is* at the limits of reality, and later God is invoked under a triune image—Father, Brother, Spirit. King understands his work under the image of the Exodus; he is leading his people on a new crossing of the Red Sea; he is a Moses who goes to the mountaintop, but who is not privileged to enter with his people into the promised land. These are major images, and for each there are others as well. What we must now explore is the proposal that in these men, indeed in all of us so far as we are religious, *such images are of the very substance of religion*; that these sacred images are not for Hammarskjöld or King peripheral to faith; that images, while not the only constituent of religion, are of central importance in it.

Now total novelty would be an argument against such a

[2] See especially Sigmund Freud, *Civilization and Its Discontents,* trans. and ed. James Strachey (New York: W. W. Norton, 1961 [1st German ed., 1930]), and *The Future of an Illusion,* trans. W. D. Robson-Scott, rev. and ed. James Strachey (Garden City, N.Y.: Doubleday, 1964 [1st German ed., 1927]).

[3] The word "religion" has a remarkable history, its present use (as in the expression "the religions of mankind") being of nineteenth-century origin. For the history, see Wilfred Cantwell Smith, *The Meaning and End of Religion* (New York: Macmillan, 1963), chapter 2, with extensive notes, pp. 203-45.

[4] See Gerhard Ebeling, *The Nature of Faith,* trans. Ronald Gregor Smith (Philadelphia: Fortress Press, 1967 [1st German ed., 1959]).

claim, for it is not likely that anything so central should have gone unnoticed. I call as witness the late Austin M. Farrer, esteemed Oxford Anglican, whose first book on the present theme, *The Glass of Vision,* appeared over a quarter-century ago.[5] Farrer, in attempting to answer the question about the place of Christ and the place of Scripture in revelation, suggested that "the thought of Christ" was expressed in "certain dominant images." These images, he says, include (1) the Kingdom of God, (2) the Son of Man, (3) Israel, and (4) "the infinitely complex and fertile image of sacrifice and communion, of expiation and covenant"[6] concentrated in the Last Supper. Farrer's claim was that we may penetrate "the luxuriant growth of apostolic teaching," and may find that Jesus historically employed these very images in his teaching, applying them to himself.[7] *He* was the presence of the kingdom; he was the exalted Son of Man who should come with the clouds of heaven; he was somehow Israel, and the twelve were his typical "sons"; he was the bearer of the role of suffering servant given by Isaiah and by Jewish tradition to Israel; and in the Supper he was the broken loaf, the wine poured out in sacrifice. It was these images thus employed, claims Farrer, which in interaction with the other events composing the history of Jesus, constitute that history as revelatory. Thus, he says,

the great images interpreted the events of Christ's ministry, death and resurrection, and the events interpreted the images; the interplay of the two is revelation. Certainly the events without the images would be no revelation at all, and the images without the events would remain shadows on the clouds. The events by themselves are not revelation, for they do not by themselves reveal the divine work which is accomplished in them:

[5] Austin Farrer, *The Glass of Vision,* the Bampton Lectures for 1948 (Westminster: Dacre Press, 1948) ; *A Rebirth of Images* (Dacre Press, 1949) ; *A Study in St. Mark* (Dacre Press, 1951) .

[6] *Glass of Vision,* p. 42.

[7] *Ibid.,* p. 41.

the martyrdom of a virtuous Rabbi and his miraculous return
are not of themselves the redemption of the world.[8]

Well, most of us can agree with that last caution, at least.
We need not pursue Farrer's bold mid-twentieth-century
view with its account of how a Thomist God enlightens natural men, nor linger over his solutions of historical problems in New Testament research, to be instructed by the
application of his work to our own problem. (For he goes
on, in *The Glass of Vision,* to say how the interplay of image and event continued in the shaping of the early church,
and pursues the role of images in theology and in metaphysics, in poetry and in prophecy, with brush strokes too
broad for us here.) [9] However it may be with his larger
claims, can we not agree that such images thus employed
are central to the 'religion' of the New Testament? That
is, the image-shaped lives of those who, employing the images, produced these writings? And if central to the writers,
then surely central to the correct reading? Our doctrine,
then, must be that men of biblical faith are those who find
in Scripture what is centrally there—great dominant images,
such as those of Kingdom of God, and Israel, and sacrifice,
and Son of Man, *and who apply them as the makers of
Scripture applied them*—to themselves.

One difference there seems to be between Farrer's account and our own—he says that Christ and his apostles
applied the images to Christ, while we can see that Hammarskjöld and King apply their images to their own century, to their own crises, to themselves. But that is too quick
a distinction. For in the New Testament writings there is
a continual blurring of the line of application between the
teacher and his disciples: *he* is the presence of the Kingdom, yet those who know their need of God learn that the
Kingdom is *theirs;*[10] *he* takes up his cross so that *they* may

[8] *Ibid.,* p. 43.
[9] *Ibid.,* chaps. 3-8.
[10] Cf. Luke 11:20; Matt. 12:28; Luke 7:22; Matt. 11:4-5, etc.; with
Matt. 5:10, 20; Mark 9:47; etc.

take theirs up and follow him;[11] the Son of Man is sometimes Jesus alone, sometimes his community collective;[12] he
is Israel, but they are the twelve tribes who constitute Israel.[13] But if it is thus with Christ's servants Peter and
James and John, may it not be so for his servants Dag
and Martin (and perhaps for us) as well?

Let us now draw a significant inference. If biblical
faith consists especially in the application to one's own
circumstances of appropriate biblical images, may not other
sorts of faith similarly consist in the application to one's
circumstances of other sorts of images? Is there anything
uniquely Jewish or Christian about this way of understanding faith? There is not, and likewise there is no reason why
a Christian must draw his images exclusively from the wells
of Scripture. Martin King, for example, was deeply influenced by the Gandhian image of the *Satyagraha*, the
truth-warrior, and by the American "dream" of a land from
whose every mountainside freedom would ring; Dag Hammarskjöld was formed by the images of the mystics, both
Christian and non-Christian.

Here then, more plainly, is our argument so far: our
biographical subjects have contributed to the theology of
the community of sharers of their faith especially by showing how certain great archetypical images of that faith do
apply to their own lives and circumstances, and by exten-
sion to our own. In doing so, they make clearer the answer
to a (preliminary) theological question, *What is religion?*
Part of the answer is that it is just such use of images. By
images, I mean metaphors whose content has been enriched
by a previous, prototypical employment so that their application causes the object to which they are applied to be
seen in multiply-reflected light; they are traditional or

---

[11] Cf. Mark 8:34 with 9:1 and parallels.

[12] Cf. Mark 8:38 and parallels with Mark 2:27-28 and parallels.

[13] Cf. Matt. 15:31, 27:42; Luke 1:54; with Matt 19:28 and parallel,
and see Farrer, *Glass of Vision*, p. 42.

canonical metaphors, and as such they bear the content of faith itself.

There will be those who question the adequacy of such a formulation. First, does it not fail to categorize biblical faith as faith in a transcendent object—as faith in God? This would be a failing indeed, and we must say more about it presently. A more immediate objection is rather different; it is that we are making too much of these images. Can so much be done by a figure of speech? Are we not confusing the coat of wax with the floor on which we stand, confusing mere words with the solemnity of solid faith?

In answer, let us note how recent inquiries in the theory of language have stressed the *powerful* role of model and metaphor. I merely mention the work of Max Black, Ian Ramsey, and Stanley Cavell,[14] and now briefly report the seminal work of John Wisdom of Cambridge.[15] In one essay, Wisdom sets out to show the way in which a metaphor, though not factually informative, may be decisive in forming a judgment or guiding our action. He says:

Someone is trying on a hat. She is studying the reflection in a mirror like a judge considering a case. There's a pause and then a friend says in tones too clear, "My dear, it's the Taj Mahal." Instantly the look of indecision leaves the face in the mirror. All along she has felt there was about the hat something that wouldn't quite do. Now she sees what it is. And all this happens in spite of the fact that the hat could be seen perfectly clearly and completely before the words "the Taj Mahal" were uttered.[16]

[14] See Max Black, *Models and Metaphors: Studies in Language and Philosophy* (Ithaca: Cornell University Press, 1962); Ian T. Ramsey, *Religious Language, an Empirical Placing of Theological Phrases* (New York: Macmillan, 1963 [1957]); *Models and Mystery* (London: Oxford University Press, 1964); and Stanley Cavell, *Must We Mean What We Say, A Book of Essays* (New York: Scribner's, 1969).

[15] See John Wisdom, "The Logic of God," in *Paradox and Discovery* (New York: Philosophical Library, 1965), reprinted in John Hick, ed., *The Existence of God* (New York: Macmillan, 1964). My citations are from the latter.

[16] Wisdom, "The Logic of God," p. 277.

Wisdom goes on to make two very important claims. The first is that, while "It's the Taj Mahal" is not descriptive in the way that "It has long feathers" is descriptive, yet the metaphor may change not only one's feelings about a hat, but his very apprehension of it, just as the words "A rabbit, there!" may make what did look like a clod look like an animal, like a rabbit.

The second is an exploration, regrettably all too brief, of the way in which a metaphor differs from a simile not only in power or force, but in the very work to be done by the words. Listen again to John Wisdom:

If for "It's the Taj Mahal" we put "It is in some respects like the Taj Mahal" we get the sort of negligible stuff that so often results from trying to put poetry into prose, from submission to the muddled metaphysics which pretends that a metaphor is no more than an emotive flourish unless and until we happen to have the words and the wits to translate it into a set of similes.[17]

Now, however, I have made my case appear a weak one indeed in the eyes of some. For they will say, how poor a claim it is that the stuff of religious faith is no more than a metaphor about a hat! Give us a red-blooded faith, that knows less of symbols and more of realities, less of form and more of content. Very well, for these I shall change my illustration, and refer instead to that ancient Christian rite, the Eucharist or Lord's Supper. What happens in that ritual meal? Is it not this: that in connection with the meal, bread is said to be, bread is seen as, is taken as, the body of the Church's Lord? And wine is taken as his blood poured out for us? Some of course will say, not "taken as" but *becomes* the body; whereupon others will be quick to reply, not "becomes" but *represents* that body. With these old disputes I have at the moment no concern—I wish rather to call attention to the disputants' common ground, that in the rite *this* is (in some sense) *that—hoc est corpus meum*,

[17] *Ibid.*, pp. 278-79.

this is my body. The whole event is an enacted imagery, and the more strongly one urges the centrality of the Lord's Supper in Christianity, the closer is he to understanding why I say that Christian faith comprises images applied to life, and the closer to seeing why the understanding of that faith must involve the examination of the role of images in actual lives, the role of images in the experience of life.

II

I must now say more fully how the visions thus produced provide insight for the theological task, not only aid in answering the question what religion is, but also in saying what its content must be. To do this, let me choose as illustration a single Christian doctrine, *the doctrine of atonement,* and point out some ways in which our subjects cast present light upon that doctrine. The doctrine of atonement is as old as, indeed older than, Christianity. Theology for nineteen hundred years, and particularly for the last nine hundred, has been at work to give this doctrine a form deemed best suited to the contemporaneous Christian community. The elements of the doctrine are well known. There is the element of estrangement, our personal distance from God our Maker and rightful Lord, from the Holy Center of life and thus from one another. There is the ending of this estrangement, the overcoming of the bars to oneness, and this overcoming is atonement (at-one-ment) itself. There is the costliness of the work of at-one-ment, the fact that no reconciliation of radically separate persons is effortlessly achieved. And there is the question of the respective roles of God, of Christ, and of ourselves the reconciled—what does each do in this work?

If these are the elements, another task of the theologian is to relate them authentically, truly, to one another. Some ways, as every student of theology in biblical perspective knows, are now debarred, however attractive they appeared in earlier ages as heightening some true aspect of the doctrine. God cannot in the atonement have been extracting a price for the redemption of the world, taking his legal pound of flesh. Jesus cannot in his suffering and death have been a mere teacher of the art of dying, setting us a model of stoic detachment. Further, we in being reunited cannot truly take ourselves to be the source or cause of our own reconciliation—we are more like the adopted sons of a new family than like those who have worked through their own therapy and been discharged, self-healed. And yet again, we are not excluded from the process of atonement —our role in it is one of crucial involvement.

The statement of the doctrine must also vary in accordance with the times and the circumstances of the community. Perhaps as clear and satisfactory a statement as any, prior to our own times, was achieved about a hundred years ago by the important American theologian Horace Bushnell. In a series of addresses and books, Bushnell laid down the main lines to be followed.[18] The human race is bound up together in its destiny. Original sin is the estrangement, the fallenness, which rests upon and blights us all. What wrong each does makes the other's plight worse. However, one member of the race, Jesus, is uniquely in position not only to be disadvantaged by his fellows because he so fully sympathizes with all, but also to aid his fellows for he is by vocation a healer of men. This healing is the point of his life; it leads him, at whatever cost to his own comfort, to forgive and by personal influence virtually to remake the blighted lives of his fellow men. But his ability to do this is the very presence of God—his is the moral power of God to men—his death, because it is in fact the consequence of his healing program, is thus the full expression of that

---

[18] For Bushnell's doctrine of atonement, I have depended upon the careful account of and generous extracts from his works on the doctrine found in H. Shelton Smith, ed. *Horace Bushnell*, in the series "A Library of Protestant Thought" (New York: Oxford University Press, 1965).

power, and his resurrection the full disclosure of it to his followers. What he has done is therefore nothing less than what God in eternity does—to engage in the intrinsically costly business of healing, by forgiveness and reconciliation, estranged men. Moreover, what he does we as reconciled are also to do—the forgiven must be forgivers, again a costly work.

So much for the statement, here much condensed. Theology is not, however, a merely historical enterprise; it is not enough for the theologian to report what the community or its best teachers have said; he must ask whether that can be said today. Our question, that is, is not merely what the doctrine of atonement has been or is, but whether there is a doctrine of atonement which we can believe today. Can we men who live in the age in which we live, having discovered what we have discovered about ourselves in the modern world, believe *this*? Is there any longer any serious use for this doctrine?

If we turn seeking an answer to the lives of Hammarskjöld and King, we find no evident interest in the formal statement of the doctrine of atonement. What we do find are dominant images—Caesarea Philippi, sacrifice, the cross, the single garment of destiny. But these images are steeped in that doctrine; they can be truly understood only in the light of that ancient doctrine; they are images whose point is the point of the doctrine, images, therefore, which *are* the theological doctrine in the only form in which it can give substance to the religion of those who live by that doctrine.

I would not be misunderstood here. This is not the lesser point, to which many would assent, that the terminology, the rhetoric, of Hammarskjöld and of King was affected by Christian tradition, just as the language of today is affected by the King James version's English, or by Shakespeare. It is rather the precise claim that they accepted, believed, were convinced by this Christian doctrine, that it was a controlling *motif* of their lives, as evidenced by what they said and did, and principally by their application of these controlling images to the events of their lives. Thus the result of our inquiry is to declare the doctrine validated, so far as it can be validated by the evidence of these lives. Atonement was not, as far as these men were concerned, an anachronism; it was not peripheral; it was a focus of the very vision by which they lived. If there were no such lives we should be imperiously urged to acknowledge that this doctrine had lost its power; if in the future there should be no more such lives, we should then have to make that concession. But as matters stand, these men with others are the vivifiers, the exemplars, of the doctrine of the cross; their lives cry out to us, in the language of *Markings,* O Caesarea Philippi!

More than this, however, is involved. For they tell us what in the doctrine must be stressed, and what may for their part be laid aside. Centrally, the doctrine is for these a doctrine of at-one-ment. Hammarskjöld and King are men of unity, the one struggling for the unity of nations, the other for that of races and classes. For both, the unity is integrally related to the at-one-ment images which shape their lives. I can illustrate this from either; let me illustrate it by three passages from Hammarskjöld's *Markings.*

The first passage is proleptic, preparatory. Hammarskjöld, ever a lonely man, is exploring in a 1950 trail mark the nature of his own hunger—a hunger for fellowship, a hunger for righteousness, he says. He writes, "the nature of life is such that I can realize my individuality by becoming a bridge for others, a stone in the temple of righteousness. . . . For this alone was man created, and he who fails to take the Way which could have been his shall be lost eternally" (53). Now "way" and "temple of righteousness" are images intimately related to sacrifice in Hammarskjöld's thought. Somehow his own sacrificial acceptance of his fate is to become a building-stone for others. But how?

The second, written when he is catching his stride as

Secretary-General (1955), refers more clearly than most passages in *Markings* to the United Nations:

A jealous dream which refuses to share you with anybody or anything else: the greatest creation of mankind—the dream of mankind.
The greatest creation of mankind, in which it is the noblest dream of the individual—to lose himself.
Therefore: gladly death or humiliation if that is what the dream demands.
Therefore: how easy to forgive. (115)

How vividly here does the "dream of mankind" link up with Hammarskjöld's markings which unite death, destiny, sacrifice, and forgiveness, under the guidance of *"one* man, and *one* man's experience" (205) —that one being Jesus, the man of the Gospels.

Finally, a trail mark from the earlier period (1945–1949), which seems already to epitomize these others:

No peace which is not peace for all, no rest until all has been fulfilled. (35)

Here again, the language of the Gospels brings their imagery of mission and fulfillment of goal into interplay with the peaceful unity of mankind. Atonement is mission; the goal of the mission is at-one-ment and peace.

In 1957, Hammarskjöld planned and supervised the transformation of the meditation room in the General Assembly Hall of the U.N. into a "Room of Quiet." The central piece of furniture in that place of "silence and inner stillness" is a great slab of rock, lit from above by a shaft of light which causes its surface to seem to float, a table in space. Hammarskjöld was at pains to point out that in a room belonging to men of many faiths "none of the symbols to which we are accustomed in our meditation could be used." [19] The rock is not, then, a table or an altar; it is

---

[19] Dag Hammarskjöld, "A Room of Quiet—The United Nations Meditation Room," in Wilder Foote, ed., *Servant of Peace, a Selection of the Speeches and Statements of Dag Hammarskjöld* (New York: Harper, 1963), p. 160.

"the Uncarved Block" (159), which symbolizes the unity of mankind centered in a God who is not unknown, but one "whom man worships under many names and in many forms." [20] Is it too fanciful to believe that Hammarskjöld himself saw the Uncarved Block in cruciform—as the altar of sacrifice, or as the stone which the builders rejected—but that he also saw it as bearing many other carvings, many other forms, just as "the sacrifice" became in his writing and in his life a sacrifice to unite diverse peoples, lands, nations, and ways of faith?

In this case a part of the experience of our subjects (for a similar case could be made for King) [21] is that the Christian doctrine of atonement must in our statement of it give room for a broader human scope than Christians have generally allowed. That doctrine cannot see the goal of atoning action as anything less than at-one-ment, an at-one-ment which breaks down the lines of creed and tribe, race, caste, and class which (also behind the facade of the cross and the gospel) we men have proudly drawn. Christian faith must not only acknowledge its own pluralism, and the need for transcending that pluralism, which in the ecumenical age we have partly done. It must also acknowledge the pluralism of convinced communities, the pluralism of faiths, in the one earth, and must find a way of faith which transcends that pluralism too. Atoning faith, in whatever religious community it appears, must find that its atonement is at-one-ment, that the man of faith by his sacrifice can become a bridge-stone in the temple of righteousness. Then, then will your light shine! [22]

Again, theology is set a task by *the role of death* in the

---

[20] *Ibid.*

[21] I have in mind the way in which the particularity of the liberation King sought for his Black brothers was always matched by his vision of the liberation of their oppressors as well. I also think of the ways in which in his preaching and teaching he reached beyond Christianity (to Judaism, to India, to the family of man) both for guidance and in concern.

[22] Cf. Isa. 58:8; 60:1; Matt. 13:43.

religion of men such as Hammarskjöld and King. At-one-ment and death have been partners in a strange dance throughout the long annals of man. How in reality are these disparate partners paired? The doctrine of atonement provides an answer, and that answer may be reinforced by the image-guided experience of our witnesses.

Every man is touched by thoughts of death, but Hammarskjöld and King seem to have been more than usually preoccupied with their own deaths. Each faced the nearness of death more than once in his career;[23] each saw his death as related to the sacrifice which was the point of life itself. Let us hear this time the witness of Martin Luther King, Jr. Toward the last days of the early and crucial 1955-57 Montgomery, Alabama, bus boycott, which set the tone for King's subsequent public ministry, the young Black leader came to the eve of his twenty-eighth birthday—and to another of the frequent mass meetings of the movement at a Montgomery Negro church. His home bombed, his life threatened, the ultimate outcome of the Montgomery struggle still uncertain, King was in low spirits and bone-tired. Then, as he stood before the congregation gathered in the church, and began to lead in prayer, King was for the first time in his life seized in public with a burst of ecstasy.[24]

Such seizures are, as King knew, a familiar part of the phenomenology of American folk religion, when the poor, the deprived, the oppressed find in the glad fellowship a release, and 'go outside themselves' in shout and trembling. For the young middle-class Boston University doctoral graduate to be so seized was another matter! The church

[23] King's life was often threatened, and once in Harlem he nearly died of a stab wound inflicted by a member of his own race. Hammarskjöld's early brushes with death are reflected in *Markings* (see especially 30), and during his U.N. days he was under constant guard to protect his life. His death may have resulted, as did King's, from malice.

[24] For King's account of this, see Martin Luther King, Jr., *Stride Toward Freedom, the Montgomery Story* (New York: Harper, 1958).

audience broke into an uproar. King, rather shamefaced, reports the incident by saying, "I broke down in public." [25] His chief biographers also curiously treat the incident as a kind of failure of their subject—"he seemed to disintegrate psychologically" is Black historian David Lewis's undiscerning phrase.[26] Must we not rather see the event as an unconscious act of identification, both with the brothers and sisters who had experienced similar visitations, and with the primal sources of energy and destiny upon which King finally depended?

In any case, the words which ecstasy then drew from that rich throat were these: "Lord, I hope no one will have to die as a result of our struggle for freedom in Montgomery. Certainly I don't want to die. But if anyone has to die, let it be me." [27] And then he falls silent and is helped by other ministers, one on either side, back to his seat. He is comforted by the brethren after the meeting, sleeps soundly, and is "unexpectedly" greatly relieved of his guilt and strain.

More familiar is the speech King gave in Memphis to the discouraged band of garbage strikers on the eve of his own death in 1968:

We've got some difficult days ahead. But it really doesn't matter with me now. Because I've been on the mountaintop. I won't mind.

Like anybody, I would like to live a long life. Longevity has its place. But I'm not concerned about that now. I just want to do God's will. And He's allowed me to go up to the mountain. And I've looked over, and I've seen the promised land.

I may not get there with you, but I want you to know tonight that we as a people will get to the promised land.

So I'm happy tonight. I'm not worried about anything. I'm not fearing any man. "Mine eyes have seen the glory of the coming of the Lord." [28]

[25] *Ibid.*, p. 155.
[26] *King, A Critical Biography* (New York: Praeger, 1970), p. 83.
[27] *Stride Toward Freedom*, p. 155.
[28] William Robert Miller, *Martin Luther King, Jr., His Life, Martyr-*

That was April 3, 1968. By seven o'clock the next day, he was dead of a gunshot wound in the neck. In Hammarskjöld's earlier words, "Acts of violence—Whether on a large or a small scale, the bitter paradox: the meaningfulness of death—and the meaninglessness of killing" (121).

Perhaps I can put my present point as a dilemma: unless theology can hear her own witnesses, unless she can take death in deadly earnest, take its grim enmity into her counsels and be shaped thereby, she ceases to be a serious discipline. Men cry peace when there is no peace (a quotation from Scripture,[29] not Virginia), they savor peace without sacrifice, at-one-ment without atonement, unity without costly death. Theology must hear her witnesses, discover her own truth, shape her doctrine in faithfulness to that truth. I do not mean that theological passion should replace thought; there must be clear thought even about passion and about death. I mean that in the community which includes the doctrine of at-one-ment in its storehouse of treasures, the community whose sacred images included the Suffering Servant, there can be no clear thought which does not think truly, and passionately, about *that* somber treasure.

The lives of King and Hammarskjöld teach us what must be included in our theology. They show us, as well, what we need not emphasize. For a century or more, theology has made much of the historicity of the portrait of Jesus in the Gospel accounts, now affirming more, now less, of that portrait. New Testament historians have agonized and spilled much ink over the literal accuracy, or the reconstruction, of at least some parts of the record. Closely allied with this diligent research has been a theology already referred to which made much of the "revelatory events," the "mighty acts of God," as comprising our knowledge of God. Now such crucial events as the cross, and such

---

dom, and Meaning for the World (New York: Weybright and Talley, 1968), pp. 275-76.
    [29] Cf. Jer. 6:14; 8:11.

teaching as the Sermon on the Mount, are irrevocably part of Christianity. Yet there is no hint in the religious experience of Hammarskjöld, or King, that these events or teachings, or any other, must be validated by historical research before faith can flourish. It was true that Hammarskjöld regarded Schweitzer's portrayal of a truly human Jesus as an important revision of the traditional Swedish Lutheran 'dogmatic' picture of Christ as a masquerading God.[30] And it was true that "the love ethic of Jesus" as found in the Gospels was normative for Martin Luther King.[31] Both Hammarskjöld and King had a place, a central place, for Jesus of Nazareth, and Hammarskjöld at least developed a profound trinitarian motif among his governing images. But for neither was the vexing question of the scientific availability of the Christ of the Gospels a central one in their apprehension of the Christian doctrine of atonement. This does not imply that Jesus was *not* a historical person or that the whole theological community should neglect the details of his historicity, but it does provide a clue, in this case a negative clue, for theological development.[32]

III

What about the place of God? So far we have treated the atonement far too much, it may seem to some, as an ethical technique, a mode of man's dealings with man. And while historic faith insists that atonement does so involve a man's own life, the historic doctrine has seen the human role, even the role of Christ regarded as true man, overtopped by the towering role of God who redeems man; the deepest element in at-one-ment is the costly act of God, restoring us to himself. Indeed the historic doctrine allows no final separation, but holds that the reconciliation Christ brings

[30] Gustaf Aulén, *Dag Hammarskjöld's White Book, The Meaning of Markings* (Philadelphia: Fortress Press, 1969), p. 50.
[31] Martin Luther King, Jr., *Strength to Love* (New York: Pocket Books, 1964), p. 12.
[32] On this see further chapter 7, pp. 197-200.

about between man and man is none other than the work of God, reconciling us to himself. In the age of the death-of-God movement, the age of secularity, how do these witnesses to faith stand on this question?

One answer is that at the discursive level each affirms the presence and power of God. "At the center of the Christian faith," says Martin King, "is the conviction that in the universe there is a God of power who is able to do exceedingly abundant things in nature and in history." [33] And Hammarskjöld, already in a 1950 trail mark, perhaps two years before his great "Yes," writes, "God does not die on the day when we cease to believe in a personal deity, but we die on the day when our lives cease to be illumined by the steady radiance, renewed daily, of a wonder, the source of which is beyond all reason" (56).

More interesting to us, we can note that of 'experience with God' narrowly conceived there is enough in these two saints to fill a new chapter of William James's *Varieties*. Finally, of experience in our sense—the lesson of life's experience, experience as life lived out under a dominant image or images—we can soberly report that 'God' does so dominate the experience of these lives. Our present doctrinal task, then, would not be complete until it seriously attempted to explore anew the "central affirmation" of God and man in confrontation via these biographies.

Now, however, there seems to be a fatal blemish in our project. For we have spoken of the primary religious data as images, metaphors with such and such a history, working in such and such a way. Yet we have said that in biblical perspective the central theological proposition is confrontation between ourselves and God—a real confrontation, a God truly God. If however "God" is in religion but a metaphor, an image, then is not the great gulf between ourselves and him unclosed, our faith mere human contrivance, our hopes unfounded in the end?

[33] King, *Strength to Love*, p. 124.

This matter requires more space than I will take here. Yet I must mention the problem lest any think it unmentionable because unmanageable. The answer, briefly, is this: to speak truly and faithfully of God is indeed to speak in models, images, analogies—we have no other way. Yet images can speak not only falsehood but also truth. Some set of images, some vision of reality, is better than all the rest because truer, more faithful, more open to hard fact and to beauty and to wonder—more open to the realms of science, of art, and of faith.[34] To note that science depends upon models, art upon abstract forms, and religion upon images, is not to reject these realms, but to open the way to the full discovery of the vision they evoke, the truth they can tell.

The vindication of vision depends in part upon the quality of life which that vision evokes. And thus we come for the time being to mention a final aid which these image-bearing lives may provide to theology—they are witnesses concerning the vision which they represent. Thus I believe that we have in the vision of Dag Hammarskjöld and that of Martin Luther King a oneness, a wholeness, a holiness not otherwise available to them or to us. Their lives witness to their vision, even as they challenge the depth of our own. So there comes the question, not so much of the suitability of their vision to their own circumstances, but of the justification of our present way of life when held against theirs. Thus theology is drawn by its biographic material to face a challenge not only to its propositions, but also to the selfhood of its practitioners.[35]

[34] With the theme expressed in this and the remaining sentences, cf. James Wm. McClendon, Jr., "How Is Religious Talk Justifiable?" in Michael Novak, ed., *American Philosophy and the Future* (New York: Scribner's, 1968); and the concluding chapters of my forthcoming book, *Religious Convictions and the Problem of Pluralism* (probable title), with James M. Smith.

[35] This chapter to this point appeared in slightly different form in *Cross Currents*, Fall, 1971.

It has been the intention of this chapter only to suggest, rather than to exhaust, the theological use of two significant contemporary lives. In the nature of the matter, the task must be left incomplete, both because we know Dag and Martin only in part, and because what we do know may stir up different questions in different inquirers. This raises forcibly the suggestion that such theological use of lives may be abuse. In the final chapter, we must consider the problem, whether the biases or presuppositions of the individual theologian make this inquiry of necessity an unfair and unhappy one. Meanwhile, it seems desirable to clarify what has been claimed here by applying the method to two further lives, those of Clarence Jordan and Charles Ives, attempting in these cases as well to discover dominant images which unlock these biographies, and to harvest some theology in the process.

Chapter Five

The Theory Tested:
Clarence Leonard Jordan—
Radical in Community

Now we need to give the method of biographical theology a
further test. The lives so far explored were already familiar
to most readers. Will we achieve comparable results by
attending to lives less well known? Must our 'saints' belong to a popular canon, if not an official one? Was the
appearance of the images in the lives so far examined a
lucky coincidence or the result of shrewd choice of subjects, or will we find matching phenomena in any compelling biographical subject we may choose? Clarence Jordan
is the first test case. Known to some Bible readers as the
writer of the regionally flavored *Cotton Patch Version* of
the New Testament, and to students of the civil rights
struggle of the fifties and sixties as the leader in a perilous
struggle to keep alive during that period an interracial
commune in south Georgia, Koinonia Farm, Jordan is
nevertheless a far more obscure figure than Hammarskjöld
or King (I, at least, brought no prefabricated image to my

study of Jordan's life). Yet here, too, the images vividly appear, and shed a remarkably penetrating light.

I

Because of its relative obscurity, it will be useful to sketch Jordan's life at somewhat greater length before asking our usual questions about it. Clarence Leonard Jordan was born in Talbotton, a county seat town in west central Georgia, July 29, 1912, the middle child among the seven children in the prosperous home of J. W. Jordan, merchant and founder of the local bank.[1] Clarence was preco-

[1] Published sources for the life of Clarence Jordan are limited. Primary sources, besides his New Testament translations (see note 8, below) include a book of sermons, *The Substance of Faith and Other Cotton Patch Sermons*, ed. Dallas Lee (New York: Association Press, 1972) ; an exposition, *Sermon on the Mount* (Valley Forge, Pa.: Judson Press, 1952 [Koinonia ed., 1970]) ; and "Christian Community in the South," *The Journal of Religious Thought* (Howard University), Autumn-Winter 1956–57, pp. 27-36; "The Sound of a Dove," *Town and Country Church*, Sept.-Oct., 1961, p. 16 (?) ; "In the Land of Great Violence—a Parable," *The Mennonite*, May 25, 1965, p. 353. See also the issues of the Koinonia *Newsletter* from 1942, and especially among these an issue headed "A Personal Letter from Clarence Jordan to Friends of Koinonia," Oct. 21, 1968. See also a published interview with Walden Howard, "The Legacy of Clarence Jordan," *Faith at Work*, April, 1970. Also there are published phonograph records issued by Koinonia Records, Tiskilwa, Ill., 61368, as follows: *Judas; The Rich Man and Lazarus and Other Parables; The Great Banquet and Other Parables; Jesus the Rebel and Jesus and Possessions;* and *Metamorphosis, also Love Your Enemies.* The preceding records are also available from Koinonia Products, Rt. 2, Americus, Ga., as are tape cassettes with the same content. From the same source other tape cassettes are also available: *Substance of Faith; The Sabbath Is a Way of Life; Incarnating Brotherhood; Christians under Pressure; Power from Parables; Episodes from Acts.* The records and tapes are valuable as conveying the emphasis and style of Jordan's thought; however I have not listened to the second list of tapes just given.

Secondary sources include especially Dallas Lee, *The Cotton Patch Evidence, the Story of Clarence Jordan and the Koinonia Farm Experiment* (New York: Harper, 1971) . This, the only biography, is journalistic, but was researched and written with care. During the intense persecution and legal assault on Koinonia 1956–58, articles on the Farm and events there appeared in *Newsweek, Time, The Petal*

cious and argumentative, earning himself the family nick-name, "Grump." The family were active Baptists, and Clar-ence took the religion offered at the Baptist church with all seriousness. He learned to sing the Sunday school song:

> Jesus loves the little children,
> All the children of the world;
> Red and yellow, black and white,
> They are precious in His sight;
> Jesus loves the little children of the world.[2]

And he came forward in a Sunday service, at about age twelve, to profess his own love of Jesus and acceptance of him as Lord and Savior.

He was serious enough to perceive, even then, a scandal-ous difference between that culturally encouraged profession of faith and the common treatment of *some* of the little children of Talbotton, the Black ones. The environment taught him, he later wrote in his journal, that "a nigger was a nigger and must be kept in his place,"[3] an awareness

---

Paper, *Christian Century, Nation, The New York Times, Action, Catholic Worker, Redbook,* and *Friend's Journal.* Reference to some of these appears below. *The Atlanta Journal* carried a six-part series on Koinonia Farm, the first part datelined April 13, 1957.

Because biographical material was so limited, in September, 1973, I interviewed persons who knew Clarence Jordan at Koinonia Farm, including Florence Jordan, Will and Margaret Wittkamper, Al and Ann Zook, Ladon Sheats, John and Diane McEntyre, and others, and consulted scrapbooks at the Farm. I interviewed C. Arthur Insko and J. Lyn Elder, who were at Southern Baptist Theological Seminary, Louisville, during Jordan's Louisville years.

Some of Clarence Jordan's papers, including his unpublished doc-toral dissertation. "The Meaning of *Thanatos* and *Nekros* in the Pauline Epistles," Southern Baptist Theological Seminary, 1939, have been deposited in the library of the University of Georgia, Athens (but I have not seen these), while still others remain in Florence Jordan's care at the Farm and have not been made public.

Where I depend in the following account on the Lee biography or on my own interviews, I will not cite them individually, except in the case of direct quotations, or in order to substantiate disputed points.

[2] Words, marked anon., from *The American Hymnal,* ed. Robert H. Coleman (Dallas: Robert H. Coleman, 1933).

[3] Lee, *Cotton Patch Evidence,* p. 8.

that struck Clarence with special horror one summer night when he heard terrible groans coming from the nearby chain-gang camp, and realized that a Black prisoner he knew, Ed Russell, was being tortured in the stretcher—the stretcher being a Georgia version of the ancient rack—used in disciplining convicts. What added irony was the boy's knowledge that the administering torturer was the same Warden McDonald who only hours earlier had been lustily singing "Love Lifted Me" in the Baptist revival choir.[4] So by the time he graduated from high school at sixteen, Clarence had decided to become a scientific farmer who would help poor farmers make a better life. Some of these would be Whites, but Blacks were at the very bottom; therefore he would especially help them.

He went away to the state agricultural college at Athens, Georgia, to learn scientific farming. A good dancer, a good mixer, Clarence joined everything there was to join at college, and its little world seemed to suit him exactly. He was of a prominent family in a rather snooty old Georgia town; his religious views harmonized well enough with those of the Baptist Student Union to secure his election, in due course, as statewide president of that organization; his banker father had given him a checkbook and told him not to worry about money. Racial concerns simply did not arise. He fulfilled a requirement of the college by joining the ROTC cavalry unit, and came proudly home to Talbotton showing his boots and spurs.

And then, in 1933, chaos yawned before him. The depression caught up with the Jordans; the bank and the general store failed in March of Clarence's senior year, and the twenty-year-old student had to close the gift checkbook for good. Financial insecurity was accompanied by anxieties about his vocation. Would "scientific farming" really meet the deepest human needs? Perhaps, then, he should be a preacher? In a melodramatic day on exercises

4 Howard, "The Legacy of Clarence Jordan."

at summer ROTC camp, this mounted officer-to-be faced and settled a central issue. He could not both believe the Sermon on the Mount, which he had been memorizing, *and* be a soldier; he could not both love his enemies and slash them with that long saber by his side. Reluctantly he explained his conviction to the colonel, who argued with him, but then engineered Clarence's release from the army, and finally told him, "Son, I hope someday you make my job impossible."

It is noteworthy, I think, that in those tense months of 1933 the issues that crowded together for Clarence were ones which would converge in every crisis of Clarence Jordan's life: the economic problem (in this case his own as well as that of the rich and poor around him), the problem of violence, and the ministry of Jesus Christ. His next move, however, was to enroll in a seminary where those three issues rarely if ever were seen as convergent and central: Southern Baptist Theological Seminary, Louisville, Kentucky.

'Louisville' was the patriarch of Southern Baptist seminaries: conscious of being older than the convention's structures of support and oversight, steeped in the biblical approaches of John A. Broadus (Broadus on Preaching) and A.T. Robertson (the Big Grammar). Robertson died while Jordan was there, but he plunged dutifully into studies with Robertson's disciples, and emerged after six years with a Ph.D. in Greek New Testament, a degree whose most notable requirement was being able to locate every Greek form and construction in every verse of the Westcott and Hort critical text. It seems a strange preparation for a future agrarian radical, but Clarence knew what he was doing. "I knew that I was going into the Southland," he said later, "and I knew that I would be coming into contact with a lot of people, both clergy and laity, who claimed to be followers of Jesus Christ, and I wanted to know what the man was saying. I didn't want some little jackleg preacher tying me up in knots. . . . I rooted myself in the

Greek language. . . ." [5] Clarence was not tied down by Southern Seminary's ambivalent involvement with traditional Southern Black-White relations, nor by its traditional Southern militarism and Baptist ecclesiasticism.[6] But he was circumscribed, I believe, by the failure of his New Testament teachers to lead him beyond their own 'conservative' conceptions of the origin and purpose of Scripture.

Yet Louisville had more to offer. For one thing, there were opportunities for service, first in country weekend pastorates, then in the city mission program, working with Negro churches. To his surprise, Jordan was asked at about the time he received his doctorate to become Superintendent of Missions for the Louisville association of (White) Baptist churches, a job which put him in position to press his ideas concerning race and ministry upon other churchworkers. Around Clarence there gathered other White seminarians who shared his vision. This included making Negro churches, not White mission stations, the center of the ministry to Blacks. It also included a brief experiment with a "Lord's Storehouse" plan—an inner-city store to sell new and used goods to the poor at low prices, or to give them to those who could not pay.

Another bonus of Louisville was that he met and married Florence Kroeger. Miss Kroeger, tall, blue-eyed and beautiful, was the daughter of a German immigrant liquor dealer who had married a Kentucky girl of German stock. Florence had gone, with her parents' encouragement, to the Baptist Sunday school, and become a Baptist. But she was

[5] Lee, ed., *Substance of Faith,* p. 108.

[6] It is worth recalling that seminaries in the South had no patent on compromising with the prevalent American racism; compare Martin Luther King's experiences at Crozer Theological Seminary (See David L. Lewis, *King, a Critical Biography* [New York: Praeger, 1970], pp. 27 ff.). On the "militarism" of Southern Seminary see Lee, *Cotton Patch Evidence,* p. 16. On its "Baptist ecclesiasticism" (whatever that oxymoron conveys to the reader) consider the role of Southern in the development of the Southern Baptist Convention as recounted by W. W. Barnes in *The Southern Baptist Convention* (Nashville: Broadman Press, 1954), pp. 120 ff.

independent enough of mind, and free enough from the
Kentucky culture, to encourage Clarence's own independence of thought and action.

So it was that by 1942 the Jordans, with one child born
and another on the way, joined with another Baptist
family, the Englands (Martin, Mabel, and their three children) to form a "missionary" enterprise, Koinonia Farm,
Incorporated, which would proclaim Jesus Christ and
apply his teachings in a kind of demonstration plot, where
"suffering, sin-stricken" Southern people of both races
could be taught productive farming, and where simultaneously there could develop a community life based "on the
teachings and principles of Jesus." [7] A site of 440 acres
southeast of Americus, a county seat town in south Georgia,
was chosen; a donor provided an unexpected $2,500 down
payment; and, as America girded for world war, Americus
saw the beginning of an experiment in peace and brother-
ly community.

When he began Koinonia Farm, Clarence Jordan, Ph.D.,
was uninformed of the history of 'intentional communities'
in America and elsewhere. He knew next to nothing of
Oneida or Brook Farm, the Hutterites or the Latter Day
Saints, not to mention the long tradition of the (locally
despised) Catholics, from Benedict of Nursia to the present, with a pattern of life shaped by an ancient and practical 'rule.' He did know intimately the congregational
shape of American Christianity, but that pattern provided
no amelioration of the twin evils of poverty and riches.
However, he also knew the text of the Greek New Testament almost by heart. Therefore, when the question of
family allowances for the Englands and the Jordans arose
on the new Farm, Clarence was adamant: there must be
common ownership of *all* things: Acts 2:44. Equally adamant was his insistence that, since God in Jesus had overcome the separation between Jew and non-Jew, every

[7] Brochure of 1942, cited in Lee, *Cotton Patch Evidence,* pp. 31-32.

separation of races was thereby abolished. "The secret," he would 'translate' Ephesians 3:6, "is that the Negroes are fellow partners and equal members, co-sharers in the privileges of the gospel of Jesus Christ" (CPV).[8] (Today's reader must remember that the presently acceptable designation "Black" was then a term of derogation, and its Latinized equivalent, "Negro," was widely considered more courteous.) Those privileges certainly included table fellowship and sharing in common worship. If Blacks wished to join Koinonia as full-fledged members, or to live and work there, they were welcome. This did not sit well with Georgia Whites, and trouble was on the horizon from the start for these communitarian preachers.

The full fury of opposition, however, did not appear for nearly fourteen years. Meanwhile, the experiment in community waxed and waned and waxed again, as assorted families and young singles were attracted to the unusual farm and came for awhile or came to stay. Most were White; most were moved by Christian concerns; many first learned of Koinonia through Jordan's wide-ranging national speaking schedule. He was an easy-going, informal speaker, with a flair for setting the human foibles and dignities of men in New Testament times alongside those of today. That was a flair not uncommon in Southern preachers, however. What distinguished Jordan's presentation was an unmis-

[8] CPV=*Cotton Patch Version*. The CPV was published in a series of booklets, as follows: *The Letter to the Hebrews or A First-Century Manual for Church Renewal in the Koinonia "Cotton Patch" Version* (Americus, Ga.: Koinonia Farm, 1963); *Practical Religion or the Sermon on the Mount, and the Epistle of James in the Koinonia "Cotton Patch" Version* (Koinonia Farm. 1964); *The Cotton Patch Version of Paul's Epistles* (New York: Association Press, 1968); *The Cotton Patch Version of Luke and Acts, Jesus' Doings and the Happenings* (Association Press, 1969); *Letters from Partners Rock, Jack, and Joe: I and II Peter; I, II, III John & Jude in the Koinonia "Cotton Patch" Version* (Koinonia Farm, 1969); *The Cotton Patch Version of Matthew and John* (Association Press, 1970); *Cotton Patch Version of Hebrews and the General Epistles,* which collects some of the segments, just noted, previously published at Americus (Association Press, 1973).

takable rocklike commitment to the "God Movement" (the kingdom of God) he preached, a plain willingness to live —or die—by the Sermon on the Mount. At first at home, and later only in other regions, people listened with mingled outrage and delight to his uncompromising radical message spoken in the unexpected accents of Georgia. One Southern lady, after hearing Clarence attack racism on New Testament premises, counterattacked. "I want you to know that my grandfather fought in the Civil War, and I'll never believe a word you say." Clarence, whose own forebears had fought the Yankees, too, replied gently: "Ma'am, your choice seems quite clear. It is whether you will follow your grand-daddy, or Jesus Christ." [9]

Organized opposition to Koinonia, perhaps fittingly, began with the church. Nearby Rehoboth Baptist, one of the successful open-country churches that had once formed the sociological core of the Southern Baptist Convention, after some consultations "withdrew fellowship from" (i.e. excommunicated) its Koinonia Farm members in 1950, the main stated reason being that "said members . . . have persisted in holding services where both white and colored attend together." This behavior, a distressing example of the "views and practices" of the Koinonians "contrary to those of other members of the Rehoboth Church" [10] meant that the offenders were no longer welcome even to attend services. The Jordans never tried to join another church; Clarence, when asked his denomination, would sometimes reply with a twinkle, "Exbaptist."

The opposition from the wider White community in Sumter County became so violent that it was widely reported in the national press. Local opinion, shocked by the 1954 Supreme Court *Brown* decision, reasoned that the decision must have been Communist-inspired; that the Koinonians, professed non-capitalists and "race-mixers,"

[9] Lee, ed., *Substance of Faith,* p. 7.
[10] Rehoboth Church recommendation adopted August 13, 1950, cited in Lee, *Cotton Patch Evidence,* pp. 77-78.

were a part of this Communist menace; and that it was only right to get them out of the county. In 1956, threatening phone calls began. Soon the persecution took the form of bombings, then rifle and pistol and buckshot shootings at Koinonia houses, farm animals, and residents, more vandalism, ominous cross-burnings, building-burnings, beatings, legal harassments, Klan caravans. Much Farm property was lost, and insurance companies canceled all Farm policies. Though children asleep in bullet-riddled buildings were sometimes missed only by inches, it was remarkable that no one was ever seriously harmed by the gunshot barrage. The Koinonians responded only by trying to speak peaceably to their assailants, by floodlighting their roads, and if possible by turning "not the other cheek but both heels." [11] Although Jordan was a man who, in Ralph McGill's phrase, "had guts when it took guts to have guts," [12] both he and the whole community lived in nightly fear.

The other threat to the life of the community was a near-total economic boycott by the business firms of south Georgia from 1956 to 1959. Koinonians could not sell their peanuts or buy gasoline for their tractors; they could not gin their cotton or buy fertilizer for their corn. No bank would handle their account; no butane dealer would deliver fuel. Jordan and his friends sought to meet this problem by witnessing in person to every boycotter. A contemporary reporter records one such confrontation.

"Why haven't you been around?" [Jordan asked a butane truck driver.]

"I can't," the man said. "If I do, I'll lose all my other customers; it'll ruin my business."

"It looks to me like you're on a spot," said Jordan in his mild voice. "You're either going to lose some money or you're going to lose your soul."

"I know," the man said, "I ain't doing right, am I?"

"I don't think so. Winter is coming on. We got a lot of chil-

[11] Jordan, phonograph record *Love Your Enemies*.
[12] Quoted by Hal Gulliver in a eulogy of Jordan published in the *Atlanta Constitution*, November 1, 1969, the paper of which McGill was publisher.

dren out there on the farm, and without gas those children are going to be cold. They'll huddle in their coats and, when they get cold, they're going to cry. You'll be sitting here in your nice warm office and when that old north wind begins to howl, maybe you'll be hearing the crying of those children in the howling of the wind."

. . . "My God, Mr. Jordan, I don't know what to do. This thing has got me so messed up I got a headache. I want to keep serving you, but I'm afraid. If I do, I'm going to get my truck blown up someday."

Jordan waited a moment. . . . "I feel sorry for you. All you got to do is stand up on your hind legs and act like a man. Maybe you'd lose your truck, but you'd lose your headache, too."

. . . "I'll tell you what I'm going to do. I'm going to get you the gas. . . . I'll get another man to sell it to you."

Jordan did not move. . . . "You mean you'd ask a friend to take a chance you're not willing to take yourself?" [13]

The conversations didn't change things much. Koinonians considered a move to a second headquarters in New Jersey, but events there proved that Christian communitarianism was as unwelcome in the North as in the South; the Northern branch had to be closed. And after three years, the opposition of Americus to these nonviolent Christians began, little by little, to decrease.

Meanwhile, there were other changes. The boycott had made growing field crops impossible and cattle-raising difficult, but pecans seemed more manageable, so in 1957 a pecan-shelling operation was started; it provided some needed funds, and cash employment for neighboring Blacks. Shaken by the violence and pinched by the boycott, the community shrank but survived. And Clarence Jordan, his mind off farming, began to think about using his poignant way of setting Bible scenes in south Georgia locales for a "Cotton Patch Version" of the New Testament.

Jordan's scholarship was circumscribed, now, not only by his teachers' limitations, but by his own limited library.

[13] André Fontaine, "The Conflict of a Southern Town." Reprinted from *Redbook Magazine*, October, 1957, copyright © 1957, The Redbook Publishing Company.

("*Not* buying books," said Florence, "was Clarence's temptation"—one to which he plainly succumbed.) He seemed to believe that the best opinion held Luke the Physician to be the author of Luke-Acts; Simon Peter to be the author of I (and II?) Peter; John, one of the Twelve, the author of the Johannine literature.[14] By Jordan's day, interpretations of the New Testament in the light of its environment were circulating which might have shed much light on the problems he was confronting in the church and in the world, but those critical interpretations seemed to have gone unnoticed, and one can surmise that in fact Jordan's library did not introduce him to them.[15]

Nevertheless, the *Cotton Patch Version*,[16] besides displaying genuine philological erudition, displayed also an uncanny knack for locating central claims of the gospel of Christ exactly in the lives of its readers. This phenomenon of bringing New Testament events alive was not aimed merely at Southern readers who would be familiar with cotton patch lingo. In fact, the language of the *Version* is not unrelieved Georgia rural, but achieves its striking effects by an artistic superimposing of ancient Near Eastern and modern U.S. Southern elements.[17] Two locales in rapid

[14] For Jordan's views on New Testament authorship, see the introductions to the *Cotton Patch Version*. Could these views have been held by so fair and open a mind had he read and reflected upon such standard works as James Moffatt, *An Introduction to the Literature of the New Testament* (3rd ed., 1918), or Edgar J. Goodspeed, *An Introduction to the New Testament* (1937), or even Kirsopp and Silva Lake, *An Introduction to the New Testament* (1st ed., 1938)? But the evidence is uncertain, since no catalog of his library is known to me.

[15] I have in mind the sort of work done by the history of religions school in Germany, or that represented by Donald W. Riddle and Harold H. Hutson, *New Testament Life and Literature* (1946). (Hutson taught at nearby Birmingham-Southern at that time.) Jordan might have found strong reinforcement for his own reading of Southern ecclesiasticism, politics, and racism in these researches, had he known of them.

[16] See note 8.

[17] Jordan was vividly conscious of this method: see the Introduction to the CPV Luke-Acts. It was his practice to purify his

and unexpected alternation manage to suggest the universality of the message as perhaps neither alone could do. This device achieves a triumph in the Jordan version.

By the middle 1960s, Koinonia community was languishing. Clarence was busy translating and speaking, while the Farm lay fallow. The orginal motivation for a demonstration plot for scientific agriculture and Christian living in the South had been superseded by the times. The rising problem in America seemed not so much poverty and segregation, though those still existed, as it did materialism and greed, a problem arising from abundance rather than from shortage. At this juncture, stimulated by newfound allies such as converted Alabama lawyer Millard Fuller, Jordan began to formulate a new set of problems, possibilities, and projects.

The new plan of 1968, called Koinonia Partners, was wide-ranging. At the Farm in the 1950s, a dedicated few had radically restructured their life histories in order to obey God. Perhaps now there were many others who would accept such restructuring, not necessarily on a farm, but in dozens of ways. Let the new structure be called "partnership with God." It would entail a system of recruitment of the "partners," a system of training for those recruited, and (always final for Jordan) a system of implementation: partnership industries, partnership farming, partnership housing, and perhaps more.[18]

For brevity, consider the last two alone. Jordan believed that economic forces were driving the world's real estate into a few large holdings. The poor man, lacking a rich father from whom to inherit, could not afford to buy enough land to make a living. In socialist land reform, this

Georgia dialect passages by reading English renderings to an old Black neighbor as she sat on her front porch, asking her "Now, how would you say that?"

[18] Clarence Jordan, "A Personal Letter from Clarence Jordan to Friends of Koinonia," *Koinonia Newsletter*, Oct. 21, 1968.

problem was attacked by seizure and forced division of the land. Was there not another way than force? In the Partners' plan, givers would donate enough money to buy up, at the start, a million acres. This would be held by a non-profit Fund for Humanity, which would *lend* the land, without interest, to the poor in small plots for farming and for dwellings. Kononia Farm's assets, $250,000, would make a start on the Fund. Thus the ideal of "usership" would replace the ideal of ownership in property; more and more, owning would become a mere arrangement to guarantee that those who lived there could use the land. Jordan believed that those benefited would be motivated to give to the Fund for the sake of others. Those involved in Partnerships, whether at the Americus site or elsewhere, would draw family allowances (Acts 2:44 to the contrary notwithstanding) for their living needs, and would encourage one another in spiritual community as well.

So went the dream. Perhaps the most remarkable fact is that the dream began to come true. The Fund grew; Koinonia land *was* farmed by Partners; industries, employing Koinonia's Americus neighbors, appeared and flourished; low-cost housing sprang up on state route 49. And then, in a year's time, Clarence Jordan was dead. In his last months, he had traveled with Florence to Africa, had seen another portion of the *Cotton Patch Version* published, had watched the partnership vision set the community on the Farm bustling with new life and activity. He died suddenly, in his translator's shack on the Farm, October 29, 1969, of heart failure. He was 57 years old; the *Cotton Patch Version* was not complete. Survivors included his wife, Florence, who carries on as a Partner; their four children, none of whom remains at Koinonia; and the brothers and sisters in the flesh and in the spirit who had understood his vision so little or so late. They included as well Koinonia's community, which is very fully alive.

II

My business now is to pick out, from this story, the image or images which will permit us to grasp Jordan's central vision and apply it to our theological concerns. We are confronted here with a rich surplus of possibilities. Clarence lived much in the New Testament; he appropriated much of its imagery. We must decide what dominated this full warehouse of images. Dallas Lee offers us three possibilities in the names he has given to three sections of the posthumous volume of Jordan sermons: "Incarnational Evangelism," "The Substance of Faith," "The God Movement." [19] The first two of these, however, lack the special force which I have claimed belongs to the canonical image. They do not, or no longer, work as metaphors. The third is a better prospect. "The God Movement," along with "God's New Order of the Spirit," was Jordan's Cotton Patch term for the kingdom of God or heaven.[20] Thus Luke 19:11 becomes in the *Cotton Patch Version:* "He told this one because they were near Atlanta, and because they were thinking that the God Movement was about to burst forth immediately. . . . ." And Matthew 19:23-25 becomes, "Jesus said to his students, 'I'm telling you a fact; a rich man finds it extremely difficult to come into the God Movement. I say it again, a pig can go through a knothole easier than a rich man can get into the God Movement.' "

Certainly, Jordan's translation of *basileia* as "movement," by which term he meant "something that gets underway spontaneously," [21] is significant. You cannot *plan* a movement, cannot 'organize' or 'enlarge' the God Movement. All you can do is be swept along by it. This means, however, that the image of "the God Movement" alone cannot fully capture what Jordan was, for while he was a man caught up by the tides of God's pur-

---

[19] Lee, ed., *Substance of Faith.*

[20] See *Cotton Patch Version,* in loc. Earlier, Jordan had used the expression "kingdom movement"; see *Sermon on the Mount,* p. 121.

[21] Lee, ed., *Cotton Patch Evidence,* p. 213.

poses, he was preeminently a planner, and a doer as well.

Another image which recurs in Lee's study of Jordan is the "disciple." Clarence was fascinated with the Twelve in the New Testament, furnishing them with remade Cotton Patch names. (Simon Peter, Bar-jonah, becomes "Simon, nicknamed Rock," or "Rock Johnson"; the sons of Zebedee become "Jim, Mr. Zebedee's boy, and his brother Jack.") "Disciples" were not a phenomenon that ended with the first century, but were being called to obedience in these days, right here. Jordan scorned the revivalist term "saved"; he spoke instead in anabaptist fashion of obedient or faithful discipleship. Threatened by the Klan in 1942 for interracial fraternizing, Jordan said, "It was not a question of whether or not we were to be scared, . . . but whether or not we would be *obedient*. The revelation in the New Testament [is] that God is no respecter of persons . . . ." [22] And Lee believes that in the last year of his life, with the bitterness of years of local opposition still hurting him, Clarence increasingly "had clung to *faithfulness* as the one and only responsibility of the follower of Jesus." [23]

As so often, a bit of remembered Jordan dialogue may come nearest to clarifying his notion of discipleship. In the early fifties, it is told, Clarence approached his brother Robert Jordan, later a state senator and justice of the Georgia Supreme Court, asking him to represent Koinonia Farm legally.

"Clarence, I can't do that. You know my political aspirations. Why, if I represented you, I might lose my job, my house, everything I've got."

"*We* might lose everything too, Bob."

"It's different for you."

"Why is it different? I remember, it seems to me, that

[22] *Ibid.*, pp. 38-39. My emphasis.

[23] *Ibid.*, p. 224, my emphasis. It is noteworthy, too, that Jordan's most enduring ally among the many who came to live at Koinonia was Will Wittkamper, a Disciple of Christ minister, for whom this image ("disciple") naturally loomed large.

127

you and I joined the church the same Sunday, as boys. I expect when we came forward the preacher asked me about the same question he did you. He asked me, 'Do you accept Jesus as your Lord and Savior.' And I said, 'Yes.' What did you say?"

"I follow Jesus, Clarence, up to a point."

"Could that point by any chance be—the cross?"

"That's right. I follow him to the cross, but not *on* the cross. I'm not getting myself crucified."

"Then I don't believe you're a disciple. You're an admirer of Jesus, but not a disciple of his. I think you ought to go back to the church you belong to, and tell them you're an admirer not a disciple."

"Well now, if everyone who felt like I do did that, we wouldn't *have* a church, would we?"

"The question," Clarence said, "is, 'Do you have a church?' " [24]

Obedient discipleship was indeed a pervasive image in the life of Clarence Jordan. But as the preceding exchange indicates, there was another image always present as well, that of the church, the Christian community, the *koinonia*. Jordan believed that the early Christians were guided in their understanding of community not only by the idea of *ecclesia* (assembly, church) but also by that of *koinonia*

[24] As the tale is told, Robert then replied, "I think you are the greatest Christian I've ever known." It is interesting that Robert Jordan, who by the world's standards did not come off so badly in this exchange with his brother, was true to his own convictions. In the 1958 Georgia gubernatorial race, opponents charged that the Vandiver forces were tainted, by Koinonia via Robert Jordan, with race-mixing, and were therefore not true to the Southern way of life. Robert, denying all connection with Koinonia, valiantly defended himself and Vandiver: Talbot County was as segregationist as any in the state, and that county's voters would never have returned Robert Jordan to the state Senate had they not known him to be the same. He, Robert, had "fought for and voted for" every segregationist measure in the Senate, and he would vouch for candidate Vandiver. The counterattack was successful; Vandiver won the election handily. See *The Atlanta Journal and Constitution*, Sunday, July 6, 1958, and P. D. East, in *The Petal Paper*, Nov. 6, 1958.

(fellowship, partnership). He felt that in America the former had come to dominate to the exclusion of *koinonia*. As a consequence, the churches were mere ecclesiastical institutions or religious clubs. He was determined to recover the notion and the practice (always both for Jordan) of *koinonia*. In the next pages, I propose to trace the role of this image in Jordan's biography, with a view to fixing more clearly the theological import of his life.

Jordan found the term *koinonia* during his encounter with the Greek New Testament at Southern Seminary, 1933–39. Built on the stem *koin-*, "common," it was translated "fellowship," "participation," "communication," "communion," in standard English versions, but none of these, he learned, captured the full force of the term. *Koinonia* was what the earliest Jerusalem Christians shared, according to Acts 2, when they shared their goods and their lives in Holy Spirit (2:42 ff.). Another use appeared in I Corinthians. The "cup of praise" which believers share is here a *koinonia* of the Messiah's blood, the broken bread a *koinonia* of his body, for all share (*metechein*) the one loaf. Eaters of a sacrifice in Israel were *koinonoi* (sharers) of that sacrifice; this is true, said Paul, even in demonic sacrifices—such participants become *koinonous* (partners) with the demons (10:14-22). Paul uses the same term of the purse being collected for the poorer brothers and sisters; such activity is ministry via *koinonia* (shared wealth) (II Cor. 8:4; cf. 9:13; Rom. 15:26).

Clarence Jordan's earliest use of this image seems to have been to provide a name for the informal band of Southern Baptist Theological Seminary students who shared in the Fellowship Center mission work in Louisville about 1939–42. These students agreed to attend Negro churches and serve within them if requested. The dozen or more, who looked to Clarence for leadership and stayed close to him, "slowly and informally evolved into an on-campus group which met several times a month for study and discussion. Clarence began to toss out his ideas about pacifism, racial equality, and the radical stewardship of complete sharing. As the group became more cohesive, they sought to define themselves. Clarence offered the Greek word *Koinonia*. . . ." [25] It is interesting that this early *Koinonia* actually established a common bank account, though there was never much money in it.

Already in Jordan's dreams during those early days was the "demonstration plot," Koinonia Farm, which the Jordans and the Englands established in 1942. In a 1956 article, he set out "some of the spiritual beliefs which hold [Koinonia Farm] together." First there was the persuasion that "any commitment to Christ is a total one, involving surrender of self, vocation, possessions—everything. It transcends all human commitments or loyalties and, like marriage, is for better or for worse." [26] Commitment to Christ was not identical with commitment to Christ's community, but it could not be separated from the latter commitment, either. Koinonians, having this double commitment, expressed it by turning all their goods over to the community. (If they had very much wealth, they were asked to dispose of it elsewhere before joining.) "This principle of common ownership characterizes any human family where a real love relationship exists, and we feel that a family of the Father should do no less." [27]

A second principle, distribution according to need, entailed a 'family' decision upon the purchase of each tractor—or of any member's new shoes. A third declared that "there must be no favorite children" in the family, "whether they are blondes or brunettes, white or black." [28] In the South, this meant no racial lines could be drawn by Koinonia. A child of God was a child of God, period. Without the interpretation provided by the second and third principles, Koinonia might have been indistinguishable

[25] Lee, ed., *Cotton Patch Evidence,* p. 26.
[26] Jordan, "Christian Community in the South," p. 29.
[27] *Ibid.*
[28] *Ibid.*

from the cultural Christianity of the South. With these principles added, however, they were "Communists" and "integrationists" in their White neighbors' eyes.

No less important was the fourth and final principle. Extending the familiar figure, this emphasized the community's relation to God as a Father who gave his qualities to his offspring. His nature was increasingly to give shape to their own character. And that nature "is redemptive love. He is not a God of violence, hate, or revenge. . . ."[29] Thus Koinonia must be a peaceable community; with such a God it could not defend itself (the year of Jordan's article saw the beginnings of the shootings, arson, bombings of the Farm) by any means save "by practicing the truth in love" (Eph. 4:15 CPV).

What was happening to Jordan's *koinonia* image was concurrent with what was happening to his life. In seminary and city mission days, *koinonia* had stood for sharing, even a brief sharing of a bank account, but the sharing was with a primary view to *service*. We might say that its focus then came from II Corinthians 8:4, where it can be translated "offering," the main form of "offering" then being the week-by-week ministerial services rendered by the Louisville student *Koinonia*. At Americus, however, *koinonia* came to stand primarily for *community,* and the problem that arose was how self-giving in community could be truly total, how it could participate in the total giving of oneself to Jesus Christ.

It may clarify this point to see that a parallel problem arose for the Koinonia Farm residents who had joined nearby Rehoboth Baptist Church. Southern Baptists were schooled in the importance of transferring membership to the church where one lived. It was painful on both sides when it began to appear that dedicated Baptists like the Jordans could not fulfill that ideal at Rehoboth. The Koinonians' "views and practices" came, they believed, from the

[29] *Ibid.,* p. 30.

very New Testament gospel to which Rehoboth also declared loyalty. Loyalty to the ideal of fellowship ran head-on into loyalty to Jesus; Jesus and his church were at odds. In that case, though, it was clear to Clarence and Florence that the church must come second, not first. Would the case of Koinonia Farm community be otherwise?

When Koinonia Farm began, its founders had no contact with, and little knowledge of, other intentional communities. Soon, however, such knowledge and contacts began. Two larger and older fellowships, the Hutterian communities and the Society of Brothers (Bruderhof), interchanged ideas and members with Koinonia during the fifties. Both of these, like Koinonia, were Christian: the Hutterites were Anabaptists who had journeyed, fleeing persecution, from medieval Europe to Russia to the Dakotas, Montana, and Canada in a centuries-long pilgrimage; the Bruderhof, begun in Germany in 1920 by Eberhard Arnold as a community of love and brotherhood, had migrated to England, to Paraguay, and to New York State, Pennsylvania, and Connecticut in a much briefer period.[30] One consequence of the contact with these groups was a challenge to the concept of community held by the Koinonians. The Koinonians had worked to draw up a "pledge" to be signed by each full member. By 1951, this had evolved into a two-sentence statement:

We desire to make known our total, unconditional commitment to seek, express, and expand the Kingdom of God as revealed in Jesus the Christ. Being convinced that the community of believers who make a like commitment is the continuing body of Christ on earth, I joyfully enter into a love union with the Koinonia and gladly submit myself to it, looking to it to guide me in the knowledge of God's will and to strengthen me in the pursuit of it.[31]

[30] An interesting recent account of the Bruderhof in sociological perspective is Benjamin Zablocki, *The Joyful Community* (Baltimore: Penguin Books, 1971).

[31] Lee, ed., *Cotton Patch Evidence*, p. 83.

As we have seen, this was understood to entail surrender of individual private property ownership, communal decisions about the life of the community, and the renunciation of all racial barriers and of all violence. What is remarkable is what it omitted: it offered no constitutional structure for the society, no officers, teachers, disciplinary procedures—in general, no 'rule' for community life. Some Koinonians moved to the Hutterian colony at Forest River, or shifted their allegiance to the Bruderhof, and then complained that Koinonia had permitted an individual autonomy that was inimical to total community as experienced in these other places.

Clarence thought long and hard about this challenge. What did total commitment involve? His response, as expressed in a 1956 letter to former Koinonian Marion Johnson, revealed his state of mind on the proper understanding of the elusive *koinonia*.

Let me say that you are right about my being thrilled at the first contact with the Bruderhof. Immediately I saw in them a sister community, produced by the same Spirit. I felt the same deep sense of kinship with Forest River when Will and I visited there, and sought to convey that to the group here both by our letters home and in later reports. And this sense of kinship with both Forest River and the Bruderhof has neither left me nor diminished. . . . I have never felt that there was an "either-or" between us, that one was above or below the other, that one was divine and the other human. True, there are differences, in some of which Koinonia excels and in others the Bruderhof excels, but that's all the more reason why we need each other, and why each can help the other to be more Spirit-led.[32]

What Jordan saw clearly then was that no pattern of community could in itself guarantee spiritual life and health, or exclude the inevitable admixture of grace and sin. To have judged otherwise, regarding some one pattern of Christian community such as Koinonia Farm as a final end in it-

[32] *Ibid.*, pp. 102-3.

self, would have been to turn the image of *koinonia* into an idol, a false god, and this Clarence was not to do.

This issue was focused by the events of 1956–58. During the hardest time of the boycott and violence in Americus, the question was inevitably considered whether Koinonia should yield to the pressure of bombs and the offers of a fair purchase price for the Farm, and move away from that antagonistic neighborhood. At that time, many friends, especially in the Bruderhof, were urging Koinonia to do just that, on the ground that it was the community itself which was supremely valuable. But in the minds of those who stayed, neither their own lives nor Koinonia's fellowship was ultimately valuable in itself; both could be risked in order to be faithful to Jesus. In Jesus' name, they had an obligation to another 'community,' the racially torn, sin-sick society in and around Americus, where they had staked out their witness and staked their lives.

> To leave or abandon an opponent is not an expression of love for him. So long as an adversary has "aught against you, Go," said Jesus, "and be reconciled to him." A man is not free to leave until that between him and his adversary has been cleared up. Therefore, we felt that Koinonia must continue the struggle for redemption and reconciliation, no matter how difficult it might be for all concerned.[33]

Jordan's vision of *koinonia* never conceived the 'church' and the 'world' as totally distinct realms. *Koinonia* meant loving your enemies, and that meant staying to be reconciled with them.

[33] Clarence Jordan, draft of letter to the editor, *Atlanta Journal*, preserved in scrapbooks at Koinonia Farm. How little Koinonia understood itself as a community separated from the outside world can also be seen in the history of the relations of Koinonia children to the public schools of Sumter County during Jordan's lifetime. The Farm never ran a weekday school, but chose to send children to the White, or often Black, public schools, which were otherwise still segregated. Indeed at one point the Wittkampers, Brownes, and Jordans filed suit in federal court to prevent their children from being excluded by local prejudice from the Americus school system.

Recapitulating, I have said that the ongoing struggle to define the role and mission of Koinonia Farm was also a struggle to define and give concrete form to one dominant image, *koinonia,* which Clarence Jordan found in Scripture, and by which his own life was grasped. It was the struggle to avoid, on the one hand, the deification of that image, making loyalty to community merely and totally identical with loyalty to Christ. And it was the struggle, on the other hand, to maintain that image in all its rightful power, not allowing it to be swept away when the life in community became inconvenient or threatening. Images have rights, too! Jordan maintained this struggle even in connection with the rupture with Rehoboth Church. When the split came, he did his best to persuade the church to reconsider its withdrawal of fellowship. Years later, he could still ruminate, in a public address: "I hope and pray that before I pass on to glory, the little church that expelled me from its fellowship will realize that I really am its son, that I really do love it and that it will gather with me, perhaps even after the crucifixion, along with the rest of the brethren. . . ." [34] He was not expressing a nostalgic desire to go back to mother church, but rather a longing to be led with that church into a truly crucified and risen *koinonia,* which would incorporate his own vision as well.

This understanding of the faithful Christian's relation to the community was also expressed in another vivid Jordan image, that of the 'church pregnant.' Mary had been pregnant with Jesus, and Jesus was God's son (a relationship Jordan took to express a religious truth but not a scientific truth; in the scientific sense, he supposed that Jesus was precisely Joseph's son) .[35] Until after the resurrection, Mary had resisted letting her son be the son of God. She "tried to keep him. She was told that he was God's son, but the mother instinct in her wanted to keep him. She wanted him

[34] Lee, ed., *Substance of Faith,* p. 16.
[35] *Ibid.,* p. 19.

for *her* son." [36] Mary, however, is typical of the church, which has the role of bearing sons in the image of God, but shrinks from that role.

Now, the early church was willing to become pregnant. But I think the trouble with God's bride today is that she either has passed the menopause or she's on the pill. Or perhaps even worse, she's gone a-whoring. It could be that she has sought other husbands, that she's trying to let someone else impregnate her. And generally when a woman goes a-whoring and becomes pregnant, she hopes that the offspring will favor her, rather than the father. And I think this is what's happening many times in the Church today. It isn't that we are failing to beget children. We are begetting children. But they are not bearing the image of the Almighty. They are bearing the image of false gods. [37]

Thus, via a little Baptist Mariology, the image of the church, like that of *koinonia,* is kept from idolatrous pretensions.

Jordan's image of *koinonia* came to its fullest development in his concept of *partnership*. Although this term appeared in his speech and writing over the years, it was not until his last year, when he had grown deeply discouraged with earlier expressions of *koinonia*—as church, as mission, as community—that the partnership idea really flowered. Partnership, as we have seen, meant concretely a grand plan, developed in 1968, for recruiting, training, and employing Partners—in Jordan's terminology it meant communication, instruction, and application. Basic to the idea of Koinonia Partners was an element also at the root of biblical *koinonia:* partnership in this sense is first of all being *God's* partner; it means taking seriously the incarnational theme. In his incarnation, God is "not in his heaven with all well on the earth. He is on this earth, and all hell's broke loose." [38] Partnership with God also means taking seriously the resurrection theme:

[36] *Ibid.,* p. 15.
[37] *Ibid.,* p. 21.
[38] *Ibid.,* p. 24.

He raised Jesus, not as an invitation to us to come to heaven when we die, but as a declaration that He Himself has now established permanent, eternal residence on earth. . . . The good news of the resurrection is not that we shall die and go home with him, but that he has risen and comes home with us, bringing all his hungry, naked, thirsty, sick, prisoner brothers with him.

And we say, "Jesus, we'd be glad to have you, but all these motley brothers of yours, you had better send them home. You come in and we'll have some fried chicken. But you get your sick, naked, cold brothers out of here. We don't want them getting our new rug all messed up." [39]

Partnership to Clarence Jordan meant accepting anew this vision of an active, earth-seeking God, and finding ways of sharing both the vision, and earth's goods, with the rich *and* the poor, the high and mighty *and* the down and out. One element seems on first examination omitted from the plan for Koinonia Partners: deliberate bringing of the Partners into spiritual community with one another. In the plan, this wealthy farmer might donate his land, and that poor laborer might find himself with a chance to own his own home, but how are the two of them to be brought side by side on their knees, or face to face sharing their evening meal and sharing their faith?

A different kind of Christian mind would have answered this question by generating a liturgical structure for the Partnership, or by laying down a new rule for faith and practice. But the free spirit of Clarence Jordan was content to leave spiritual community to the Spirit. After all, "the wind blows as it will, and you listen to its sound, but you have no idea where it's coming from or where it's going. It's like that when a person is fathered by the Spirit" (John 3:8-9 CPV). Perhaps that was too bold a trust. But the fact which any critic must concede is that Koinonia community does live on, on the Farm and elsewhere, providing Partners with a spiritual. *koinonia* as they work at their

[39] *Ibid.,* p. 28.

common tasks. Maybe Jordan knew what to leave to the Spirit.

III

Jordan's changing theology was never fixed in a single pattern. At the beginning, he was closest, save on a few issues (but those were crucial ones), to the traditional orthodoxy of the Baptist South. By the time of his death, biblical study fertilized by a life of profound Christian action had reshaped many of his convictions. Three strands seem prominent throughout this development. (1) Jordan was, as his biographer Lee emphasized, an "incarnationist." But this did not mean that his Jesus was a God-man, a masquerading deity. Rather, in the man Jesus we learn that God is not an absentee landlord. Jordan sometimes put this point with a totality and force that might have satisfied Thomas Altizer. God is not *there,* in heaven; he is *here* in Jesus and his brothers.[40] This theme provided a doctrinal backbone, as far as I can tell, through all his thought. (2) He made "faith" central in Christian life, but "faith" had neither the rationalist's sense of belief in the improbable, nor the Reformation sense of self-abandoning trust in God. Faith is always understood as the ground of *action:* it is "a life in scorn of the consequences"; it is "conviction translated into deeds."[41] In brief, he did not believe it was faith unless it was what one lived by. The well-known characterization of faith in Hebrews 11:1 came out in the *Cotton Patch Version:* "Now faith is the turning of dreams into deeds." (3) As the image *koinonia* has shown us, the faith with which Jordan was concerned was faith-lived-in-community; it was (to coin a word) koinonic faith, and Jordan's ethics was always a koinonic ethics, which valued community, under God, highest of all. No one community

[40] *Ibid.,* pp. 12-38; cf. Lee, *Cotton Patch Evidence,* p. 186.

[41] Lee, ed., *Substance of Faith,* p. 43; Lee, *Cotton Patch Evidence,* p. 143.

or form of community was essential, but God intended the disciple to be together with his brothers and his neighbors.

We are of course under no obligation to replicate these or any of Jordan's own beliefs. Our task is rather to ask about our own theological vision in the light of what we learn of him. The central question, it seems to me, with which Jordan's life story confronts us is: what are we to make of life together in the light of our life with God? The communities we enter may not be Jordan's community; our heritage may not be Baptist or Southern, or focus as did his in anabaptist fashion on the Sermon on the Mount. Yet we find ourselves, whoever we are, living in a world in which some are richer than they need to be and some poorer, a world in which class, caste, race divide men, a world in which "men of violence seize the kingdom" of man, if not the kingdom of God. If, as suggested in the preceding chapter, the central theme of a theology in the biblical line must be the meeting of God and man, their encounter, their having to do with one another here and now, then Jordan's life asks us: given that primal meeting, in what manner are we to meet our neighbors?

Chapter Six

Expanding the Theory: Charles Edward Ives— Theologian in Music

By now the music of Charles Ives is as familiar to concert-goers as that of any American composer. His *Concord* Sonata for piano and his great Fourth Symphony have become part of the standard fare. It is also known, at least to musicians, that this acclaim represents a profound shift in musical taste for which Ives himself is partly responsible, for during the years when he was actively composing them (1895–1915) he was unable to have any of his major works performed in public. Thus he endured many years of apparent total failure in music prior to his ultimate success. Ives's musical innovations include radical departures from traditional harmony and tonality: 'discord' is music, too. They also include use of materials drawn from the sounds of America: rural nature, city streets, marching bands, Stephen Foster melodies, and "What a Friend We Have in Jesus"—the whole without precedent in serious composition.

Those who have studied his biography know that during the years of composition Ives devoted himself also to the insurance business and made a fortune in it, and that later he wrote short but passionate tracts and essays on social, political, and aesthetic topics. Very few, however, are aware that behind Ives the musician, Ives the pamphleteer, and Ives the insurance executive stands still another Ives, whom we may tentatively call Ives the theologian, in whose thought his activity in business, in politics, and in music has a common root. This chapter will therefore explore the religious basis of the career of Charles E. Ives and will ask how the understanding of this life, seen in terms of its central or dominant images, may contribute to the clarity of our own theological vision.

In doing this, we will have to expand the idea of the 'image' which we have so far employed, that of a metaphor in language which illuminates a life and thereby may illuminate our own faith. For Ives, though he made considerable use of the written word in insurance, in politics, and in musical criticism, made his chief medium of expression not words but music itself. His words were eloquent, but it is impossible to treat his music as peripheral to his life. So we are confronted here with the question of whether the tonal images of Ives's music (or of any music, ever) can be 'translated' into verbal images, whether there can be a transmigration of images: whether dominant metaphors can be seen to unify not only Ives's literary and financial and political activities, but also his musical compositions. Will it be possible to *say* what his music means, to say what *he* means by it, and thus to say what Charles Ives, that human person, means or is?

I

Present purposes aside, the story of Ives's life, full of drama, agony, and final delight, is worth telling in its own right.[1] He was born in Danbury, Connecticut, October 20, 1874, the son of George Ives, a Yankee bandmaster, and Mary Parmelee Ives, a farmer's daughter. The Ives family were old New England settlers; more recently Charles's father had soldiered under U. S. Grant as an army bandmaster during the Civil War. Charles had no sisters; his only brother, Moss, born fifteen months later than he, would become a well-known Connecticut lawyer.

Charles's boyhood was full of the things small-town America afforded boys: school, baseball, summer revival camp-meetings, church, playing 'store' in his grandmother's backyard, weddings, funerals, country excursions, books, friends—and home. It was America's first Gilded Age, and Mark Twain (whom Ives was later to know) was writing satirically of its phony glitter, but Charles Ives's

[1] The principal source for Ives's life is a series of autobiographical memoranda which he prepared in the 1930s and which have been published, together with much other useful biographical information, as Charles E. Ives, *Memos,* ed. John Kirkpatrick (New York: W. W. Norton, 1972). There are also autobiographical data in Ives's other writings. The longer of these pieces have been gathered up in Charles Ives, *Essays Before a Sonata, The Majority, and Other Writings,* ed. Howard Boatwright (New York: W. W. Norton, 1962). (The first part of this book was separately published, under the title *Essays Before a Sonata,* by the same publisher in 1961.) Ives wrote introductions to many of his compositions when they were published and frequently scrawled comments of biographical value in the margins of his score sheets, and some of the latter have been published with the music as well. Many of the scrawls are collected in John Kirkpatrick, compiler, *A Temporary Mimeographed Catalogue of the Music Manuscripts and Related Materials of Charles Edward Ives, 1874-1954* (Yale University, 1960). The unpublished writings, together with some letters and other materials, are available in the Ives Collection at Yale University, but I have not examined these.

The chief biography of Ives is Henry and Sidney Cowell, *Charles Ives and His Music* (New York: Oxford University Press, 2nd ed. with added material, 1969). This contains a partial bibliography of articles on Ives and passages on him in treatments of modern music, to 1969. A critical biography, with full access to the sources, has yet to be written. In what follows, I will note sources only where I believe the facts I report cannot readily be found in Cowell or in Kirkpatrick's *Memos,* or where my interpretation demands backing.

boyhood hometown was closer in type to Hannibal, Missouri, than to the coruscations of the capitals and the young American cities. As a boy Charles read Thoreau and Emerson and found the virtues they espoused confirmed in the texture of life in Danbury, Connecticut.

A simple setting, however, does not insure a simple childhood. The two preoccupations of the boy were baseball and music. Baseball meant the male brotherhood, team spirit, personal glory. Music meant instruction from his talented and clever father, long hours of practice indoors, praise from old ladies—and perhaps a degree of sissy softness. How to avoid the latter? Luckily his father started Charles on that masculine instrument, the drum, and soon he was discovering that a piano keyboard could be made to play drum notes, too! But we have here touched on a lifelong tension: Charlie would be obliged to scorn "men in skirts," effeminacy in musical taste, and any sign in himself or others of being "a God damned sissy." One wonders, looking long at the photographs of Charles's father, whether George Ives the bandmaster—though in 1885 he wore a U. S. Grant Civil War beard—was the original of this abhorred sissy *imago,* and whether Charles's own music and manner were efforts to reject in his father, and thus in himself, the aspect of softness he associated with musicianship. In any case, when young Charles's compositions were admired, and he was asked what he played, he chose to reply, "Shortstop."

Nevertheless, his education was preeminently a musical one. At home, George Ives expected the major band instruments to be learned and played, and theory mastered. Moreover, George was a Yankee innovator, gifted with perfect pitch and a flair for invention, fond of inventing machines to make sounds not ordinarily heard from bandstands—a system of waterglasses to play quarter-tone tunes, for example. George was always trying to stretch the family's ears to new sounds: he would make them sing a hymn in one key while the accompaniment was played in another. Thus Charles was forced to learn the 'rules' of harmony and interval by learning also what it was like to break these rules; foundations were being laid for later creativity. Meanwhile Charlie was busy as organist at the Baptist church (beginning on his fifteenth birthday), member of his father's town band, composer of pieces for band and for organ, and, as time permitted, member of the Danbury Alerts baseball team. He also attended Danbury Academy and Danbury High School, and at eighteen went away to Hopkins Grammar School in New Haven to prepare for Yale.

Growing up in Danbury meant religious opportunity as well. Church attendance was at First Congregational for the Ives, but Charlie was sent to the Methodist Sunday school, his mother having been brought up Methodist.[2] When he began his organist jobs, he began a circuit that took him, during adolescence and young manhood, to the Baptist, Episcopal, Congregational, and Presbyterian churches. More memorable than church, though, were his experiences of attending the summer camp meetings which had become a feature of late nineteenth-century rural New England. Naturally, Charlie remembered his father leading the music, and the grand singing:

I remember, when I was a boy—at the outdoor Camp Meeting services in Redding, all the farmers, their families and field hands, for miles around, would come afoot or in their farm wagons. I remember how the great waves of sound used to come through the trees—when things like *Beulah Land, Woodworth, Nearer My God To Thee, The Shining Shore, Nettleton, In the Sweet Bye and Bye* and the like were sung by thousands of "let out" souls.[3]

And did the singing and the preaching take inward hold? Did he profess his faith, or join a church? Alas, his biographers have not learned, or have not told. What we do know is that unforgotten experiences of an inward sort came also: one of them linked not with church or revival

[2] Letter from John Kirkpatrick to me dated June 5, 1973.
[3] Ives, *Memos*, p. 132.

meeting, but with his father's marching band: "In the early morning of a Memorial Day, a boy is awakened by martial music—a village band is marching down the street—and as the strains of Reeves' majestic *Seventh Regiment March* come nearer and nearer . . . a moment of vivid power comes . . . an assurance that nothing is impossible, and that the whole world lies at his feet." [4]

A later experience must be dated between the ages of nineteen and twenty-three. It gathers up the first, but places it in a Christian context, deeper than the first, and truer to the reality Ives sensed.

Later in life, the same boy hears the Sabbath morning bell ringing out from the white steeple at the "Center," and as it draws him to it, through the autumn fields of sumach and asters, a Gospel hymn of simple devotion comes out to him—"There's a wideness in God's mercy"—an instant suggestion of that Memorial Day morning comes—but the moment is of deeper import—there is no personal exultation—no intimate world vision—no magnified personal hope—and in their place a profound sense of a spiritual truth—a sin within reach of forgiveness. And as the hymn voices die away, there lies at his feet—not the world, but the figure of the Saviour—he sees an unfathomable courage—an immortality for the lowest—the vastness in humility, the kindness of the human heart, man's noblest strength—and he knows that God is nothing—nothing—but love! [5]

The sum of Charles Ives's home years is undoubtedly positive on any scale we have considered. He was a good ballplayer and was to get better, pitching for Hopkins in a memorable defeat of the Yale freshman team. He was a good organist ("youngest in the state," said the Danbury *News* in 1888) and his music won his father's praise and trust. While he was no virtuoso in the Danbury schools, he was not a dropout, either. To any chronicler who looked in upon Danbury *circa* 1892, eighteen-year-old Charlie Ives

[4] Ives, "Emerson," in Boatwright, ed., *Essays Before a Sonata* . . . , p. 30.
[5] *Ibid.*, pp. 30-31.

must have seemed secure in his family, in the world of his peers, and in the rise of his art.

Yet there was in that very success the yeast of costly failure. Let Sidney Cowell tell the story:

At thirteen he composed a band piece, *Holiday Quick Step*. This was the first of Charles Ives' compositions to win comment in the public press; it was approved and the young composer applauded. When a little later the piece was performed by the band for the Decoration Day parade, Charlie was too overcome to appear in his usual place at the snare drum. Instead, when the band came marching down Main Street past the Ives house playing Charlie's piece full tilt, the boy was discovered nervously playing handball against the barn door, with his back to the parade.[6]

Why this turning of the back when the father's band plays the son's tune? Why the refusal of the unavoidable risk of blame or praise? Is there not here a premonition, a first experience of the great and costly risk which making music entails? And is it not significant that what his sure young ear told him in 1888 was musical success was just as painful, in its way, as what his businessman's judgment would tell him in 1919 was, though not musical failure, yet failure in music, failure in winning an audience for his work? [7]

Yale College was certainly weighted with many kinds of failure for Charles Ives. John Kirkpatrick says that only in music, his major, did Ives ever rise above a gentleman's C,[8] but that seems too generous a summary: dullard's D would be nearer the actual achievement of his four-year course. How can we explain that one of the deeper and more wide-ranging American minds of its time did so poorly? There are some reasons. Charles's beloved father died suddenly during his freshman year, and the shadow of

[6] *Charles Ives and His Music,* p. 27.

[7] Cf. *ibid.,* pp. 90-91, and Kirkpatrick, ed., *Memos,* esp. pp. 114-27. The psychodynamics of failure and success in Ives's biography deserves exploration. These feelings were evidently intense, yet so masked that friends like the Cowells and Henry Bellamann could speak of Ives's "curious indifference."

[8] Kirkpatrick, ed., *Memos,* p. 182.

that death hung over his college stay.[9] His college music courses seemed to him repetitive of what he had already learned from George Ives; however Professor Horatio Parker seemed determined to allow no experimental nonsense in classroom compositions. Every note must be by the book. There was also substantial competition for young Ives's attention—work as a church organist, playing with the Hyperion Theater Orchestra, days writing music for fraternity shows. More noteworthy still, during these years he was busy composing first versions of both the First and the Second Symphony, and the First String Quartet.

After college, Ives went to New York City to look for a job in the business world. Virgil Thomson, the composer, has severely faulted Ives for choosing, after college, a career in business, not music. Ives, claims Thomson, is a "maimed" composer, and what is at fault is character itself: he did not give his all to his art. He should have become not a successful businessman but a music teacher; then he would have been a whole man.[10] Ives's own retrospective explanation of his choice was that his boyhood had indeed left him "partially ashamed" of an occupation as musician—was it not too much an emasculated art?

Father felt that a man could keep his music-interest stronger, cleaner, bigger, and freer, if he didn't try to make a living out of it. Assuming a man lived by himself, and with no dependents, no one to feed but himself, and willing to live as simply as Thoreau—[he] might write music that no one would play, publish, listen to, or buy. *But*—if he has a nice wife and some nice children, how can he let the children starve on his dissonances —answer that, Eddy! [11]

Perhaps in any case it is too much to impute vile money-grubbing motives to the college graduate of 1898 who goes

[9] Cf. *ibid.*, p. 227, note 30, and pp. 257-58.
[10] Virgil Thomson, "The Ives Case," *New York Review of Books,* May 21, 1970, p. 9.
[11] Ives, *Memos,* p. 131. "Eddy" is one of the fictionalized *personae* whom Ives uses as foils in his writing; cf. "Arthur," "Rollo." See the entry "Eddy" in the index of names in *Memos.*

to New York City, lives in Poverty Flat, composes all his free time, and supports himself with a five-dollar-a-week job in an insurance office. But the real difference between Thomson and Ives, I think, lies in their view of business. Ives regarded neither musicianship nor business as inviolate vocations. He did regard business as potentially a widener of Emersonian sensibilities. Being thrown with thousands of people of all sorts for many years, his friends believed, gave him a "high respect for the average man's mind and character." [12] Ives said business gave one access to the great issues of life: "tragedy, nobility, meanness, high aims, low aims, brave hopes, faint hopes, great ideals, no ideals," and enabled one to "watch these work inevitable destiny." [13] In brief, we have here a hint that business work was for him a means more than an end, and that his end was something other than the money to be earned in downtown Manhattan.

The story of the following twenty years (1898–1918) has been told and retold on many a record jacket and in not a few articles and books.[14] Ives continued to compose, writing and rewriting huge stacks of music manuscript, perhaps 150 songs of the musical seriousness of Schubert *Lieder,* 5 symphonies (counting *Holidays* Symphony), 2 orchestral sets (including *Three Places in New England*) and a Theater Orchestra Set, 2 string quartets, 4 or 5 violin-and-piano sonatas, 2 piano sonatas (the second being the *Concord* Sonata), choral settings for 12 of the Psalms, and a shower of smaller pieces for band, orchestra, organ, piano, etc. He wrote these at a furious pace, sometimes during hours at the office when fragments occurred to him, more often at home or on vacations. He wrote in an awful scrawl, tossing the paper over his shoulder onto a pile, to be copied later (if ever) by a paid copyist. He continued as

[12] Henry Bellamann, "Charles Ives: The Man and His Music," *The Musical Quarterly,* Jan., 1933, p. 46.
[13] *Ibid.,* p. 47.
[14] See note 1.

church organist in Central Presbyterian Church, New York, until 1902, when he resigned seeking more time for composing. Meanwhile he met and married Harmony Twichell, a Hartford minister's daughter noted for her beauty and character. And he formed a firm with Julian Myrick which became Ives and Myrick, in its day the largest-volume life insurance brokerage house in America, representing Mutual of New York in Manhattan.

Ives and Myrick became a prestigious business and made a mint of money. Though stable, it was far from staid. Ives was responsible for promotion, training, and sales. In a day when government social security was only a dream, he believed that life insurance should provide a decent minimum for the workingman's widow, and he trained agents to go out to help the plain man meet his family's need for financial security. Ives had other, more radical ideas for income redistribution as well, but that did not keep him from pressing his insurance ideas for all they could produce. He peppered his partner, the parent company, and the insurance trade with memos designed to revise the business in line with its human function as opposed to its role as a guardian of the assets of the investors.[15] He salted these two fast-paced decades of simultaneous musical composition and commercial management with convictions drawn from the American Transcendentalists, from his own boyhood experience, and from the radical faith which had somehow merged these two into one. And then, in late 1918, disaster struck. When it had done its work, he had to retire from business and from music as well.

The full details of Ives's crippling illness have not been published. The first unmistakable sign of trouble was a disabling heart attack. There were other symptoms, however: a type of nervous disorder which caused sounds to be heard in a distorted way; an emotional affliction which made it difficult for the genial Ives to meet even friends,

[15] See Ives, "Correspondence with Darby A. Day," in *Essays Before a Sonata . . .* , pp. 240-42.

far less strangers. Diabetes set in, and cataracts. As these troubles began, Ives found it impossible to continue sustained composition. It seemed his career was ended in his mid-forties. He took leave from Ives and Myrick and later withdrew from the firm. He tried repeatedly to sit down at the piano, but his nervous symptoms were intensified by composing.

In fact, however, halted on two fronts Ives merely opened a third and began to publish—both music and essays. All his life he had been deeply influenced by Thoreau and Emerson. He now set out to write about the Concord men and women whom he had celebrated in the Second Piano Sonata (*Concord, Mass., 1840–90*) —Thoreau, Emerson, Hawthorne, the Alcott family. This collection of essays ended with a long serious reflection on the source of artistic intuition—the relation holding between art and the ever-flowing stream "partly biological, partly cosmic, ever going on in ourselves, in nature, in all life." [16] Ives published these essays at his own expense in 1920. (Simultaneously he privately published the *Concord* Sonata, and in 1922 his *114 Songs,* and distributed these works to libraries and to whoever asked for a copy, without charge.)

Meanwhile, the invalid was also at work on another idea. Long reflection had led Ives to believe that unchecked 'representative' government (concentration of political power) and unlimited private property rights (concentration of wealth) were profound and interlocked evils, which had led the nations into a World War only a minority had wanted or intended. His essay "The Majority," published posthumously,[17] served to organize these radical political ideas.

The 1930s saw the widespread acceptance of Ives's major insurance concepts—agent training and "estate planning."

[16] *Essays Before a Sonata* . . . , p. 71.

[17] Ives, "The Majority," Boatwright, ed., *Essays Before a Sonata* . . . , pp. 139-99. See also Ives, *Memos,* pp. 205-28, for an important supplement to the Boatwright text.

This decade also saw the first tentative performances of his major works, as a few performers and conductors risked boos and cat-calls to give his innovative music, with its distinctively American (and therefore in urban America unacceptable?) sounds a public hearing. After World War II, the musical atmosphere changed. Ives's technical originality had by then been matched by that of important Europeans, notably Arnold Schönberg. A major series of programs was devoted to the work of these two composers in the 1944–45 Los Angeles season. All this was accepted, or rather ignored, by the aging Ives with majestic equanimity; his struggle for musical acceptance was now more than half a century old, and he seemed no longer to be concerned about it. When he was given the Pulitzer Prize in 1947 for the Third Symphony (which he had completed in 1904!) he said laconically that "prizes are the badges of mediocrity" —and he gave the money away. The gruffness suggests the old pain of failure or of success; one remembers thirteen-year-old Charlie bouncing a ball against the barn as the band paraded by, playing his march. And so amid rising (and ignored) acclamation, the bittersweet life of "our first really great composer . . . our musical Mark Twain, Emerson, and Lincoln all rolled into one" [18] was lived out. He wrote and dictated his *Memos* ("no one but the President of a nice bank or a Golf Club, or a dead Prime Minister, can write 'Memoirs'" [19]). He helped musicians who were struggling to understand his music. He wrote peppery letters to Presidents of the United States, and profane ones to old friends. He continued to labor upon a *Universe* Symphony, begun in 1911, whose performance would require several orchestras at once, "the underlying plan of which was a presentation and contemplation in tones, rather than in music (as such), of the mysterious creation of the earth and firmament, the evolution of all life in na-

[18] Leonard Bernstein, on two separate jackets of his recording of Ives's Second Symphony, Columbia Records, n.d.
[19] *Memos*, pp. 25-26.

ture, in humanity, to the Divine." [20] The work was never completed. Ives died in New York in his eightieth year, and was buried in West Redding, Connecticut.

Perhaps the most glaring omission from the preceding sketch is adequate note of the winsome, puckish, sometimes zany charm of the man. It appeared in the erratic notes scrawled on the pages of his music manuscripts—to himself, to future performers, to the copyist, e.g., "Mr. Price: Please don't try to make things nice! All the wrong notes are *right*." [21] Or it may appear in his insisting, to performers he believed understood his music, that they might do things their *own* way. There was no single 'right' way to perform his work, and the performer just might need to improvise and thus become a partner in the creation.[22]

II

Our present business, however, is to discover the religion of Charles Ives, and to show, if we can, the sense in which it underlies and unifies his life. By "religion," as before explained, I mean life lived out under the governance of a central vision. I will seek, therefore, some central image, or cluster of images, by which our subject understood himself and his horizons, and through which that vision may be expressed.

But where shall we find these central images in Ives's case? Shall we examine his relation to the Congregational and Presbyterian churches which he attended most of his life, and which partly served as proving grounds for his early musical experiments? There can be no doubt of his lifelong church loyalties, made even stronger, no doubt, by

[20] *Ibid.*, p. 163; cf. Cowell, pp. 201-3.

[21] Marginal note on MS of "The Fourth of July," cited in Kirkpatrick, *A Temporary Mimeographed Catalogue*, p. 11.

[22] John Kirkpatrick, letter to me dated June 5, 1973. "However, do whatever seems natural or best to *you*, though not necessarily the same way each time," Ives wrote to Kirkpatrick about performing Ives's music, in a 1935 letter (*Memos*, pp. 200-201).

his filial affection for his father-in-law, the Reverend Joseph Twichell of Hartford. But it seems that this loyalty did not in itself evoke Ives's deepest convictions or express them. For Ives the church was instrumental, not central. He went to church, belonged to churches, but the church was false to itself if it regarded itself as anything more than "the symbol of the greater light," that is, the "Christ-light." He could reproach Emerson, and himself as a youth, for summarily discarding the church, but not too harshly, for that discarding had its own truth still.[23]

What then of Emerson and Thoreau? Do we find the central images of Ives's life and work in the American Transcendentalist school? Here indeed is one of the sources of Ives's own mature character. It is important to note, however, that with this as with every source, Ives took what the Transcendentalists gave him, and recomposed it as his own. Emerson, for example, in his essay on the over-soul, had taught again his own confident individualism—the soul of each man participates in the great over-soul itself: "within man is the soul of the whole; the wise silence; the universal beauty, to which every part and particle is equally related; the eternal ONE." [24] Alternatively, Emerson refers to the soul's participation in "universal mind," and argues that therefore no consensus is relevant to the soul's knowledge of (religious) truth—each man must "greatly listen to himself." [25]

Ives picks up the Emersonian theme of universal mind or over-soul, but in Ives's interpretation, Emerson's univer-

[23] See Ives, "Emerson," in *Essays Before a Sonata*, p. 19: "But every thinking man knows that the church part of the church has always been dead—that part seen by candle-light, not Christ-light. Enthusiasm [by which, the context shows, Ives meant the youthful Emerson, and his own college-age Emersonian views] is restless, and hasn't time to see that if the church holds itself as nothing but the symbol of the greater light, it is life itself; as a symbol of a symbol, it is dead."

[24] Ralph Waldo Emerson, "The Over-Soul," in *The Selected Writings of Ralph Waldo Emerson*, ed. Brooks Atkinson (New York: Modern Library, n.d.), p. 262.

[25] *Ibid.*, p. 26.

sal mind is identified with the minds of the majority. Even the actuarial tables seemed to him an expression of universal mind, operating in the experience of many individuals. The individual interest alone may be the merely private interest, as when a Senator Fall (Albert B. Fall, later Secretary of the Interior under Harding; of Teapot Dome notoriety) or a Mr. Hearst (William Randolph Hearst, the publisher) pushes through Congress a bill that will protect his millions in copper mines.[26] Against this "minority mind" type, of which Ives as a Manhattan insurance broker must have had frequent experience, he set the image of the *Majority Mind*.

In an essay dating back to the critical 1919–20 turning point, he unfolds his conception. "The Majority" [27] is an old-fashioned political tract in the grand style. In Ivesian fashion, it begins with highly abstract or metaphysical principles, connecting the Majority Mind with God and the over-soul. The essay's central section is an exploration of a political mechanism whereby a nation might exchange the style of government by personalities (a style sure to produce domination of the Majority by some minority) for a system of national selection of key questions of the times, which will then be put to the people in periodic national referendums. One such question, Ives thought, might be whether there shall be a limitation of personal income and an absolute maximum property limit for each person or family unit. The result of the referendum would become stated policy and a guide for legislation until the next ballot. After explaining the principle of income limitation in some detail, Ives closes his essay in a fiery burst of prophetic hope for the Majority: "And what will the picture be? . . . A caricature, or a Velasquez? . . . We know not.

[26] Cf. Ives, "Emerson," pp. 33-34; on Fall and Hearst, see Kirkpatrick, ed., *Memos*, p. 212, and Boatwright, ed., *Essays Before a Sonata* . . . , pp. 180, 257.

[27] Ives, "The Majority," pp. 142-99.

But as it approaches maturity, there will come, we believe, a radiance such as the world has never seen!" [28]

Although Ives emphasized that he regarded the question of the limitation of wealth as separable from the issue of rule by the people, it is evident that the former, too, was a cause close to his own heart, and one which he strongly believed the Majority Mind supported. Ives himself had advanced from a five-dollar-a-week clerk to the control of a considerable personal fortune—how large is not known certainly.[29] In the various versions of his wealth and income limitation plan,[30] he proposed that the maximum wealth limit in America should be between $50,000 and $150,000 per family unit, the maximum annual income between $2,500 and $7,500,[31] with some or all the excess wealth going to give assistance to those who had not yet themselves attained the maximum in either category. Kirkpatrick suggests we triple these figures to convert from 1920 to 1972 values;[32] the significance of such conversions is difficult to specify, but an economist friend informed me that a tenfold increase might more accurately show the force of Ives's 1920 proposals in 1974. On that reckoning, it is clear that Ives was not envisioning poverty as the goal of justice!

It is interesting to ask whether Ives, on the principle he loved to quote from Thoreau ("the silent example of one sincere life . . . has benefited society more than all the projects devised for its salvation" is one version[33]) divested

[28] *Ibid.*, p. 199.

[29] John Kirkpatrick assumes (letter to me, June 5, 1973) that the $1,800,000 mentioned in *Memos*, pp. 210, 224, is autobiographical, but George G. Tyler, Ives's son-in-law and executor, doubts this (letter to me, May 14, 1974).

[30] See Ives, "The Majority," p. 172; *Memos*, p. 207; Cowell, *Charles Ives and His Music*, p. 94.

[31] It is interesting to note that the income figures are just what the maximum wealth figures would yield if invested at a conservative 5 percent, lower figures corresponding to lower, etc.

[32] *Memos*, p. 207.

[33] "Thoreau," in Boatwright, ed. *Essays Before a Sonata* . . . , p. 59; cf. *Memos*, p. 211; "The Majority," p. 161. The quotation, Boatwright says, is from *Dial* (*Essays Before a Sonata* . . . , p. 247, note 27).

himself of his own "unnatural coagulation" of wealth. The evidence is indecisive.[34] It would be stirring to claim, as Sidney Cowell does, that Ives indeed acted as a "silent example" in this matter, by returning his "excess" to the firm of Ives and Myrick. Regrettably, the New England reticence of the Ives family seems to have made the verification of that fact, if it is a fact, very difficult. It may be enough here to note that the Ives family lived as if he were fulfilling the principle. Charles's and Harmony's life-style, all agree, was severely modest, and much of his wealth went into anonymous contributions for the publication and performance of new music, both his own, and equally that of other little-known composers.[35]

So far, we have traced one living image, "The Majority Mind," noting its rooting in Ives's Transcendentalism, and have seen how he transformed the image, and how its application precipitated his convictions about wealth and equality. These convictions, in turn, led both to a definite political theory about income redistribution and property limitation, and at the very least to a life-style oriented toward that principle.

Still other images—"Nature," for example—could be

[34] On the one hand, Sidney Cowell writes, "He never drew from the business more than was needed to keep his family comfortable in their unostentatious way, and he provided against illness and retirement by means of an annuity" (p. 119). And again, "[Ives] limited his own income to what he calculated an individual's share of the country's wealth should be, taken in relation to the rights of other citizens. The surplus, which in Ives' case was large, was returned to the business. Ives believed a man who had a great deal more money than his neighbors was in moral danger, and he pointed out that too rich manuring of the ground is as damaging to crops as too little" (p. 94). Moreover, Ives in 1919–20 wrote, in the course of discussing the property limitation proposal, "For our own part, we hope some day to obtain our maximum and retire *to* business on ten acres and dig potatoes and write symphonies." ("The Majority," p. 170.) On the other hand, John Kirkpatrick and George G. Tyler doubt that this divestiture occurred (letters to me from Kirkpatrick, June 5, 1973, and from Tyler, May 14, 1974). I believe Cowell to be correct, but do not know.

[35] Cowell, *Charles Ives and His Music,* p. 119.

traced to Emerson and Thoreau. However, we have another, more difficult quest to follow, the quest for, or the question of, Ives's *musical images*. At once a problem of nomenclature appears. In music, what best corresponds to the canonical metaphors in spoken language which I have dubbed "images"? What in Ives corresponds to the verbal images of Hammarskjöld, King, and Jordan? In a sense, we might call a single chord or interval an image; in another sense, the entire Fourth Symphony images forth the reality Ives apprehends. I intend, however, to focus upon the snatches of melody and harmony which Ives borrows from the musical past—the 'quotations' from Beethoven and Wagner and Brahms, but especially from American songbooks: "Columbia, the Gem of the Ocean," and "Yankee Doodle," Stephen Foster songs, hymn tunes, and gospel songs—"What a Friend We Have in Jesus," "Come, Thou Fount," "Bringing in the Sheaves," "O Happy Day," "Beulah Land." John Kirkpatrick's *Catalogue* shows that Ives drew far more on hymns and gospel songs than on any other source,[36] and it is to them in particular that I will now turn. Songs such as "Work, for the Night Is Coming," "In the Sweet By and By," and "Beulah Land" *are* Charles Ives's images, by which, with others already mentioned, we can find our way to the center of his convictions and his life.

I am aware of the dangers involved in that claim. For one thing, it can be argued that, as Ives himself would have agreed, no one national corpus of music can be an exclusive avenue to the full human truth which music expresses. For another, there is the question (which Ives frequently addressed) whether music is 'translatable.' And not least, there is the danger that someone may find in what he supposes to be the simple gospel hymns a too-simple version of the complex and often enigmatic person of Charles Edward Ives.

Addressing the first of these, Ives certainly held that the

[36] Kirkpatrick, *A Temporary Mimeographed Catalogue*, pp. 264-66.

mere adoption of local material, whether Indian, American Negro, or African, could not make the composer's work more profound unless the composer in question happened to participate significantly in that source.[37] This goes to Ives's distinction between manner (the mere externals of artistic style) and substance (the inner truth, or vision, of the creative artist, whether poet, prophet, painter, or musician). A given substance, since it participates in the universal and divine, has itself a universal quality. But the man "born down to Babbitt's Corners," i.e., Ives himself, "may find a deep appeal in the simple but acute Gospel hymns of the New England 'camp meetin'' of a generation or so ago." [38] Such a man, then, may find *his* way to substance, and to the universal, through just these images. If

the Yankee can reflect the fervency with which "his gospels" were sung—the fervency of "Aunt Sarah," who scrubbed her life away for her brother's ten orphans, the fervency with which this woman, after a fourteen-hour work day on the farm, would hitch up and drive five miles through the mud and rain to "prayer meetin'," her one articulate outlet for the fullness of her unselfish soul—if he can reflect the fervency of such a spirit, he may find there a local color that will do all the world good.[39]

And that, I would submit, is just what New England Yankee Charles Ives did do. But can we *say* anything about it? *Is* Ives's music 'translatable'? Certainly the question of program and cognitive content in music in general is beyond our present scope. If such content were in the nature of the case impossible, it would be impossible here as everywhere else. On the contrary, I must risk assuming, as Ives did assume, that the possibility at least exists, and ask whether it is realized by Ives's music, and by means of his musical images. Ives believed "music could 'proclaim' any part of human experience," [40] but he did not think it was easy. Indeed, he believed that traditional music theory had set

[37] *Essays Before a Sonata*, pp. 78 ff.　　[39] *Ibid.*, pp. 80-81.
[38] *Ibid.*, p. 80.　　[40] *Memos*, p. 61.

artificial limits upon musical expression, and that these severely limited the desired 'proclamation.' Yet he hoped that the century would come, aided perhaps by his own quarter-tone and other musical experiments, when the subtler shadings of human experience might become expressible.[41] Men have a multitude of conceptions of God, so of course they have trouble understanding one another when they speak of God—the problem of language, Ives pointed out, is not limited to the problem of music. But Ives's hope was that "music is beyond any analogy to word language, and that the time is coming, but not in our lifetime, when it will develop possibilities inconceivable now —a language so transcendent that its heights and depths will be common to all mankind." [42]

Regarding the translatability of Ives's music, however, we have one great advantage, which is that he regularly quoted tunes with which familiar words can be associated. We know what Ives is singing about when the violins repeat a snatch of "America" or the trombones blare "Columbia, the Gem of the Ocean," because we know those songs. Ives's father had taught that one should *think* the words while playing songs on an instrument,[43] and in his larger compositions, Charles often wrote the words in the margin alongside his musical quotations so musicians unfamiliar with them could know what it was they were playing. It is such clues as these which give us hope that, knowing the message of some parts of his music, we may conclude to the message of more, or even most, of it.

Certainly, Ives's quotations are not to be read as mere telegraphic repetition of the message or sentiment of old hymns or patriotic songs. Rather Ives, in taking these materials in hand, knows them for what they are and transforms or recomposes them into his own message. I will take as a single example Ives's use of the camp-meeting song

[41] *Essays Before a Sonata*, p. 71.
[42] *Ibid.*, p. 8.
[43] *Memos*, pp. 46, 127.

"Beulah Land."[44] Just as the "universal mind" of Emerson's concept is transformed by Ives, so is "Beulah Land" transformed.[45]

This song (see next page) is one Charles Ives would have heard his father, George, lead in the summer camp meetings. The word *Beulah* is Hebrew for "wedded"; in Isaiah it is a prophetic image of the promised reconciliation between God and his people after their exile:

> No more shall men call you Forsaken,
> no more shall your land be called Desolate,
> but you shall be named Hephzi-bah [my
>   delight is in her]
>   and your land Beulah [wedded];
>   for the Lord delights in you
>   and to him your land is wedded.
>
> (Isa. 62:4 NEB)

In the hymn, the imagery shifts from present to promised consummation of God and his people: the singer first is, then is to be, fully blessed. Beulah in the hymn is said, then, to be a "borderland" between the already and the not-yet. The music of this rather subtle song, on the other hand, is not subtle at all, but rollicking, in a major key—a children's song, or a song for a childlike people indeed. In it, an old biblical image has transmigrated to become a new, musical one.

[44] "Beulah Land," words by the Rev. Edgar Page Stites (born 1836) and music by John R. Sweney (born 1837), was already included in the familiar Ira D. Sankey *Gospel Hymns Consolidated*, published in New York by Biglow and Main, and by John Church & Co., 1883, when Charles Ives was 9 years old.

[45] Denis Marshall has shown that Ives's quotations clearly belong to the "substance," not merely the "manner," of his music. Marshall's argument is a musical one, based upon the formal and melodic structure of the hymns in relation to the compositions into which they are introduced. Thus his conclusion that the quotations are of the substance of Ives's work is an important undergirding element in the present argument, which attends instead to the elements of cognitive and emotive content in these elements and in the resulting compositions. See Denis Marshall, "Charles Ives's Quotations, Manner or Substance," in *Perspectives of New Music*, Spring-Summer, 1968, pp. 45-56.

No. 192. **Beulah Land.**

E. P. STITES. JNO. R. SWENEY.

1. I've reach'd the land of corn and wine, And all its rich - es free - ly mine;
2. The Sav-iour comes and walks with me, And sweet commun-ion here have we;
3. A sweet perfume up - on the breeze Is borne from ev - er ver - nal trees,
4. The zeph-yrs seem to float to me, Sweet sounds of heaven's mel - o - dy,

Here shines undimm'd one bliss - ful day, For all my night has pass'd a - way.
He gent - ly leads me with His hand, For 'this is heav-en's bor - der-land.
And flow'rs that nev - er fad - ing grow Where streams of life for - ev - er-flow.
As an - gels, with the white-robed throng, Join in the sweet re - demp-tion song.

CHORUS.

O Beu - lah land, sweet Beu - lah land, As on thy high - est mount I stand,

I look a - way a - cross the sea, Where mansions are prepared for me,

And view the shin - ing glo - ry shore, My heav'n, my home for - ev - er-more.

From "Goodly Pearls," by per. John J. Hood.

No. 193. **Bringing in the Sheaves.**

KNOWLES SHAW. GEORGE A. MINOR, by per.

1. Sow-ing in the morning, sow-ing seeds of kind-ness, Sow-ing in the noon-tide
2. Sow-ing in the sunshine, sow-ing in the shad-ows, Fearing nei-ther clouds nor
3. Go - ing forth with weeping, sow-ing for the Mas - ter, Tho' the loss sustain'd our

186

From Gospel Hymns No. 5, ed. Ira D. Sankey, James McGranahan, and Geo. C. Stebbins (New York: Biglow & Main, and the John Church Co., 1887). See original attribution on cut.

161

For Ives's generation, Beulah represented God's link with ancient Israel. But Ives could not understand that link as excluding God's presence with other peoples: there was the Bible, but there were also the *Vedas*—and Emerson. "Beulah Land" was America, too, and expressed that American dream, a new land, God's land, where sturdy Puritans dreamed and their grandchildren might live to see the dream fulfilled. But how could Ives, with his universal vision, incorporate that national dream in his vision? Let us see.

Ives quoted "Beulah Land," along with many other such materials, frequently throughout his twenty years of active composing. Its first appearance, as far as I know, is in Ives's first major work, a string quartet originally composed for a revival service in Center Church, New Haven, and prefaced by a fugue. This fugue of the First String Quartet was based on two standard hymns, "From Greenland's Icy Mountains," and "All Hail the Power of Jesus' Name" (Coronation tune). Musically, the fugue is rather traditional. Next comes the Prelude, a movement as bouncy as a barn dance. And it is here that "Beulah Land" appears, briefly quoted, but already "recomposed," and made to answer the main theme of the Prelude. One feels that in this quartet Ives is exploring his constructive powers in musical composition. He uses his familiar themes here (the third movement employs "Come, Thou Fount"; the fourth, notable for many key changes, uses "Stand Up, Stand Up for Jesus") in order to celebrate the existing vision of the religious community, rather than to revise it.

Come next to the Second Symphony. Still a product of college days, this work shows Ives fully in command of his distinctively musical powers. The symphony is notable for its lyrical beauty, somewhat in the style of Brahms, and is perhaps the most accessible to the musical beginner of all the major Ives works. Significantly, its quotations bring together Ives's American heritage with allusions to the European literature—Beethoven, Brahams, and Wagner—

alongside "Bringing in the Sheaves" and "Turkey in the Straw"! The deeper message of the Second Symphony, if there is one, is hard to decipher at this point. At least there is here the sheer joy of musical sound, all kinds of musical sound—joyfully combined by a youth whose father was now tragically dead, but who found music still alive for him. And in this symphony too, "Beulah Land" appears, tenderly quoted throughout the third movement and interwoven with quotations from "O Mother dear, Jerusalem" (to the tune of which a later generation would sing "America, the Beautiful"). These two seem to gather up all the beauty and good the young Ives had ever known into a rhapsody of Christian hope.

Passing over the interesting use of "Beulah Land" in the Third Violin and Piano Sonata[46] as well as other instances, we come to the Fourth Symphony, composed 1910–1916 (but first performed complete in 1965, almost eleven years after Ives's death, and fifty years after its composition). I shall say a bit more about this final Ives symphony, for I believe it incorporates his main musico-theological insights more clearly than does any other work.

While Beethoven had ended the last movement of his Ninth Symphony with human voices in chorus, Ives chose thus to end the brief first movement of his final symphonic work. Only it was not Schiller's "Ode to Joy," but a hymn from the nineteenth-century revivals, "Watchman, Tell Us of the Night," which Ives has his chorus sing.

[46] There can be little doubt that the Third Violin and Piano Sonata, dated 1905–1914 in most Ives lists but with a first movement based on Organ Preludes of 1901 (*Memos*, p. 163), is a deliberate evocation of the camp-meeting religious past to which I have referred in chronicling Ives's boyhood. Ives wrote: "The sonata is an attempt to express the feeling and fervor—a fervor that was often more vociferous than religious—with which the hymns and revival tunes were sung at the Camp Meetings held extensively in New England in the 70's and 80's. [C.E.I. was born in 1874.] The tunes used or suggested are: *Beulah Land, There'll Be No More Sorrow,* and *Every Hour I Need Thee.* Common themes are used with or against the hymn tunes." (*Memos*, p. 69.)

Watchman, tell us of the night,
What the signs of promise are:
Traveler, o'er yon mountain's height,
See that Glory-beaming star!

Watchman, aught of joy or hope?
Traveler, yes . . . it brings the day,
Promised day of Israel.
Dost thou see its beauteous ray? [47]

In these words, and in its music, the ominously shaded first movement asks its question. I suggest, from what we know of Ives as pamphleteer, as transcendentalist, and as Christian believer, that it is a question about America, and (since for Ives the local opens to the infinite) about the infinite in the local. Which way, America in 1914? What is your promise? What is your destiny under God? And what is yours, humanity?

The second movement of this symphony is one of the most striking anywhere in the literature of modern music. Utterly complex, rich with superimposed layers of sound, confused with changes in key and meter, it nevertheless strikes the listener (if not always the struggling performers) with a strong, tough unity, not of musical form, but of idea, intuition, purpose.[48] Its dominant sounds are the sounds of twentieth-century America—the roar of cities and factories, the clash of musics—and the inner sounds of yearning, anticipation, frustration, anxiety, perhaps madness.

From time to time we hear in this movement the hymn tunes which we have learned to recognize as Ives's familiar trade marks—"till we meet, till we meet, till we meet at Jesus' feet," "Jesus, lover of my soul, let me to thy bosom

[47] These are the words (minus repetitions) Ives writes out for the voices and trumpet in the first movement. It is altered from the text of John Bowring (1825), but I do not know what text Ives was familiar with. Used by permission of Associated Music Publishers, Inc.

[48] On the Ivesian notion of unity, see Aubrey Davidson, "Transcendental Unity in the Works of Charles Ives," *American Quarterly*, Spring, 1970, pp. 35-44.

fly," and, clearer than any, the first violins sing "I've reached the land of corn and wine . . . Beulah land." It is noteworthy that each hymn Ives chose for this movement is eschatological—the hymns of pilgrims, he told Henry Bellamann.[49] But whenever the hymns appear, they are promptly drowned out by the crashing sounds of America on the go. (Ives achieves these crashing effects by a variety of unprecedented musical techniques—sometimes as many as seventeen different rhythms going at once.) And then there are musical sounds clearly political, indeed clearly jingoistic. America is marching, boys, and don't stand in her way! "Columbia, the Gem of the Ocean," which appears joyfully in the Second Symphony as a song of innocent celebration, here takes on the tones of monster power monstrously used. A Stephen Foster tune ("down in de cornfield, hear dat mournful sound") appears, but it seems to speak of the travesty of White supremacy and Black suffering in America.[50]

O Beulah Land, what are you doing in such company as this? Is the message of the movement tragic—do you come to have your violin voice trampled beneath heavy feet, beneath the venalities of the industrial city, the chauvinisms of small-town America with its blaring booster bands, beneath the ambitions of *imperium Americanum?* Or is your presence ironic—its violin sweetness the reminder that religion shares complicity in the American tragedy? Or . . . ? The answer is in doubt as the second movement ends.

In the Fourth Symphony's third movement, what seems an optimistic answer appears. In form, this movement is our old friend, the fugue built upon "From Greenland's Icy

[49] Henry Bellamann's program note of 1927 contains this comment: "The occasional slow episodes—Pilgrim's hymns—are constantly crowded out and overwhelmed . . .". Quoted by John Kirkpatrick in Preface to Charles Ives, Symphony No. 4 (New York: Associated Music Publishers, 1965), p. viii.

[50] Ives's address to American anti-Black racism, and nevertheless his (New England–style) participation in that racism, is worthy of separate investigation.

Mountains" and "All Hail the Power," taken from the First String Quartet of Ives's college days and made richer by concert orchestration. From the opening statement in the trombones to the concluding trombone quotation of the Handel Christmas hymn, "Joy to the World,"

> And heaven and nature sing,
> And heaven and nature sing,

it is triumphant. Now, if ever, I think, we must take Ives's concern with the texts of the tunes he quotes seriously. These are missionary hymns—"From Greenland's Icy Mountains" is one of the great hymns of the nineteenth-century Protestant missionary advance around the globe, and "All Hail the Power of Jesus' Name" exalts that vision. Now Ives is affirming this movement. He is neither cynical nor mocking (and certainly he knew how to be both: hear his organ Variations on "America"). The themes of the missionary hymns are celebrated in a fugue of classical proportions. I believe that in this reorchestrated fugue, Ives is paying full tribute to the church religion of his young manhood—to Harmony's father, the Reverend Joseph Hopkins Twichell; to Doctor Horace Bushnell of Hartford, to Center Church, New Haven; and to Central Presbyterian, Manhattan.

And yet, something is wrong. Ives did not, in this movement, depart in any interesting way from traditional music theory. Thus he was not here fully Charles Ives, though there is much of Ives in the fugue. He himself expressed the discomfort we sense by saying that the answer of the third movement to the question of the first two (here rephrased as the question, "Whither, America?") was "an expression of the reaction of life into formalism and ritualism." [51] Perhaps we could say that in music Ives has declared the Christianity of his day valid only if it can escape the prison house of its own forms, its own inherited theology.

[51] Kirkpatrick quoting Henry Bellamann reporting Ives; see Preface to Symphony No. 4, p. viii.

Musically and theologically, then, the fugue, however satisfying as a self-contained musical utterance, has proved unsatisfactory as an answer to the question put by "Watchman, Tell Us of the Night." What is wanting will now be supplied by the fourth movement, marked *largo maestoso*. Musically, this movement is characterized by Ivesian complexity. Three independently conducted instrumental groups are to be stationed about the performance hall, and at the end of the movement a fourth group, a chorus, reenters. The scoring is complex and on a grand scale. This vast battery achieves its purpose in a bare eight minutes' time—an immense concentration, not of volume, but of flexible aesthetic power.

And what of the message? This is the transcendental movement—the answer of the fugue will be transcended, in Emersonian fashion, by another, broader, deeper, truer answer. But wait—the theme of this pilgrimage to the transcendent is another familiar gospel hymn, "Nearer, My God to Thee," a hymn which evoked for nineteenth-century churchgoers Jacob who left home and the god of home, only to find a God he knew in a strange place:

> Though like the wanderer,
> The sun gone down,
> Darkness be over me,
> My rest a stone;
> Yet in my dreams I'd be
> Nearer, my God, to thee . . .[52]

The journey to the transcendent is in Ives a journey to a divinity, to an infinite, already near, already known, to the home God rediscovered.

Two other theological clues to the meaning here are worth noting. When the movement is elaborated, a subsidiary theme is "Ye Christian Heralds" (Zeuner's Missionary Chant tune)—another of the great Christian hymns of

[52] "Nearer, My God to Thee," Stanza 2, text by Sarah Adams, 1841.

mission. So the missionary theme is not abandoned with the third movement, but taken up in the final one, not as the whole, but as a distinct part. And Ives has besides this one more surprise. He who loves texts so much, when he comes to the choral finale, has the chorus sing the pilgrim hymn on which the movement is based, "Nearer, My God to Thee." But they sing it, or rather hum it, without any words. It is as though Ives is saying that at this level all words fail, music alone can speak, and we do not yet know the words of our eschatological hymn of praise to God. One remembers Hammarskjöld's Meditation Room at the UN, and the uncarved block which is (in imagination) carved with many symbols.[53]

We do not know the words, but we already know the melody, and it is "Nearer, my God to Thee, nearer to Thee." And so the work ends.

III

In a chapter already too long in proportion to others, how can we assess, in sum, the theological contribution of the life of Charles Ives? Let it be remembered that our goal is not to accept as *dicta* the convictions of our subjects. Rather, our attempt must be to ask what it means to the received heritage of theology to have the witness of *this* particular life, lived as this life was lived.

It seems to me particularly important that we should see in Charles Ives a living lesson to theology about how it is to go about its work. He is, as it were, a theologian in music. Let me see if I can now make that single point clear. First, consider that Ives's continual reappropriation of the small-town American religion—revivalist religion—of his boyhood points to a way in which theology may recover and reintegrate a strand of religion to the health of both religion and theology. It must be clearly said that neither Ives's own thought, nor the religion he experienced in boyhood

---

[53] See chapter 4, pp. 103-4.

and found expressed in the gospel hymns, was fundamental-
ist religion. Fundamentalism is not easy to define, but a part
of its (evil) genius is that it seeks to recover a past that
never was, and turns the mysteries of faith into literalistic
absurdities. The gospel hymns, on the whole, were never
either of these in their intention or their power. They
spoke not of a past, but of a present faith, and they were
not (and are not, for the tradition is not dead) literalistic.
"Beulah Land" did not need to be demythologized by Ives,
for it was already rich with paradoxical but profound religious insight.[54] The man "born down to Babbitt's
corners" might already have a religion as deep as sin, as
profound as grace, as rich as the infinite God. It was Ives's
business, not to parrot that religion (which parroting could
only make it something it was not), but to take it up into
his own musico-theological vision. I suggest that theology
has a like task in this (and every) generation.

The God whom Ives celebrates is the God of Americans,
but he is not an American God. The religion Ives responds
to, born in the meeting houses and camp meetings of New
England (though, like every babe, of older pedigree),
sublimated in the passionate Transcendentalism of Emerson
and Thoreau, lived out in the painful but triumphant experience of Charles Ives's own defeats and discouragements,
is a religion which goes to church without being churchy,
which worships Christ without being christomonistic. It is
a religion which Ives took into his own deepest reflections,
and expressed musically in ways which both criticize that
religion, refine it, and perpetuate it for his generation of
Americans. Ives the musician thus became Ives the musical
theologian, and shows the theologians how they may do
their work as well.

[54] The sense of "demythologize" used here is that which I take to
be Rudolf Bultmann's—the rejection of objectivizing talk about God
and his ways, the refusal to talk of God as if he were another object alongside earthly objects, and of his acts as if they were other
acts alongside of, and like, our own.

Chapter Seven

Toward a Theology of Life

If the preceding pages have achieved their purpose of stimulating biographical investigation in theology, the few pages to follow can in no important sense conclude that investigation. There are many more lives of our times (to say nothing of those of other times) deserving such investigation, and the theological harvest as we have seen must be made row by row or (to drop the figure) life by life rather than in some more sudden or more decisive way. The matters to which we can now attend, without turning to fresh lives, are of a subsidiary nature, and they are quite varied, so that this final chapter will seem less unified than the others. Some explanation of its loosely connected parts at this point may be helpful. Part 1 of the chapter will reflect on the difference, if any, made by bringing the two latest lives into our focus here. In a sense, Part 1 will bring the constructive work of the book to a close. Parts 2 and 3 will take backward and forward looks, respectively: Part 2 will attempt to find the connections, such as they are, between biography as theology and some of the main Protestant and Catholic theologies of the recent past; Part 3 will attempt to sketch in the outlines of the theoretical work which in my judgment needs next to be done in connection with biographic theology. The unity of the three parts lies in the contribution each may make toward a more exact answer to the question of Chapter 1, "Where are we now in theology?" The general answer of the book, of course, is that we are at a point where biography as theology can make a most significant contribution; more for its rhetorical force than for any new contribution this chapter may make I have here designated that goal as a "theology of life."

I

Consider, then, the difference which is made by examining not only the lives of Hammarskjöld and King, but also those of Jordan and Ives. Have we now any reason to change the tentative conclusions expressed in Chapter 4, "Biography as Theology," as a consequence of this modest doubling of the number of investigated lives? In the earlier chapter we explored especially the contribution of the lives of Hammarskjöld and King to the Christian doctrine of atonement, arguing that by instantiating atonement as a central motif of their own image-governed lives, these two had powerfully reinforced the viability of that doctrine for Christians in our times, but that by living out this motif in the forms in which they did, each of those lives also demanded certain changes in the received form of the doctrine. In particular, each of them showed us that atonement must be more broadly conceived than the doctrinal tradition might require. Atonement entails nothing less than reconciliation of human beings to one another across the lines of race and nationality and economic class and religious tradition. Each life also reinforced certain older aspects of the doctrine. The atonement or reconciliation which gave meaning to their lives cost them profound personal suffering. Moreover, this suffering as they experienced it was intimately bound up with the archetypical suffering of Israel the people of God and of Christ the Servant. It was in their experience an atonement which God was achieving through them rather than one which could be understood adequately apart from God and his purposes. There were also distinctive individual emphases: King's life was more nearly formed by atonement images drawn from the Old Testament (Moses) and from the Black Southern church ("free at last"); Hammarskjöld's was formed from the New Testament via Schweitzer (Jesus the adamant young man) and from the unity symbols of Western and Eastern mysticism.

Now we are able to address similar questions to Jordan's life, and to Ives's. To keep the comparison before us, I will again turn to the same doctrinal locus: atonement. A little reflection will make plain that these Christian lives as well are profoundly involved with the atonement-work. Jordan's is a life so biblically centered that it would be difficult to conceive this doctrine's not entering imaginally into his life story; Jesus and his cross were in fact recurrent themes in his thought and were deliberately chosen models for his action. But Jordan lived in a region where "Jesus" was a mantric charm, where "the blood" was proclaimed by radio evangelists and cross-roads preachers as patent medicine effective without cost or obligation to the taker—and yet where militarism, materialism, and racism continued to grind Black faces and White ones into the Southern dust. In such circumstances, Jordan turned from preacher talk to prophetic action, founded a "demonstration plot" based upon the living out of the gospel, made that plot a working emblem of the reunion of men with their neighbors, with God, and with the good earth—and called it Koinonia, "Sharedness." Thus he transformed the local Baptist gospel from a magical word into a shared event, and brought atonement, oneness, *koinonia,* to life in south Georgia.

In Ives's life and work the quest for atonement (or, as he would have preferred to say, for *unity*) took a different form. Whether in social theory or in music, Ives's struggle was to defend the rights of the many against a too swift or too imperious domination by the one. He remembered the old New England town meetings of his boyhood, where any citizen could stand up and have his own say, saying it in his own way. He remembered as well the camp meetings of the late nineteenth-century religious awakening, where many a preacher preached the faith, each in his own style and with his own emphases. In the camp meetings this pluralism was made vivid in the singing, as individual worshipers sang the common songs the way *they* had learned them. Ives learned from his father not to despise the 'wrong' notes some singers sang, or the unconscious key changes entire congregations, exalted, sometimes made, but to accept these as contributions to the larger musical and spiritual whole. From Emerson and Thoreau he learned to see these pluralities philosophically, and philosophically to unite them into a transcendental whole.

When it came to his own music, there was no discontinuity with the lessons of unity Ives had learned in these ways. His music would have a unity, not one achieved through an orderly progression of key changes and back home again by the book, but through a rugged plurality mightily heaped together so that its unity reflected nothing smaller than the grand plural unity of the cosmos. In such unity 'disharmonies' were overcome not by filtering them out but by enclosing them in a whole perhaps not fully or finally seen. Nor was the unity of this music to be seen in isolation from all else. Ives believed "that an interest in any art-activity from poetry to baseball is better, broadly speaking, if held as a part of life, or *of* a life, than if it sets itself up as a whole—a condition verging perhaps, toward a monopoly or, possibly, a kind of atrophy of the other important values, and hence reacting unfavorably upon itself." [1]

If it be asked whether this struggle for a unity in music and beyond music had anything to do with atonement as conceived in Christian theology, one must invite the questioner first to listen to Ives's music—to the Fourth Symphony or to the Third, or to the two string quartets, or to the songs collected in *114 Songs*—and then to ask that question. In more pedestrian fashion, the questioner must be reminded of Ives's insistence that his own concern in music was primarily with "substance," not merely with "manner"; he must examine, as we have done, the links between the substance of Ives's music and his life story, and most particularly, he must follow the clues provided by Ives's images, such as "Beulah Land," as they lead to the connections between the substance of Ives's music, the thrust of his politics, and the deepest convictions of his life. These investigations yield an affirmative answer: Ives's quest for unity is of a piece with the Christian work of atonement.

In the lives of both Ives and Jordan the atonement work is linked in Christian fashion to the larger community of God's people, to the historic movement of faith (Jordan's "God Movement"), and, though these last two are less prominent in Ives's case, to Jesus the pioneer of faith. Neither of the two made any easy attachment to churchly Christianity, yet each made important and deliberate contributions to the churches, and each recognized his own work as part of a larger historical process both past and future. These links, as I have suggested, are easier to single out in Jordan's life than in Ives's. In the latter case, there is indeed an affirmation of Christian tradition expressed both in music and outside it, but there is also, in Ives's discipleship to Thoreau and Emerson, a deliberate attempt

[1] Charles Ives, last page but one of *114 Songs*, privately published by Charles E. Ives, Redding, Connecticut. These last pages are named "Postface" and reprinted in Howard Boatwright, ed., *Essays Before a Sonata, The Majority, and Other Writings by Charles Ives* (New York: W. W. Norton, 1962), pp. 123-31. My quotation is from p. 124.

to transcend the limitations of historic Christianity. (The same sort of yes and no can be seen in Ives's relation to his American ideological heritage; yet he is properly hailed as a musician of America; also properly, I believe, as a deeply Christian thinker.)

More telling is the way in which both Jordan's life and Ives's exhibit the ancient connection between suffering and atonement. In each of these men the struggle to realize the sort of unity or *koinonia* they sought was a source of great anguish. Although the etiology of Ives's convergent and destructive illnesses remains obscure, it seems difficult to believe that their relation to the central struggle of his life was merely coincidental. However that may be, there is no longer any doubt that his long-failing attempts to give his musical vision to the world were the source of costly pain for him. In Jordan's case, the link between his commitment to "the God Movement" in Georgia and the persecution he and his friends endured is self-evident. In both these cases, as in those of King and Hammarskjöld, "If any man would come after me, let him deny himself and take up his cross and follow me" (Mark 8:34 RSV) regains its meaning in our times.

I have repeatedly noted that the point of these biographical investigations is not to discover the beliefs of these examined subjects with a view to recommending the beliefs when discovered as beliefs for all. That would be a simpler but far less satisfying task than the one undertaken here. At the same time, it would seem a curious policy to ignore these beliefs if they are in any way relevant to the basic structure of the examined lives. Certainly each of the four men investigated here, in his life work for the reconciliation of men to one another or to a greater unity than any yet realized, projected some exact model of men in community or of the good society. These projects stand before us as challenges: to the extent that these lives do show forth the Christian work of atonement we are compelled to consider the concrete application of their work as they conceived it. But we may see the coherence of their projects with their own lives without being compelled to adopt them for our own. What we cannot escape in these lives is the compelling suggestion that reconciliation is at their center, their theological center, and that it therefore *must* find adequate expression in every political, social, economic realm in which their lives are engaged.

So we can answer, yes, the witness of these lives, as well, is found related to that ancient Christian doctrine. This discovery has grown not from an artificial forcing of each life examined into a preconceived pattern, but from a respectful and humble inquiry into the life seen in its own terms. This result could in principle be overturned by showing that the biographical studies I have undertaken are misconceived or misconducted—that they do not in fact fairly represent the lives examined. I have attempted to correct the interpretations others have offered of my chosen saints; still others may in turn correct mine; such ongoing hagiographic revision is a part of the ongoing task of biographic theology.

A more general objection to this conclusion might be expressed as follows: "What you have so far shown is at best related analogically to the actual Christian doctrine of atonement. The lives you have reported may indeed be inspired by the biblical concept, and that, if true, is an interesting fact about Hammarskjöld, King, Jordan, or Ives. However, it goes no distance at all to showing that the objective, biblical doctrine is true—to showing that Christ died for our sins, or that in him the world is truly redeemed. Yours is an account of inspired men, who might even inspire others. But the true Christian doctrine claims to tell us what is true about the world, what is true about and in all history. Is atonement merely a subjective truth about Hammarskjöld and others, or is it, as Christians claim, a doctrine about mankind summed up in Christ the last Adam?"

This objection, though mistaken, is not merely wrong-headed, and answering it should make it possible to clarify what is being claimed for the biographical approach to theology. First we might note that this objective/subjective distinction has not proved satisfactory in modern theology. I referred in Chapter 4 to the writing on atonement by Horace Bushnell as an effective brief summary of the received Christian doctrine. His nineteenth-century theological opponents who regarded themselves as orthodox Calvinists accused Bushnell of holding a "subjective" doctrine of atonement, while his Unitarian opponents regarded Bushnell's approach as mistakenly "objective." Bushnell found it necessary to reject both of these criticisms: his approach, he said, was "subjective-objective." [2] That is, Bushnell saw that two false ways, not one, must be overcome. On the one hand, the beneficiaries of Christ's salvation must not regard themselves as the source or cause of their own reconciliation: gratitude, not self-congratulation, is the appropriate Christian response to Christ. But on the other hand, these same beneficiaries must not suppose that they are excluded from personal participation in the atoning work. And that supposition is the mistake which "objectivist" theories of atonement are likely to make.

That Jesus died by crucifixion in first-century Palestine is as well established as any fact in his disputed life history. That his first-century followers testified to having been redeemed by him, and particularly by his death and resurrection, is an even better documented historical fact. The issue is whether these facts are to be seen as mere antiquities, like the facts that Caesar crossed the Rubicon and was subsequently hailed as Emperor by the Romans, or whether the Christian facts just cited are to be seen in vital developing continuity with the living witness of persons of our own time. If the latter is true, we must hold that these lives tell us that the redemptive reality is not a mere phenomenon of the historical past, but is a significant way of life today. Of

[2] See H. Shelton Smith, ed., *Horace Bushnell* (New York: Oxford University Press, 1965) , pp. 276-77.

course, the mere existence of such testimony does not settle the issue—our witnesses just might be themselves deceived concerning Christian truth, or we might have misunderstood what their lives are really saying to us. The existence of their witness, however, makes Christian atonement a real issue, a live option, and confronts us with that issue here and now.

Our hypothetical objector protested that the experience of Hammarskjöld, King, Jordan, Ives (and by implication many others) was merely their private experience; that it did not tell us how things are in the world, how things are in history. Now perhaps there is somewhere experience so private, or so singular, as to deserve that categorical rejection. I cannot say. It does seem evident by now that it would be false to treat the lives of the men studied here in this privatistic way.

Of course, the doctrine of atonement does not mean simply a motif embodied in contemporary life stories; it means a motif which can be spelled out in the form of propositions, as was done by Anselm, by Schleiermacher, by Bushnell, by Barth. Biographical theology need not repudiate and should not ignore the propositional statement of theological doctrine. What it must insist is that this propositional statement be in continual and intimate contact with the lived experience which the propositional doctrine by turns collects, orders, and informs. Without such living contact, theological doctrine readily becomes (in a pejorative sense) objective—remote from actual Christian life, a set of empty propositions more suited to attacking rival theologians than to informing the church of God. With this living contact, theology may develop its propositions in the confidence that their meaning is exemplified in contemporary Christian experience.

So far we can argue, and I believe the argument to be sound. There remains, however, a theoretical question about the logical priority of biographic over propositional theology. For the advocate of the latter might claim that the attention to biography, while pleasing enough, is no more than a stimulus or corrective to propositional theology. Is there something about the stories of lives which is not merely prophylaxis or therapy, but which should and must determine the shape of Christian theology? I will say a little more about this question in Part 3, section 1 of the present chapter. First, however, it may be helpful to examine the recent theological past to see the role it has assigned to biographical theology.

II

If we turn to the recent history of theology in search of biographical inquiry, we find relatively little to guide and even less to reassure us. On its Protestant side, theology since World War I (in America, since World War II) was dominated by the theological tendencies loosely described as neo-orthodox. On this view, any contribution to theology from 'experience' was considered pernicious. It may be helpful to say something about this aversion.

Even in neo-orthodoxy, attention was paid to the onion-layered pseudonymous self-analyses of Sören Kierkegaard, and neo-orthodoxy certainly encouraged a rereading of the autobiographical theological writings of Luther and Augustine. Moreover, theological existentialists such as Rudolf Bultmann attended to the special sort of subjectivity associated with Heideggerian existentialism. But these special interests did not lead on to the general conclusion that there might be concrete theological gain in the close exploration of particular lives.

More typical is the case of the pivotal neo-orthodox theologian Karl Barth. In the first part-volume of the *Church Dogmatics* a long subsection was devoted to "The Word of God and Experience." [3] Barth conceded that experience (*Erfahrung*) —roughly, for Barth, the acknowledg-

[3] Karl Barth, *Church Dogmatics*, vol. I, part 1, trans. G. T. Thomson (Edinburgh: T. & T. Clark, 1936 [German ed., 1932]), pp. 226-60.

ment of the Word of God *as* Word of God constitutes Christian experience—occurs, and is thus a genuine human possibility. Having made this concession to the logic of his own language, however, Barth devoted the remainder of his subsection to a strident protest against any latter-day Pelagianism which might seek comfort from this concession. *This* 'experience' cannot be set alongside other human possibilities as one additional possibility. Its possibility belongs not to religious talent or genius, but only to God, to God alone. All Barth's energies at this point were directed to defending the unqualified deity of God, and he saw experience as a potentially dangerous enemy of that deity. While in his later work Barth said some things slightly more positive about the response of man to the Word, and while in apparent contradiction of his general principle he made frequent and sometimes extensive biographical and autobiographical excursuses in the volumes of *Church Dogmatics*, "religious experience" remained for him a red flag of warning.

This polemic is best understood as Barth's attempt to overturn the liberal theological heritage epitomized by Friedrich Schleiermacher (1768-1834), widely recognized as the father of modern theology. Schleiermacher had enjoyed a warm evangelical awakening under the Moravian Brethren in his own boyhood, and although the course of his education led him to reject the old-fashioned orthodox tenets of the Brethren, he never forgot the determinative experience of his early years, experience which he regarded as truly Christian. However, in his major theological writings, Schleiermacher was rarely if ever openly autobiographical.[4] Instead, he sought to describe the essence of religious feeling (*Gefühl*) as an awareness which would be in content the same for all men, although its form would naturally vary depending upon the cultural and religious circum-

---

[4] The nearest exception to this reticence is the *Soliloquies,* trans. H. L. Friess (Chicago: Open Court Publishing Co., 1957 [German ed., 1800]). In these five brief essays, Schleiermacher attempts to describe his own romantic character, and at least alludes to actual events.

stances in which the awareness arose.[5] This original quest for the universal essence of religion, made in the spirit of the Enlightenment tinged by the emotional coloring of Romanticism, was widely imitated in religious thought in Europe and America in the nineteenth century. That search has not ended, continuing to the present day in spite of, and now sometimes in reaction to, the Barthian revolt of the early twentieth century.

However, the classic liberal movement was scarcely more supportive of biographical theology than was neo-orthodoxy. If the essential religious experience, or the essential Christian experience, as Schleiermacher's mature work, *The Christian Faith,* sought to define it, is the same for all people in all important respects, the *differentia* which biographical study might bring forth could hardly be worthy of the liberal theologian's attention. An interesting exception to this generalization was the influence of Schleiermacher's biographer and disciple, Dilthey.

Wilhelm Dilthey (1833–1911), a German philosopher of history, has had an influence on the development of philosophy and especially of sociology. Dilthey borrowed from Schleiermacher the emphasis on inwardness as the clue to understanding man in history, but was also under the influence of British empiricism and German idealism, combining these in a distinctive way in his philosophy of history. He regarded autobiography, by which one seeks the "meaning" of life (the patterns, connections, relationships which give a point to that life), and biography, in which one thus seeks to understand another's life, as crucial for historical investigation. History, however, was not according to Dilthey the mere sum of great lives; for each life's pattern must in turn be understood via the historical interconnections of its own place and time. Dilthey's work might well have opened the door to biographical study in theology as

[5] Friedrich Schleiermacher, *On Religion, Speeches* (Torchbooks; New York: Harper, 1958 [German ed., 1799]), Second Speech, pp. 26-118; *The Christian Faith,* trans. H. R. Mackintosh & J. S. Stewart (Edinburgh: T. & T. Clark, 1928 [2nd German ed., 1830]), props. 3, 4, 6.

well, but in fact the fragmentary nature of his writings, together with the theological shift away from liberalism soon after his death, limited his influence.[6] While biographical theology has not sprung up in his wake, it may certainly learn something of value from his thought.

More influential so far as an exemplar of exact biographical inquiry for theoretical purposes was Dilthey's American contemporary, the philosopher, psychologist, and religious theoretician, William James (1842-1910). Influenced by his success in the employment of empirical methods in developing the fledgling science of psychology, James turned, in the *Varieties of Religious Experience*,[7] to a case-by-case examination of the lives of persons whose religious experience was primary and personal, rather than secondary and imitative of others. Not only did James pay careful attention to the *differentia* displayed in the lives of his 'saints' (the persons he chose included some he found repulsive as well as some he found winsome) but he extracted from his subjects, as I have done here, data they did not intend to yield in order to draw his own theoretical conclusions.

James was quite sophisticated in dealing with the problems created by the interaction of the investigator's mind and the personal data upon which he worked. On the one hand, he was prepared to allow the appearance of the data to determine his own understanding of them. For example, it was in attempting to understand and organize the experience of his subjects that James made the distinction between the "once-born" and the "twice-born" personality—a distinction we have had occasion to remember in the present work.[8] On the other hand, James recognized that the "science of religions" he sought to establish would not be able to neutralize the inevitable effect of the grand sur-

[6] On Dilthey see H. P. Rickman, ed., *Meaning in History, W. Dilthey's Thoughts on History and Society* (London: Allen & Unwin, 1961), esp. pp. 83-94.

[7] William James, *The Varieties of Religious Experience* (New York: Modern Library, n.d. [1st ed. 1902]).

[8] See chapter 2, pp. 49-50.

mises, the "over-beliefs" of its several investigators, and he took pains to identify his own over-belief in a (finite) God. James hoped that the parallel work of different investigators with differing over-beliefs might provide the needed corrective to the inevitable bias of any one of them.[9]

While there is a sense in which the powerful example of James's work stands behind the present work, we should not overlook important differences in James's outlook and goals and those displayed here. On the one hand, he sought deliberately to separate himself from theological inquiry as such, was a member of no church, and had no intention of bringing his conclusions into line with Christian tradition, while none of these is here the case. On the other hand, he was most concerned with answering questions which from the vantage point of today give the flavor of a reverent nineteenth-century agnosticism: is there a spirit world? Or is materialism true? Is religion found in one, or perhaps two, main types? What are the higher powers, and how if at all may we have contact with them? The task of biographical theology may look to James for scientific passion and for imaginative employment of materials, but cannot be content with his presuppositions or his formulation of the questions.

Meanwhile, Roman Catholic theology pursued its own, independent intellectual paths in the period (1800 to the present) now being reviewed.[10] Perhaps we should be surprised to learn that these paths were hardly more friendly to biographical theology than were those of leading Protestants of the period. This is surprising because Catholic theology more than Protestant emphasized the heritage of all the Christian centuries, and because Catholic popular piety, preaching, and hagiography continued during the period up to Vatican II and beyond to emphasize the veneration of the saints. Countless biographies of St. Theresa

[9] James, *Varieties,* Lectures XVIII, XX.

[10] For the following paragraphs, I am especially indebted to Mark Schoof, *A Survey of Catholic Theology 1800-1970* (Paramus, N.J.: Paulist Newman Press, 1970).

of Lisieux (the Little Flower of Jesus) and of the heroic Ignatius Loyola were published and read, to say nothing of the cultic activities attached to the many apparitions or visions of the Blessed Virgin Mary. Meanwhile the Bolland- ists, a Jesuit group founded in the seventeenth century, continued its scientific-historical investigations of the life stories of the saints in the Roman calendar, publishing these critical biographies in an *Acta Sanctorum* which by the 1960s was still incomplete in 67 folio volumes!

None of this activity, however, was called (or considered to be) theology by Roman Catholics. One might have supposed that Catholic theologians, noting this enormous body of religious energy and belief-guided biography, would have seized upon the phenomenon as of central theological importance. Instead, theological work was mainly given either to continuing, in the face of modernity, the neo- scholastic tradition springing from Thomas Aquinas, or to investigating those special theological problems created by the new age.

This latter effort was epitomized in the work of those condemned as the modernists, but modernism was by no means alone in its opposition to traditional neo-scholasti- cism; it was rather the visible tip of a theological iceberg comprising among others the Catholic Tübingen school, Newman and von Hügel in England, "reform Catholicism" in Germany, and, especially after 1945, the schools of Le Saulchoir and Fourvière in France. (We might see in the transcendental Thomists, Bernard Lonergan and Karl Rahner, an attempt to reunite these divergent streams of Catholic theology.) In all these varieties, however, it was rare for biography to play a central role in theological work.

The most striking exception to this neglect[11] was in

---

[11] Friedrich von Hügel is another noteworthy exception: his best work, *The Mystical Element of Religion as Studied in St. Catherine of Genoa and Her Friends,* 2 vols. (London: J. M. Dent & Co., 1908), was an attempt to derive and form a just estimate of "the mystical element" on the basis of the experiences of Catherine and her circle.

Germany, where Romano Guardini developed a distinctive style of theological thought which (with that of his fellow German Catholic Karl Adam) has been dubbed a *theology of life* (whence the title of the present chapter). The theology of Guardini and Adam turned especially to the human life of Jesus and to the shared life of the contemporary Catholic community as its foci. Romano Guardini (1885–1968), though born to a noble Italian family, was educated in Germany and became influential in the German youth movement in the years before the First World War. He was a competent scholar who had also a flair for popular writing; he published studies of Socrates, Plato, Dante, Hölderlin, Dostoevski, Mörike, Rilke, Pascal, Kierkegaard, and (perhaps most important to him) Augustine. In 1923 he was appointed Professor of Catholic Philosophy at the University of Berlin. He was so deeply identified with Christian life in Germany that he was silenced after the Nazis came to power, but returned to teach at Tübingen and Munich after the war.

Despite the title arranged for his Berlin post, Guardini's foremost interest was theology. His approach, however, was neither neo-scholastic fine tuning of Thomist propositions, nor sweeping system-building of the sort exemplified by his contemporaries Barth and Tillich. Rather his goal was "to view the pattern of Christian existence as a whole," and his model was Augustine, who, said Guardini, drew

no methodological division between philosophy and theology or, in philosophy, between metaphysics and psychology, within theology, between theoretical dogma and practical Christian life but his mind proceeds from the whole of Christian existence to consider the total pattern and its different parts.[12]

This goal led Guardini to philosophical reflections in a personalistic mode and to theological-practical studies on the Catholic Church and its liturgy, as well as to the biographical-literary sketches mentioned above. It also led him

[12] Romano Guardini, *Freedom, Grace, and Destiny,* trans. John Murray, S. J. (New York: Pantheon Books, 1961), p. 9.

to think and write about the meaning of "saints" in the Catholic Church and about the significance of sainthood for theology and life.

Late in life Guardini wrote a brief introductory volume for a projected series of lives of the saints.[13] *The* saints, he noted, are not to be sharply distinguished from saints in the New Testament sense. "Viewed in this perspective, a saint is simply a man to whom God has given the strength to take this primal commandment [the 'great commandment' of Matt. 22:37 and Deut. 6:5] with utter seriousness, to understand it profoundly, and to bend every effort to carry it out." [14] However, with the legitimation of Christianity under Constantine, there had come a corresponding dilution and paganization of the church. No longer could all Christians be considered saintly. Thus a "saint" came to be regarded as one who fulfilled the great commandment to an extraordinary degree, notably by dying for his faith. It is just this quality of extraordinariness which became the test of sainthood. "Sanctity is the love of God and of men carried to a sublime extravagance." [15] Thus the lives of saints

are diverse, but always of an extraordinary character. They come from all levels of society . . . [but] all have one thing in common: the demands which the love of God makes upon their hearts causes them to transcend the ordinary mass of human beings and to accomplish something altogether exceptional.[16]

The key point here is that saints serve as models for new styles of being Christian, opening paths which many others will follow.

So Guardini turns to speak of "a new kind of saint," who can embody sanctity in this generation. In effect, his

[13] Romano Guardini, *The Saints in Daily Christian Life* (Philadelphia and New York: Chilton Books, 1966) .

[14] *Ibid.,* p. 29.

[15] *Ibid.,* p. 17.

[16] *Ibid.,* p. 46.

book is an evangelistic summons to take up the way of practical holiness in daily life. This way, however, is not nowadays to be that of detachment or asceticism; it is to be fulfilled by a self-abandoning obedience to God's directives just as these are mediated by the secular situation in which one finds oneself. The saint's way is therefore not to be extraordinary; no one will easily identify a modern saint.

Their surroundings are standardized: they work in laboratories, in factories, in administrative agencies . . . live in homes which are often the same to the slightest detail . . . dress the same . . . are subject to uniform "packages" of education, entertainment, legislation. In such an environment, how could they lead a Christian way of life which had to express itself in extraordinary religious practices and experiences? They would have to become strangers to their own ways of existence; they themselves would have to recognize their lives as absurdities.[17]

Nevertheless, there is a particular saintly task for today's man, and that is the task of changing or reshaping the world with which God has entrusted him. For even today

man is still answerable for the world, and the world is entrusted to man. . . . His mission is not a "profane" task paralleling the religious one. It is of itself and as such religious or rather Christian. In the final analysis there is one obedience, one service which man owes God in his faith and in his work.[18]

At the end, Guardini frets lest this secular vision of sainthood might seem to someone indistinguishable from no sanctity at all, as if "the objective of the saints is . . . to render the world just a little more efficient every day." [19] I think, though, that that worry is misplaced. It is not too surprising that in the generation busy with the reconstruction of bomb-ravaged Europe, Guardini's thoughts, as those of Bonhoeffer had earlier, turned to a secular Christianity which would concern itself with the reshaping of God's earth. What seems surprising is this: Guardini seems

[17] *Ibid.*, pp. 77-78.
[18] *Ibid.*, p. 82.
[19] *Ibid.*, p. 103.

just to lose sight, in his essay, of the possibility that in this generation, too, there might be models, men and women who "transcend the ordinary mass of human beings and accomplish something altogether exceptional." [20] It is interesting to contrast that neglect with Guardini's own rather exceptional life story: except for arbitrary exclusion of theology professors, his own colorful and exceptional life might well have been included in this book. And on the other hand, the lives included here, Hammarskjöld and the others, might be thought to display, not in ordinary but in exceptional ways, the very earth-rebuilding role which Guardini lays down as the task of sainthood in our time.

What follows is that with the exceptions noted the theological generation just ended provides no ready models for the work which now needs to be done, and toward which a beginning has been made here. If a theology of life is now to grow from the examination of life stories, we must in large measure find our own way, discovering for ourselves the distinctive elements of this mode of theological work.

III

This part has the task of indicating work still needing to be done in connection with biographical theology. I will merely note seven loosely interrelated areas of possible investigation. Since what I will say is of a preliminary and programmatic nature, it will be brief in each case.

(1) We need to examine very carefully two related implications of the preceding pages: the suggestion that some theology may be expressed via narrative, and the stronger suggestion that narrative or *story* is a means of expression uniquely suited to theology or at least to Christian theology. At first glance such claims seem radically at odds with traditional 'propositional' theology. Yet, in addition to the evidence of the preceding pages, there are some further bits of support for one or both of these claims.

[20] *Ibid.*, p. 46.

One consideration is the current rebirth of interest in story and theology—the new openness to religious myth as an indispensable means of human expression,[21] the discovery of attention long since paid to story in a number of other religious traditions, for example in Hasidic Judaism,[22] and the new attention to both of these in some theological discussions currently in progress.[23]

Alongside these phenomena one may note that Stephen Crites has lately urged, via an argument in Kantian style, that human experience necessarily has a narrative form.[24] He seeks to show that the time-defying strategies of modern intellectual work (conceptual abstraction; phenomenological contraction of attention) cannot ever really overcome this necessary form, so that the "sacred stories," by which primitive people live their lives, are representative of the dwelling places of all human being; we all live in some "story" or other.

Biography is of course one form of story—a form distinguished by being always a human story, and always (in intention) a true story. Perhaps these two marks of biography make it the form of story most nearly suited to Christian faith. In favor of this conclusion is the recurrence of the form (or its predecessors) in earliest Christianity: the *Confessions* of Augustine, the *Acts* of the martyrs (and of the Apostles), and, even more central than these, the various *Gospels* of Jesus Christ each tell a human story.[25]

[21] Cf. W. Taylor Stevenson, *History as Myth, the Import for Contemporary Theology* (New York: The Seabury Press, 1969).

[22] Cf. Maurice Friedman, *Touchstones of Reality* (New York: Dutton, 1972); and Ira Friedlander, *Wisdom Stories for the Planet Earth* (New York: Harper, 1973).

[23] Cf. John S. Dunne, *Time and Myth* (Garden City, N.Y.: Doubleday, 1973).

[24] Stephen Crites, "The Narrative Quality of Experience," *Journal of the American Academy of Religion*, September, 1971, pp. 291-311. See also my reference in Part 2 to Dilthey, who held apparently similar views of temporality and humanness.

[25] Concerning the special problem of biography and the Gospels see section 6 below.

What seems most interesting to me is that, if biographies be taken as the smallest discrete units in which experience can be reported, we are confirmed in the assumption that (*contra* Schleiermacher) "experience" is to be understood, not in the abstract or compressed form which the rejection of story would require, but only and exactly in the durational form of a narrative. In this sense, when philosophers have asked whether we can have experience *of* God, they have perhaps misleadingly assigned a cognitive priority to the compressed, the non-durational, the abstracted products of actual or durational experience. (Examples of this notion of experience are found when philosophers speak of "experience of yellow" or "experience of heat.") Our question must rather be whether the life-experience of a Hammarskjöld or an Ives is or is not understood better when it is treated as experience *with* God; that is, whether the ongoing story of their lives makes more or fuller sense when the involvement of God in that story is recognized or when it is bracketed.

(2) I have referred already in this chapter to the *compelling* quality of the lives of the persons whom biographical theology may study. It is just this quality, of course, which has led the Christian church to single out some of its members as saints in a special sense—as deserving honor and emulation.[26] This phenomenon is by no means limited to Christianity; every culture and tradition has its compelling or awesome heroes, and outsiders are very often as apt as are Christians to note the compelling Christian figures, whether Francis of Assisi or Dag Hammarskjöld. These facts should weigh neither for nor against acceptance of the Christian phenomenon. Rather, our task is first to understand this compelling quality theologically. It is just the limits of this understanding on my own part which have caused me to be very slow to answer the question: how are the biographical subjects to be chosen? I have avoided giving more than the vague answer that we are to

[26] On the veneration or worship of saints, see Appendix.

like our saints if we are to claim their stories for ourselves. Yet "liking" may be misleading: perhaps we should say we are *struck* by them; there is sometimes an element of strong repulsion which signals the claim these lives make upon us.

Guardini speaks of something prodigious in the saints, of "sublime extravagance," of *that which goes beyond*,[27] in language which suggests a numinous element in these lives which so powerfully attract us. And we remember that Otto found the numinous to combine elements of attraction and repulsion—the aweful and the facinating.[28] While not wishing to deny these elements which may lie below the threshold of awareness in our response to our chosen figures, I have preferred to seek the dominant images which seem to shape the life of the subject and which relate that life to the tradition in which the subject stands and to ourselves to the extent that these images speak to us.

Karl Rahner emphasizes the creative role of the saints' lives:

> canonized saints are the creative models of sanctity who have set a concrete example, each for his own particular age, of a new way to be Christian and so have shown others how to accept Christianity creatively and with new understanding. The image of these models may fade with the passage of time or emerge with new clarity, as is shown by the fact that certain saints cease to be venerated or even disappear from the catalogue of the saints.[29]

On this reckoning, there might be an inclination to regard the saints' lives as *useful,* but if we could show that they were, we could presumably also say what they were useful for; that is, we would have discovered features or aims of Christian faith and life which were *logically* prior to

---

[27] *The Saints in Daily Christian Life,* pp. 17-18.

[28] Rudolf Otto, *The Idea of the Holy,* trans. John W. Harvey (London: Oxford University Press, 1943 [1st German ed., 1917]), pp. 1-41.

[29] Karl Rahner and Herbert Vorgrimler, *Theological Dictionary,* ed. Cornelius Ernst, O.P., trans. Richard Strachan (New York: Herder and Herder, 1968 [1st German ed., 1965]), p. 479.

the lives which so usefully exhibit these features or expedite these aims. In this case biographical theology would necessarily depend on this prior knowledge, and biographical investigation might be remanded to the realm of illustrations for theology lectures or sermons. But I suspect that usefulness is not a prime feature of saints' lives, and I know that the compelling aspect of the lives to which we are drawn is often more powerful than the propositional religious goals we are in position to formulate. Jesus compels, St. Francis compels, I think Clarence Jordan compels; the doctrine we may draw from their life stories, if it is compelling, is so just because it had prior embodiment in them and may be embodied again.[30] It is this last feature which Rahner properly recognizes.

(3) I have just mentioned *images* as the primary medium or form of that compelling quality in the lives we (therefore) choose, yet the role of the image is another of the aspects of the present work requiring further reflection. My own acquaintance with the notion of images in literary studies is slight. I have depended especially upon the seminal work of Austin Farrer, who said that "holy images" were the very mode of the inspiration of scripture, their metaphoric force turning what would otherwise be flat narrative into the inspired prose and poetry of the Bible.[31] I claimed that such images were the property not only of holy books but even more of holy lives such as we were considering here. These images combine to give a life its characteristic flavor. Images come into a life from the

[30] My sometime student and associate Terrence Tilley thinks that I ought to adopt the self-disciplining procedure of letting the Christian community commend to me a wider range of saints than I am likely to choose according to my own likings. His reason is that otherwise my faith and my theology are likely to be one-sided. I need some soldiers to match my pacifists, some women to match my men, etc. That might be (partly) sound moral advice, but my goal above is to discover how I, or the community, recognize a saint in the first place, not to decide how widely saints' lives should be attended to once discovered. On community and theology see section 7 below.

[31] See Chapter 4, pp. 94-96.

tradition in which that life participates, but different Christians are formed by different sets of images within the larger manifold. As the images converge in a particular life they both shape that life and, making themselves known, reflect its shape to others. Thus, to know its images is so far to know a life, particularly to know it in connection with its creative sources (its 'scripture' and 'tradition') and its creative possibilities (the influence that life may have on others' lives). The saints both belong to communities of the past and shape communities of the future, and the images are a central means of this communication.

Farrer's verbal notion of images was not broad enough even for the present studies; the case of Charles Ives obliged us to seek images which were primarily musical rather than linguistic. "Beulah Land" is a text as well as a tune; its role in Ives's life suggests that images possess both cognitive and noncognitive aspects. Such a possibility deserves closer exploration. Paul Tillich made central the notion of the "symbol," and it might be profitable to see in what way Tillichian symbols differ from our images, and what differences thereby arise. Carl Jung's understanding of the place of images in human life might contribute to the clarification of our own task. And there are still other understandings of image and symbol which may be even more fruitful realms for investigation in biographical theology.

(4) My own interests run, it is only honest to remark, in a quite different direction from these. Images are a clue to character, just as metaphors are the illuminators of speech. But to treat speech as if it were all metaphor is a stultifying strategy, and so is it folly to treat character as if it were only a bundle of images. Thus the discussion of "character ethics" in Chapter 1 spoke of character traits (honesty, fidelity, and the like) and also of *convictions* as forming human character. Images are vital for they help us to discover in the vision of our subjects that which may have escaped our own vision; like other metaphors they work to shift the way we see things. But images can be

made to lead us to the discovery of the central or formative convictions, the rock-ribbed beliefs which, if a man is something or stands for something, show us more precisely what he stands for and what or who he is.

Now "convictions" is a term in common religious use, and in a rough way, we all understand this everyday term. But what, more exactly, are convictions? How may they be defined, identified, and separated from the other things one knows, or believes, or believes one knows?

In Chapter 1, it was said that convictions may be distinguished from principles—the latter are of the head, the former of the gut; principles are more often consciously formed, convictions more often unconsciously lived by or lived out. Convictions in this view are affective and volitional as well as cognitive; they represent the stake of the convinced person (or the convinced community) in the world; his bet in life. Now how are these gutsy tendencies of the self to be conceived? Why are their cognitive, affective, and self-involving elements seemingly so inseparable? What laminates a given conviction into its own wholeness, or into the wholeness of a set of convictions (for hardly anyone lives by just *one* conviction)? And what has that set to do with the life of the person, with his formed character?

These are not easy questions, and simple answers are therefore suspect. One significant clue, I believe, is this: convictions, like principles but unlike at least some images, are capable of being expressed in sentences with subject and predicate—they are expressible in propositions. Very often human language is treated by the analyst of character as a smoke screen behind which the essence of humanity lies in wordless silence. But on another view, while deceit (and self-deceit) are possible, their possibility presupposes that words can also be used to tell the truth. Man is *homo loquens*. Our convictions may be suppressed, they may be hidden even from ourselves, but it is the true business of words to reveal, and every conviction is in principle expressible. If this second view is correct,[32] certain aspects of the general structure of language may provide us with a way to understand the structure of convictions generally, and the intellectual tools with which we analyze language are or correspond to those with which we discover the shape of particular human character and particular human community.

So generally stated, this parallel between life and speech may seem unlikely or even tedious. Yet if a better analysis can enable us not only to understand what a King or a Hammarskjöld means by what he says, but also to know how what he or his religious community *says* is related to what at heart each *is*, the difficulties and risks of such inquiry are as nothing compared to its gain. As said in Chapter 1, the fact that human life is lived by convinced men is the central fact which makes what we call theology possible. Theologians are concerned with convictions not as bare propositions but as those propositions by which men live. Therefore theology in attending to convictions is in position not only to learn which convictions govern particular men and groups but also to discover which ones we must live by. (In more conventional terminology, Christian theology seeks to understand the faith by which we are justified, if justified we are.)

(5) It may have caught the attention of the reader that in the present work no special attention has been paid to *autobiography*. I have examined whatever autobiographical material was available from the lives I investigated but unlike Wilhelm Dilthey have assigned no special status to that material. The assumption has been that autobiography was simply one more useful source of knowledge about other persons. It is only fair to note that theology generally has not been so impartial, and has found in autobiography a peculiarly important source of illumination. Augustine's

[32] For this view, see my forthcoming book, with James M. Smith, probably to be titled *Religious Convictions and the Problem of Pluralism.*

Confessions was not only a penetrating theological document, but the foundation of a new genre of literature, and Kierkegaard's multi-layered self-examinations brought that type to a new level of theological importance. It is significant that confessional writing appears in the Christian movement whenever one man finds its necessary to take his stand against the dominant thought-patterns of his day: Augustine against pagan philosophy; Kierkegaard against nineteenth-century culture-Christianity.

One must distinguish here the study of one's own life (which study, if recorded, becomes autobiography), and the study of (others') autobiographies. I have not treated the former; the latter, if done with theological intent, is a special case of biography as theology. It has been pointed out recently[33] that this latter specialty offers special opportunity for the study of the very important moral phenomena of *self-deception.* How is it that we are able to deceive ourselves? The most common accounts of self-deception seem to have treated it, on the analogy of the deception of others, as a deliberate hiding of the truth from oneself.[34] But is such a description meaningful? How does one do this? Perhaps a better account, then, is one which treats self-deception as a narrowing or rather a non-enlarging of our consciousness or conscious awareness. According to this account, the self-deceived person is one who has not yet learned a skill, a certain capacity for awareness. The best analogy to this is the procedure of 'spelling out' a certain part of the contents of our consciousness. In such spelling out we often become aware of that which was previously only latent in consciousness. The virtues which the self-deceived person (such as Speer, the Nazi chief whose autobiography tells us that he "should have known" that the

[33] Stanley Hauerwas and David Burrell, "Self-Deception and Autobiography: Theological and Ethical Reflections on Speer's *Inside the Third Reich," The Journal of Religious Ethics,* Spring, 1974. Hauerwas and Burrell in turn depend especially on Herbert Fingarette, *Self-Deception* (London: Routledge & Kegan Paul, 1969).

[34] Fingarette, *Self-Deception,* chap. 1.

Hitler regime was demonic, but did not) lacks, then, are not integrity or sincerity, but courage and skill to come to terms with the reality around him. As Hauerwas and Burrell put it,

we all have encounters that we do not know how to describe. Our basic stories and images determine what we discover, but often, like Columbus, we insist on describing our engagements with an image that misleads or lies. The neurotic's problem is exactly that he cannot make anything of what he is doing and therefore he cannot make his life into anything. Columbus could not understand what he had done because he did not have the skills to get it right. Fortunately we can keep sending out our ships to explore the coast lines of our engagements in order to learn the limits of our past descriptions and begin to develop more adequate skills to say what we have done.[35]

They go on to say that the problem the autobiographer faces is like the problem each of us also meets:

Autobiography is the literary form that mirrors the moral necessity to free outselves from the hold of our illusions through truer images and stories. . . . Christians claim that the truth that provides the skill to confess the sin that we do is to be found in the history of Jesus Christ. . . . The saints formed by this story testify to its efficacy in purging the self of all deception as it forces the acceptance of the truth mirrored in the cross.[36]

The autobiographical data, and autobiographical inquiry by the theologian looking at his own life, may have a special contribution to make to the larger task of biography as theology; yet this material must not become the only datum for biographical theology. If Christian theology is to be concerned always with shared faith, with community, we must hear from others' experience as well as our own, and must examine self-told stories by external as well as internal light.

(6) Theology is truly Christian only as it bases itself

[35] "Self-Deception and Autobiography," p. 112.
[36] Ibid., pp. 112, 114.

afresh upon its own origin; nothing can replace the primacy of the primitive in this community of faith. In deciding how this primacy is to be exercised, however, we meet again the contest between a propositional theology whose focus is upon abstract concepts and a theology which focuses upon lives in the round. For propositional theology, the center may be upon the Bible (though propositional theology acknowledges that the Bible speaks much of persons) or the message of the Bible duly transformed for the modern age. For a biographical theology (though it acknowledges that the lives it attends to each incorporate convictions) the center must be the lives themselves, or more accurately must be one life, *the life of Christ*. Propositional theology may take the uncritical form of Catholic scholasticism or Protestant fundamentalism, or it may take the highly sophisticated form of some modern theologies of the Word. A telltale clue in either case is abandonment of the attempt to confront, and be confronted by, Jesus of Nazareth as the Christ.

As much as any theme touched in these closing pages, this is one which cries out for full treatment or none at all. I will come as close as I can to the latter goal, and say very little here. Theology makes a distinction, already reflected in the preceding paragraph, between the life of Christ (the one who rose and lives in his community, in his world), and the life of Jesus (the man who lived and died in first-century Palestine). The stories of the saints' lives are thus a part of the life of Christ; they are not in the same way a part of the life of Jesus. The story of Jesus is a subject for historical investigation.

Now it is a well-known fact that the history of Jesus is problematic in our era. A cartoon strip I saw several years ago has three pictures. The first, labeled "the Protestant Jesus," shows a fair-haired smiling man of gentle countenance. The second, "the Catholic Jesus," wears a crown of thorns and a halo, and weeps great tears. The third, labeled "the real Jesus," shows merely a robber chieftain with a scowling face and a club. That all of us, conservative or liberal, radical or reactionary, at least get the point of the cartoon tells us something about the widespread uncertainty concerning Jesus' historical actuality.

In fact, modern biblical scholarship is not so skeptical as the cartoon suggests, or rather its skepticism is differently directed.[37] What scholarship cannot attempt is an old-style liberal or conservative 'life' of Jesus, complete with chronology, psychological development, and perhaps dramatic unity. Nothing like T. R. Glover's *Jesus of History* or Romano Guardini's *Lord* is a possibility of historical studies. (Nor, for that matter, are Hugh Schonfeld's *Passover Plot* or Nikos Kazantzakis' *Last Temptation of Christ* possibilities.) What scholarship can do is critically to examine the sources to recover a few indisputable facts (Jesus lived, drew disciples, ate at public banquets with 'sinners,' encountered opposition, was betrayed by a follower, was executed on a cross by the Romans), and a few crucial teachings. Whatever in his reported teaching in the New Testament can be ascribed neither to contemporary Judaism nor to later Christianity should probably be assigned to Jesus: there is a considerable body of material which is thus known as authentic. Certain literary stylistic considerations guarantee still other sayings.[38] And finally, the impact of its founder upon early Christianity is evidence about the founder as well as about the movement he founded, though not, of course, uncomplicated evidence.[39]

My own judgment is that the quantity and reliability of the information thus shown to be available about Jesus is sufficient to enable biographical study of him to proceed in

[37] For what follows in this section I depend (not uncritically) upon the excellent summary of Jesus research by Hans Conzelmann, *Jesus,* trans. J. Raymond Lord (Philadelphia: Fortress Press, 1973). This little book is translated from Conzelmann's article "Jesus Christus" in *Religion in Geschichte und Gegenwart,* 3rd ed., 1956–62, with added English-language bibliography.

[38] *Ibid.,* p. 16, *passim.*

[39] *Ibid.,* chap. 12.

the spirit of the present work;[40] indeed some recent and thoroughly critical 'lives' have appeared which seem to fill that bill.[41] Cautions against such confidence issued by Protestant and especially German scholars are in verbal disagreement with my judgment; thus Hans Conzelmann warns us that

> not only are the gospels in their entirety witnesses of faith, but this is true already of the individual pieces of tradition. For that reason they have no interest in the "portrait" of Jesus. One discovers nothing about his appearance, his human character, his habits, nothing about the commonplace things in his life. Insight into this character of the tradition prevents psychological-biographical evaluation of a great part of the material.[42]

Clearly, however, the term "human character" (*menschlichen Charakter*) is being used differently by Conzelmann and me here. For he goes on in his excellent survey to show us the many things we can know about what Jesus taught and meant, what images (e.g., Kingdom of God) he employed and lived by, what he did and what he suffered. But from such knowledge as this we can form, as we have seen in preceding chapters, not, to be sure, a "portrait" of the literal sort, but a clear sense of the character of any person. We know where he stood; we may be permitted to know where we stand with respect to him. And that is what matters for Christian theology.

[40] For example, it seems to me that the amount of secure historical knowledge we have about Jesus is roughly as great as the amount I have been able to secure for the study of Clarence Jordan contained in this book; though obviously there are differences in the availability of further documentary evidence, eyewitnesses, etc., in Jordan's case, these are more than matched by the critical vigor which has been exercised upon the Jesus material.

[41] I have in mind Gunther Bornkamm, *Jesus of Nazareth*, trans. I. and F. McLuskey with J. M. Robinson (New York: Harper, 1960 [German ed., 1956]); Eduard Schweizer, *Jesus*, trans. David E. Green (Richmond: John Knox Press, 1971 [German ed., 1968]); and Herbert Braun, *Jesus, der Mann aus Nazareth und seine Zeit* (Stuttgart: Kreuz-Verlag, 1969).

[42] Conzelmann, *Jesus*, pp. 15-16.

(7) How does biographic theology take account of *community*? The preceding section makes a distinction between the life of Jesus and the life of Christ. While the centrality of Jesus of Nazareth is necessary for Christian theology, it is not sufficient. What is lacking in a theology concerned only with Jesus may be fulfilled in attention to Christ. To be sure, Jesus *is* the Christ; that is to say, there is a moment in the economy of redemption when everything God is doing and will do is invested in that one life. He goes to the cross—alone; he dies—alone—for us. There is, however, another moment in the economy of redemption. Out of death Christ arose. The shared life which is oriented to and grows from that new fact is continuous with the solitary life of Jesus (it is *Jesus* Christ who rose from the dead) ; yet it possesses a fibrous dimension of breadth which the single thread of Jesus' life does not (it is Jesus *Christ* who arose). The solitary life is now the shared life of those whom he redeems. They are in Christ; Christ is in them (Gal. 1:22; Rom. 8:10). The life of Christ cannot be told without the whole New Testament, without the whole history of the "God Movement," without the whole human story *annis domini*—in the years of the Lord. In this sense, the lives of our saints significantly participate in the life of Christ; telling their stories is a part of telling *that* story.

In Chapter 4, it was acknowledged that a theologian who attends to particular human lives, seeing these from his own point of view as he must, is especially open to the accusations of subjectivist bias in theology and biographical distortion in the stories he tells about his subjects. Now we can see how this charge must be met. Of course any theologian has his bias; this will be true whether he does biographical theology or some other kind. If, however, he thinks his way into the Christian lives he seeks to know, their participation in the redemptive life of Christ becomes a redeeming element of the investigation and in the investigator. The images he discovers need not be mere metaphors, the convictions he finds mere propositions. They cannot be. To discover them in these lives is in some measure to incorporate them into one's own.

The remedy for bias, then, is participation, and as the circle of participation widens, the center from which one began becomes ever less important. I do not mean that good theological work will increasingly lose its personal and individual flavor. Our circles of work overlap without becoming identical. Others will certainly attend to other life stories than I. It matters less that these other stories will be of persons who are, let us say, Asian, or female, or drawn from other time spans than the twentieth century (though all these changes will make some difference) than it does that each life examined will have its own gift to bring to the whole Christ. The unity thus produced by the joint work of many workmen may be Ivesian, composed of disparate elements often juxtaposed in unexpected ways, and often displaying no resolution prior to the resolution of the cosmos itself. That it will nonetheless be unity is an assertion made in faith, but faith drawing some reassurance from the work represented in these pages.

The character we investigate in a biographical study is always character-in-community. None of the persons we examine can be understood unless we understand his participation in ("participation" does not exclude controversy with and alienation from) communities of faith, and other human communities as well. Thus the convictions of our saints are convictions formed in connection with life in community; the theologian in examining such a life must have this communal dimension of his study always in mind, and the theological results of the inquiry are normally addressed to the community from which his interest first grows. So the lives which impinge on our own need not be limited to those we have time and skill to examine personally. Moreover, theology in this mode is not isolated from propositional theology. The communion of the saints includes some saints who are propositional theologians! They, too, will have their say. My insistence is exactly that we not *a priori* exclude from our attention this school or that—hearing only liberals, or only conservatives, or Protestants, or Catholics, or Christians, or Christians and Jews, or . . . If the voice is human, we can understand it at least in part. If it is interesting, let us listen. If it is not, no argument for its legitimacy will compel our attention.

If this way of combatting narrowness, subjectivity, and bias still seems constricted (for to exclude uninteresting voices may be a very large exclusion indeed) it must at least be remembered that this comports with the steady insistence of this book that theology be a self-involving task. I have written about Charles Ives so that those who read may hear his musical call to America to find her true way—to us Americans to find our way; about Clarence Jordan so that the accents of the cotton patch may call the children of God to acknowledge God's other children; about Martin King so that some who remember him, and others who do not, may understand the liberating force of his life—and be free at last; about Dag Hammarskjöld in order that we may also, though in our own words, say, "For all that has been—Thanks, to all that shall be—Yes." Theology as self-involving means that the quest for an ethics of character and a theology of character makes a demand upon the character of the theologian, and upon those who, reading, share his task. We are called thus to find our selves, our own true selves, in the meeting with God which Christian faith celebrates. And these selves are irremediably *varied* selves. In this sense, we return from the lives we have examined to our own lives; the examiners become the examined, and our claim on our 'saints' becomes their many-sided claim upon us.

Appendix

Christian Worship
and the Saints

Biographical theology by its nature raises a practical question which concerns everyone who is interested in saints ancient or modern: what is the relation of the saints to worship? The Christian church in several of its main branches sponsors saints' days on which the life and witness or the martyrdom of officially chosen saints is remembered and incorporated into worship. Roman Catholic and Orthodox churches in particular make large use of such days in their church year, but to a lesser degree others do so as well, and even those Christian fellowships which minimize the church year and disown the concept of saints' days nevertheless have special days upon which the faithful ministry of a founding pastor or the sacrificial career of a missionary is made the occasion of thanksgiving and the basis of financial appeals.

Many a Protestant is dissatisfied with so restricted a fare and might be glad to share in a wider communion of saints, perhaps including those considered in this book as well as those honored in traditional churches. He is perhaps aware that his own faith was kindled by the faith of others at first hand—a parent, teacher, or friend—and is willing to widen the circle of such exemplars or models. At the same time, he is put off by his inherited (and historically not groundless) suspicion of practices associated with sainthood. Prayers to the saints, the concept of salvific merit and its transference, the exalted role assigned to the Virgin Mary—these seem to him to rival faith in God and to challenge salvation through Christ alone. Even if he is more knowledgeable about present Catholic teaching on these matters, the Protestant may still be discouraged by another aspect of Catholic practice, for the Catholic calendar attends to so many and to such obscure figures as often to make their practical effect nugatory. Even Mary the Virgin seems a somewhat forlorn, neglected figure in today's ever-reforming Catholicism. While Roman Catholic practices in all these matters no longer provide present-day Protestants with a ready example of the way not to go, these practices do not provide a clear model for adoption, either. Indeed, Protestant ambivalence concerning the proper role of the saints is often matched by Catholic ambivalence on this subject.

What is wanted is a clearer rationale of the relation of 'the saints' to worship. No full-scale account is possible here, but by making some assumptions about worship and its purpose I may be able to show the lines I would take in developing such an account. Christian worship (I will assume) is to be directed to God alone. Clearly, then, no saint is to be the *object* of that worship. Yet attention to saints may direct, enhance, and encourage our worship of God. How is this so?

In broad outline we know the history of the notion of sainthood in Christian communities.[1] One of the earliest martyrdom narratives after the New Testament, the Martyrdom of Polycarp, tells how Polycarp, bishop of Smyrna, said to be a disciple of John the disciple of the Lord, when he was arrested and required to renounce Christ by the local authorities in Smyrna, bore faithful witness to the last and was burned to death in the stadium. The narrative goes on to tell how one Niketas warned the magistrate not to give the body of Polycarp to the Christians.

[1] See Ernst Lucius, *Die Anfänge des Heiligenkults in der Christlichen Kirche,* ed. Gustav Anrich (Tübingen, 1904; photo-offprint ed., Frankfort on the Main: Minerva GmbH, 1966); Hippolyte Delehaye, S.J. (Bollandist), *Les Origines du Culte des Martyrs,* 2nd rev. ed. (Brussels: Société des Bollandistes, 1933); Delehaye, *The Legends of Saints, an Introduction to Hagiography,* intro. R. J. Schoeck, trans. V. M. Crawford (Notre Dame, Ind.: University of Notre Dame Press, 1961); Jacques Douillet, *What Is a Saint,* trans. Donald Attwater, the Twentieth-Century Encyclopedia of Catholicism (New York: Hawthorn Books, 1958), chap. 4.

"Else," said he, "they will abandon the Crucified and begin worshiping this one." This was done at the instigation and insistence of the Jews, who also watched when we were going to take him from the fire, being ignorant that we can never forsake Christ, who suffered for the salvation of the whole world of those who are saved, the faultless for the sinners, nor can we ever worship any other. For we worship this one as Son of God, but we love the martyrs as disciples and imitators of the Lord, deservedly so, because of their unsurpassable devotion to their own King and Teacher. May it be also our lot to be their companions and fellow disciples!

And it concludes the story by saying:

The captain of the Jews, when he saw their contentiousness, set it [i.e., his body] in the midst and burned it, as was their custom. So we later took up his bones, more precious than costly stones and more valuable than gold, and laid them away in a suitable place. There the Lord will permit us, so far as possible, to gather together in joy and gladness to celebrate the day of his martyrdom as a birthday, in memory of those athletes who have gone before, and to train and make ready those who are to come hereafter.[2]

The historical accuracy of several elements in this tale (for example the introduction of Jews to charge that the Christians practice an idolatrous worship of men, not God) need not detain us save to remark that at the time of its composition (late second century) Christians, having made transcendent claims for Jesus their master, were clearly alert to accusations of sponsoring idolatrous or superstitious practices, while nevertheless they had their special saint-heroes and honored them in anniversary celebrations.

What may still seem difficult to explain is how, given the initial cautions and the primitive innocence of which this account gives evidence, the cult-practices associated with martyrs and others so inexorably grew from these beginnings to their later proportions. In fact, though, the transition to these practices was made without recorded obstacle. This occurred in connection with such funeral devotions as the Smyrnans in their narrative were proposing. The second-century Christians who lost faithful leaders and members to the persecutions did not shun their victimized brothers and sisters. Boldness was gained by adherence to the bold. And had the Lord himself not died to show them the way?

As it happened, there was solid precedent in Greco-Roman

---

[2] "Martyrdom of Polycarp," trans. Massey H. Shepherd, Jr., in *Early Christians Fathers*, ed. Cyril C. Richardson, Library of Christian Classics, I (Philadelphia: Westminster Press, 1953), pp. 155-56.

paganism for gathering at cemeteries to honor departed family members. Such commemorative rites would thus arouse no suspicion in neighbors or authorities if practiced by the Christians as well. So at the burial place of Polycarp, or of similar victims in many other places, the church would gather on the anniversary of his death, not to mourn so much as to rejoice. The service would likely be the Eucharist or Lord's Supper, already tinged with memorial motifs, and it would include special prayers to honor the local martyr. A church with several martyrs would keep a list, and these lists of names and dates, later augmented by lists of confessors, ascetics, and bishops, became the canon or list of saints regularly memorialized in the churches of ancient Christianity. This development was full-fledged by the fifth century.

One crucial step has yet to be recounted. At these celebrations, prayer might be offered not only to God for an exemplary saint's life, but to the departed saint directly. In an age when both Jews and pagans believed in a personal afterlife, and in which prayers were readily addressed to the departed, at least in pagan lands,[3] it might seem perfectly natural for Christians to do the same. Had not Jesus according to the Gospel of Luke told a story in which a rich man in hades calls out to Father Abraham in heaven and is answered by Abraham (Luke 16: 19 ff.)? With such invocation of the departed dead, the veneration of saints acquired its final element.

With the passing of centuries and the Constantinian legitimation of Christianity, the practices and their supporting rationale of doctrines developed into the well-known pattern of the veneration or cult of saints in medieval and later style. The list of martyrs, as already mentioned, became the canon of official saints. The remains of the departed were the authentic beginning of an ever-proliferating clutter of traveling relics, donated, sold, stolen, or fabricated, which acquired the status of fetishes in popular practice. Days commemorating martyrdom were extended at certain shrines and centers into a *cultus* which might last throughout the year. And 'prayer' addressed to martyrs at their tombs mushroomed into private and public devotions, the angelus and the rosary being two current examples addressed especially to the Virgin Mary. These enlargements in Christian practice, however understandable in historic perspective, surely produced their own reaction. The Protestant Reformation of the sixteenth

---

[3] But a certain cultic development did occur in Judaism. See II Maccabees 15:6-16; see also the exaltation of the nine martyr-heroes of IV Maccabees.

century focused that reaction, while the cultural situation of the present day makes meaningful veneration of saints a difficult practice for many Roman Catholics as well.

If as recipients of this long heritage we turn again to the Bible, what light is shed on the question of the place of the saints in worship? The introduction to Paul's major doctrinal writing, Romans, provides a handy way of access into biblical teaching on this theme. Three relevant themes appear there, and these recur in Paul and with variations throughout the New Testament, while they remind us of what is found in the Old as well. (1) The address (1:7) salutes all the "Romans beloved of God" as "saints" (*hagioi*). This corresponds to the regular use of the Greek Old Testament, where *hagioi* translates *kadoshim* (holy ones). This Hebrew term was used both of God's angelic host in heaven and of his covenant people on earth. Toward the end of the Old Testament period, it was used along with *hasidim* (loyal ones) to refer to the faithful nucleus of God's people. As such a remnant, of course, New Testament Christians identified themselves. So the saints, the *hagioi* (rarely singular in Scripture), are the faithful generally, in Paul's use and throughout the New Testament. An exception is the infrequent cases (e.g., Jude 14) where the *hagioi* are the angelic host. The designation "saints," like the designation "priests" (*hieroi*) is given to the whole community of the new covenant. All God's children are his saints—all, and not a special or exemplary class.[4]

(2) Romans goes on to express Paul's hope that "we may be mutually encouraged by each other's faith, both yours and mine" (1:12 RSV). This concept of interdependence and mutual aid is set against any private or individualistic concept of salvation, both here and throughout Paul's teaching. "Agree together, my friends, to follow my example. You have us for a model; watch those whose way of life conforms to it," he says in Philippians (3:17 NEB). Such attention to models—Paul as a model, those who imitate Paul as further models—leads back in the other direction to the model of models, Jesus Christ: "Be imitators of me, as I am of Christ" (I Cor. 11:1 RSV). In the sainthood we share through Christ we are to be strengthened by one another's faith. This pattern runs through the New Testament writings, and illustrations could be multiplied indefinitely: in the late-Pauline letter, I Timothy, the addressee is advised to "set the

[4] See Karl Gustaf Kuhn and Otto Proksch, *hagios*, etc., in Gerhard Kittel, ed., *Theological Dictionary of the New Testament*, trans. and ed. G. W. Bromiley (Grand Rapids: Eerdmans, Vol. I, 1964), pp. 88-115.

believers an example in speech and conduct, in love, in faith, in purity" (4:12 RSV), while in the Gospels it is Jesus himself whose deeds and words show the way of the gospel as it enters human life. In the sainthood we share through Christ, we are to be strengthened by one another's faithfulness.

(3) Third, the introduction to Romans announces a gospel which overcomes human sinfulness, notably the sinfulness of those who "exchanged the truth about God for a lie and worshiped and served the creature rather than the Creator, who is blessed forever! Amen" (1:25 RSV). Beginning as a sect of Judaism made it imperative for the Christian movement to avoid this idolatry, and the New Testament never abandons its heritage from the Old in this regard. Acts, recounting the spread of Christianity into Gentile lands, tells how when Paul and Barnabas came to Lystra and there healed a cripple,

when the crowds saw what Paul had done, they lifted up their voices, saying in Lycaonian, "The gods have come down to us in the likeness of men!" Barnabas they called Zeus, and Paul, because he was the chief speaker, they called Hermes. And the priest of Zeus, whose temple was in front of the city, brought oxen and garlands to the gates and wanted to offer sacrifice with the people. But when the apostles Barnabas and Paul heard of it, they tore their garments and rushed out among the multitude, crying, "Men, why are you doing this? We also are men, of like nature with you, and bring you good news, that you should turn from these vain things to a living God who made the heaven and the earth and the sea and all that is in them." (Acts 14:11-15 RSV.)

As in Paul's thought in Romans, the doctrine of creation is held by Acts to rule out creature-worship absolutely. It is interesting to compare, in this regard, the restrained funeral of the martyr Stephen in Acts (8:2) with the joyous acclaim which greeted Polycarp's burnt bones in the passage quoted above from the *Martyrdom*. Acts does not lack for exemplary figures: Peter, Paul, Stephen, Philip the evangelist; but with the whole biblical tradition it resists a cult of the dead.

Whether we wish to avoid, in our own thinking, a too-sterile Protestantism or a too-fecund Catholicism, the biblical principles suggested in the preceding paragraphs may form a useful guide for our own belief and practice with regard to the saints and worship.

1. The saints are *all* of God's children, the people of God collectively and therefore individually. There are better and worse saints, saints more and saints less celebrated or deserving of celebration, saints who serve better as models and pioneers for

the Christian community, and those who serve less well for whatever reasons; but the commonality of the saints is here crucial; the ground is level at the foot of the cross, and that ground is the only standing place in the kingdom of God. Holiness in its full sense is God's gift to all his sons and daughters. Non-saints there may be; that there are is the mystery of evil, but non-saints (like non-sinners, who are perhaps the same) have no role to play in the drama of repentance and redemption and sanctification.

The worship of God, therefore, must celebrate that commonality and not conceal it. The saints whose life-stories we tell are counted in our own number; they are flesh of our flesh. Here the urgent drive of the historian to tell the truth can make an irreplaceable contribution. The natural tendency of the hagiographer is to conceal the blemishes of his chosen subjects; I have often felt that temptation in the preceding pages, and others must judge whether I have too often succumbed to it. Iconography is not biography. The drive to historic biography is the drive to tell the truth. But to tell the whole truth about our saints is in the end to unite them with ourselves; if we see them as we are in our blemishes, weaknesses, temptations, we can see what is in store for us in their strengths and achievements.

The biblical writers, with their strong sense of communal solidarity in salvation, rarely (yet sometimes) used "saint" in the singular; we may do well to follow their example. It is not false to say that Paul or Francis (or Dag H. or Clarence J.) is a saint, but it is more helpful, at least in the church's teaching and worship, to say that they are among the saints, as is every child of God. So we may better say "a reading from Paul's letter," not "from St. Paul's letter"; and not "St. Francis' Day" but "Francis' Day," "Martin Luther King Day," "Charles Ives Day," and the like.

2. For alongside the commonality of saintliness there is a second principle which, if the first is accepted, can be exploited to the full in Christian worship: others' life stories can be made to serve as encouragement and guidance for our own lives in the presence of God. Worship is our address to God; that is to say, it is the address made by creatures whose lives are inescapably narrative or story-like; we are living out a tale, are on a journey from yonder to there. It was the great achievement of Puritan preaching to have perceived this aspect of worship and to have exploited it in sermons which permitted the listeners to orient themselves anew in their own life journeys. Our preaching can

do the same, but it must use elements suited to our own time. One possibility is the biographical sermon.

A special difficulty is that preaching at least in the Western world has come to seem as irrelevant as collar buttons and spinning wheels to the demands of daily life. Sermons based on lives lived under contemporary conditions are especially suited to meet this difficulty, though once an appetite for biographical preaching has been developed in a congregation, it will not be difficult to satisfy it with sermons based on the lives of earlier saints as well. If, as the present work suggests, Christian life-stories are often built around images drawn from Scripture, it will be easy to link those stories with preaching-texts which illuminate, and are illuminated by, the biographies.[5]

Consider this plan for a church not traditionally furnished with saints' days. Choose a significant life to be explored in a given period of time, say a month. Arrange learning activity which will bring that life into focus at a variety of levels: children's stories, games, posters, field trips, dramatic presentations, adult reading and discussion groups, films, visits to the church by persons familiar with the life, leadership investigation of ways to reflect in common life the life under study. (A choir might study Charles Ives's music; a preacher might draw a passing sermon illustration from his life; an insurance man might explore and explain Ives's economic convictions, a politician his populism, a woman Ives's pioneering feminism.) Then at a planned time after the month's work, let the best of this harvest of inquiry and action be re-presented in a Sunday of recollection and celebration of *this* one among the saints, with scripture, song, visual art, sermon, and prayers of thanksgiving bringing this life before the people as a sign to all of life lived in the presence of God. Then in a later month, choose another life, until the church's fellowship widens to embrace a number of familiar exemplars of faith in our time. Such a policy certainly contains the seeds of church conflict: *which* lives shall be studied, which passed by in silence? But such conflict is potentially on gospel ground, and should not be shunned. To ask about the lives we will celebrate is to ask what is the character of life worth celebrating—in the end it is to ask about the character of the Christ. To evoke such controversy is to bring the church face to face with the question: what do you think about Christ?

[5] This concept is already employed in the poetry and scripture passages assigned to saints' days in service books of the Eastern and Western traditional churches.

(Cf. Matt. 22:42.) So healthy a question should not be confined to the circles of free church faith and practice; similar teaching and worship procedures may healthily be employed in the churches of fixed calendar and liturgical tradition. They, too, have great freedom to honor among all the saints those whom they will, and the appropriate adaptations of procedure can easily be made.

What is here proposed would—let us not shrink from the term—be a veneration of saints. It would not be a veneration for the sake of the dead, but in order that "we may be mutually encouraged by each other's faith" (Romans 1:12 RSV). Exactly because such veneration or honoring is not the worship of our fellow saints, it may contribute to the worship of God, and in that sense be a part of our worship of him.

Roman Catholic theologians make here a helpful distinction between the devotion properly rendered to saints, called *dulia*, and the devotion properly given only to God, called *latria*. The former is worship only in the sense that

to venerate the saints is always to praise and glorify God, since the quality of the saint which is recognized as worthy of imitation was the gift of God's grace. The "intercession" of the saints on our behalf is not to be considered a new historical initiative independent of their historical life [as if 'St. Jude' could more effectively than we tug at the Lord's coat sleeve for us], rather it is simply the enduring validity of their life for the world before God's countenance.[6]

Rahner's distinction between the historical life and the continuing life of the *communio sanctorum* takes seriously the terminus which is human death, and therefore we must treat requests to living friends, and the invocation of the dead, in radically different ways. As will appear below, this brings the latter practice into question.

3. This concept of veneration just advanced brings clearly before us the last of the three biblical principles by which we are to be guided in this matter, the demand made by the undiminishable majesty of God, which no service to the creature is to rival: "You shall have no other god to set against me" (Exod. 20:3 NEB); "they exchanged the truth about God for a lie and worshiped and served the creature rather than the Creator" (Rom. 1:25 RSV). I should want to say, in agreement with Karl Rahner in the work just quoted, that while the Christian "easily feels misgivings about the veneration of saints because it is di-

[6] Karl Rahner and Herbert Vorgrimler, "Veneration of Saints," in *Theological Dictionary*, p. 480.

rected to a reality that is not the Absolute," he must further reflect

that the religious act, if it is really perfect [or, as I should put it, to the extent that it is an act of *faith*], can also discover creatures *in* God, since the validity of ·creatures does not diminish but grows as one draws near to God. Popular piety, it is true, often regards God as no more than one reality among others and in many cases does not accept the saints as concrete models (always a kind of judgment on those who revere them) but yields to unbridled sentimentality and is impressed by religious trash; but such phenomena in Catholicism should not be thought any objection to a sensible veneration of the saints.[7]

That, I think, is well said, and reminds us of the principle, as crucial to the Baptist as to the Catholic version of Christian theology, that the abuse of a practice does not invalidate its use. But we have still to ask whether *prayer* to departed saints as this is taught or practiced in some branches of the Christian family contravenes our basic principle of worship. I hold that it can.

First, let us note that as pure phenomenon, addressing words to the departed is a common human experience, not confined along religious lines. It is quite natural for us to exclaim in words addressed to our absent but living friends concerning anything involving strong feeling: "Oh, Jonathan, why did you leave the workshop so crammed full of junk!" "Susan, you should be here to see these beautiful tomatoes you set out!" In doing this we need not assume that Jonathan or Susan hear or will respond; we are simply expressing our feelings. Indeed, we might not express them so freely if our friend could hear us.

The same phenomenon occurs when we address our feelings to those we know are now dead, and once again such cries arise quite naturally, and without regard to religious or metaphysical belief: "Mama, why did you put up with so much nonsense from me!" is a natural utterance of a grief-stricken son; again, whether Mama 'hears' is hardly to the point. Finally, if departed persons not known to us during their lifetimes have come to occupy a large role in our imaginal processes, have become our heroes or models, a similar phenomenon may occur: "What would you (or, do you) think of this, Albert Einstein?" I at least have noted such behavior in myself. Again, the disclaimers apply: the phenomenon in itself presupposes no doctrine of an afterlife or of thought transference; taken in itself it can be fully

[7] *Ibid.*

described as an inner dialogue. If, however, my church had taught me such doctrines, and if the luminary were a 'saint' in my church's canon, I might find the experience classifiable as prayer to a saint. Our present question is whether such naturally occurring 'prayer' is to be held up as a practice of Christian devotion.

In spite of the common qualities of experience just delineated, it seems quite difficult to answer the question because of the great differences in ethos which distinguish separate Christian traditions. How can the same practical advice avail the pious monk on Mt. Athos and the perhaps equally pious Presbyterian church member in the hill country of eastern Oklahoma? With some diffidence, then, I offer my own judgment in the matter. Nothing must rival prayer to God, or lead us astray concerning its nature. If 'prayers' to saints take away time or importance from prayer in the proper sense of the term, prayer to God, then the former had best be laid aside. If on the other hand they encourage and enhance true prayer, they are all to the good.

To make that judgment clear, I will now offer three suggestions for the devotional practice of Christians in those churches which do have a tradition of canonical or listed saints, just as earlier I have offered a program to a church without such a tradition. Only now, since I am speaking outside my own immediate circle, my suggestions will be of necessity more tentative. First, then, I could wish that address to saints was never called "prayer," but always by some other name. If we distinguish the term for devotion to God as alone properly "worship," while saints are rendered mere veneration or honor, could we not similarly reserve the term "prayer" for address to God, for our *ascensus intellectus in Deum,* as Thomas Aquinas puts it? Then we could call the other practice by whatever name best describes it—*cri de coeur,* ejaculation, invocation, or whatever is better than these. This is merely a terminological request, merely a matter of words. Yet the words we choose go far to make our practices what they are, and anyone who has practiced both prayer and these other cries of the heart knows that they are profoundly different, whatever similarities may also exist. Prayer and *God* belong together in Christian faith.

I could further wish that such cries or addresses were altogether omitted from the liturgy of the Church of Rome and her sister Catholic churches. Such an omission would involve revision in ritual (for example, in the *Confiteor* changing "I confess to almighty God, *to* the Blessed Virgin Mary, . . ." to read instead "I confess to almighty God, *in the presence of* the

Blessed Virgin Mary, . . ." but this revision would surely be a contribution to Christian unity in prayer.

Finally, I could wish that the churches when they teach might neither encourage *private* devotions addressed to saints (as some Catholics do encourage it), nor disdain these (as some Evangelicals do), but rather maintain with Scripture a (difficult, but) truly evangelical silence, leaving it to each Christian consciousness to learn whether such devotions pass the test proposed here—that is, whether they encourage or rival true devotion to and worship of the Creator, who is blessed forever. Amen.

To the preceding, someone may understandably object that I have neglected to apply the procedure which this book as a whole sponsors: the application to doctrine of the insight found in continuing biographical study. Should I not have looked to the lives of saints in examining the question of the veneration of saints? I would agree with such a complaint, and would hope that whoever is moved to such further inquiry would carry it out, with whatever consequent correction and enrichment of our common doctrine of worship that study may provide. I would be committed to revise my thinking in the light of such work. Meanwhile, I had not wanted to conceal my present view of the matter here.

Index

Index of Scripture References

Genesis
1-3 91
Deuteronomy
6:5 186
Isaiah
58:8 104
60:1 104
62:4 161
Jeremiah
6:14 107
8:11 107
II Maccabees
15:6-16 207
IV Maccabees 207
Matthew
5:39 69
13:43 104
19:23-25 126
22:37 186
22:42 212
25:31-46 .... 19, 22
Mark
8:34 175
Luke
16:19 207
19:11 126
John
3:8-9 137
Acts
2:42 129
2:44 .... 118, 125
8:2 209
14:11-15 209

Romans
1 .... 33, 208
3:17 208
8:10 201
12:1-2 33
15:26 129
I Corinthians
10:14-22 129
11:1 208
II Corinthians
8:4 .... 129, 131
9:13 129
Galatians
1:22 201
5:19-24 33
Ephesians
3:6 119
4:15 131
5:3-5 33
6:14-20 33
Philippians
2:5 33
4:8 33
Colossians
3:5-15 33
I Timothy
3:2-13 33
4:12 209
Hebrews
11:1 138
James
3:13-18 33

I Peter
  3:8 33
Jude
  14 208

Revelation
  22:9 91

Index of Names and Topics

Abernathy, Ralph, 74, 75
Acts of martyrs, 189
Adam (everyman), 91
Adam, Karl, 185
Altizer, Thomas, 138
America, 86, 97, 164, 165, 166;
  God of, 169
Anabaptists, 132-34
Anselm of Cancerbury, 178
Antinomians, 18
Aquinas, Thomas, 19, 26, 184,
  214
Aristotle, 19, 22
Arnold, Eberhard, 132
Atkinson, Brooks, 153
Atonement, 99, 172, 176-77, 178;
  elements of, 99; Bushnell on,
  100; Hammarskjöld on, 101-4;
  King on, 101, 104-7; valida-
  tion of the doctrine, 102;
  changes in the doctrine of,
  171; viability of the doctrine,
  171; as koinonia, 172-73; as
  quest for unity, 173; and Ives,
  174-76; and Jordan, 174-76;
  and suffering, 175; objective/
  subjective distinction, 177
Auden, W. H., 42, 52, 59
Augustine of Hippo, 33, 88, 179,
  185, 189, 195-96
Aulén, Gustaf, 42, 49, 52
Autobiography, 180, 181, 195-97

Baptist(s), 67, 70, 74, 85, 90,
  91, 114, 117, 120, 129, 136,
  138, 172
Barth, Karl, 13, 17, 90, 178,
  179-80, 181, 185
Bellaman, Henry, 146, 148, 165
Bennett, John C., 17, 24, 25
Bennett, Lerone, 67, 71
Bentham, Jeremy, 14

Berger, Peter, 48
Beskow, Bo, 42
"Beulah Land," 160, 161, 162,
  163, 165, 169, 174, 193
Bible, 91, 94, 198. See also
  Scripture, Old Testament,
  New Testament
Biography, 102, 181, 189-90. See
  also Theology, biography as
Black, Max, 97
Black(s), 24, 65, 68, 69, 71-72,
  73, 74-75, 80, 81-82, 85, 115,
  117, 119, 134, 165, 172
Blackness, 73, 78
Boatwright, Howard, 142, 150,
  155, 174
Boehme, Jacob, 91
Bollandists, 184, 205
Bonhoeffer, Dietrich, 17, 59, 187
Bornkamm, Gunther, 200
Braun, Herbert, 200
Brightman, Edgar S., 67
Bruderhof. See Society of
  Brothers
Brunner, Emil, 17
Buber, Martin, 57
Buddhism, 50
Bultmann, Rudolf, 169, 179
Bunche, Ralph, 65
Bunyan, John, 50
Burrell, David, 196-97
Bushnell, Horace, 92, 100, 156,
  177-78

Caesarea Philippi, 62, 102
Calendar, liturgical, 205
Calvin, John, 76, 90
Calvinists, 177
Camp meeting, New England,
  144, 158, 163, 173
Catherine of Genoa, 184

Catholicism, 209. *See also* Theology, Roman Catholic
Cavell, Stanley, 97
Character, 14, 29, 77, 193, 200; theology of, 14; elements in, 21; ethic of, 22, 33-35; having character, 30; traits, 34; and community, 202
Characterless person, 30
Children, moral education of, 22
Christ, 33, 94, 169, 201, 202 (*see also* Jesus); character of, 33, 38, 211; the servant, 172; life of, 198-201
Christian experience, 85, 180
Christianity, 50, 175; social, 74; secular, 188; Constantinian legitimation of, 204
Christomonism, 169
Church, 126-29, 135, 169, 174, 183, 204. *See also* Community, Koinonia
Civil disobedience, 76
Community, 20, 91, 134; convictional, 32, 34-35; linguistic, 32; national, 32; religious, 32; intentional, 118; Christian, 130; spiritual, 137; faith lived in, 138, 197; vision of the, 162; models of, 175; Catholic, 184; and saints, 193; and character, 202; and salvation, 208
Cone, James, 82
Congar, Yves, 13
Conscientiousness, 21
Context, ethical, 18
Convictions, 32-37, 193-94, 202
Conzelmann, Hans, 199-200
Cordier, Andrew, 42
Cotton Patch Version, 112, 119, 122-24
Cowell, Henry and Sidney, 142, 146, 155, 156
Cox, Harvey, 18
Criteria for biographees, 39
Crites, Stephen, 189

Cross, the, 60-63, 90, 172, 175 177, 201; ethic of, 63
Cunningham, Robert, 8, 18

Daley, Richard, 70
Dante Alighieri, 185
Davidson, Aubrey, 164
Death, 66, 104-6, 107; role in religion, 104; and theology, 107
Decisionism, 14, 17-18. *See also* Ethic
Delany, Martin, 72
Delehaye, Hippolyte, 205
"Demonstration plot," 172
Demythologization, 169
Destiny, 61, 62
DeWolf, L. Harold, 67
Dilthey, Wilhelm, 181, 195
Dostoevski, Fëdor, 185
Doty, William, 33
Douglass, Frederick, 72
Douillet, Jacques, 205
DuBois, W. E. B., 72, 80
Dulia vs. latria, 212
Dunne, John S., 48, 189

Ebeling, Gerhard, 93
Eckhart, Meister, 55, 57
Ecstasy, 105
Ecstatic Protestant, 90
Education, moral, 32
Edwards, Herbert, 24-25
Edwards, Jonathan, 31, 90, 91
Elder, J. Lyn, 114
Ellsberg, Daniel, 28
Emerson, Ralph Waldo, 143, 150, 151, 153-54, 167, 173, 174
England, Martin, 118
England, Maybel, 118, 130
Erikson, Erik, 74
Ethic, 13-38, 83, 138, 193; love, 24, 108
Eucharist. *See* Lord's Supper
Evangelism, 32
Experience of God vs. with God, 190
Experience, religious. *See* Religious experience.

Facts, 7, 110, 177

Faith, 53, 66, 93, 95-99, 138, 141, 167, 195, 197, 202, 213
Faithfulness, 127
Fall, Albert B., 154
Farrer, Austin, 94-96, 192
FBI, 66, 72
Feuerbach, Ludwig, 89, 91
Fingarette, Herbert, 196
Fletcher, Joseph, 17, 18, 19, 23, 27
Fontaine, André, 122
Foote, Wilder, 42, 44
Francis of Assisi, 190, 192, 210
Freud, Sigmund, 88, 89, 92
Friedman, Maurice, 57, 189
Frontiers, 51, 63
Fuchs, Joseph, 17
Fuller, Millard, 124
Fund for Humanity, 135
Fundamentalism, 169, 198
Furnish, Victor, 33

Gandhi, Mohandas K., 79, 96
Garvey, Marcus, 72
Glock, Charles, 18
Glover, T. R., 199
God, 26-27, 48, 49, 54-60, 75, 85, 86, 91-92, 97, 99, 100, 101, 104, 107-10, 130-31, 135-39, 145, 154, 159, 161-62, 167-69, 172, 174, 190, 203, 205, 207-10, 212-14
"God Movement," 120, 174; and persecution, 175
Gospels, 50, 60, 61, 103, 189, 211
Gregg, Richard Bartlett, 70
Guardini, Romano, 185-88, 191, 199
Gustafson, James, 17, 29

Hägerström, Axel, 54
Hagiography, 176, 183, 210
Hammarskjöld, Dag, 7, 38, 39-64, 91, 105, 157, 171-72, 176, 188, 190, 195, 203, 210; biographical sketch 40-44; "Old Creeds in a New World," 44, 54, 55, 60; early despair, 45-49; 'conversion' of, 49-53; and

Hammarskjöld, Dag (continued) God, 54-59; and faith and action, 55-64; vision of God, 58, 109; images of, 89-93; and atonement, 101; and "Room of Quiet," 103, 168. See also Markings
Hampshire, Stuart, 15-16
Harding, Vincent, 83
Häring, Bernard, 17
Hauerwas, Stanley, 8, 29, 31, 196-97
Hawthorne, Nathaniel, 150
Hearst, William R., Sr., 154
Heidegger, Martin, 179
Hölderlin, J. C. F., 185
Howard, Walden, 113
Hume, David, 89
Hutterites, 132-33
Hymns, 159-60, 166, 169

Idolatry, 209, 212
Ignatius of Loyola, 184
Images, 85, 89, 93-96, 95, 110, 141, 156-57, 192-93, 200; Hammarskjöld's, 57-59, 89, 93, 102-4, 168; national, 77; King's, 84-85, 89, 93; religious, 93-96; application of, 95; archetypal, 96; mystical, 96; and God, 108-10; dominant, 109; life lived under, 109; Jordan's, 126-29, 135-37; 'translation' of, 141; Ives's, 153-57, 193; musical, 157, 193
Indochina, 27-28. See also Vietnam
Insko, C. Arthur, 114
Invocation of saints, 205, 207, 212-14
Israel, 94. See also Jews
Ives and Myrick, 149, 156
Ives, Charles, 8, 38, 140-69, 171, 172, 173, 174, 175, 176, 179, 203, 210-11; as musical theologian, 140-41, 145, 168-69; Fourth Symphony, 140, 157, 163, 174; biographical sketch, 141-52; and New England

Ives, Charles (*continued*)
camp meeting, 144, 158, 163; failure and success, 146, 151; *114 Songs*, 150, 174; income redistribution, 149, 154-56; and Transcendentalism, 149, 153-54, 164; insurance concepts, 148-49, 150; political essays, 150, 154, 164; on church, 152; religion or central vision of, 152-68; musical images, 157; and 'translation' of music, 157, 159; manner vs. substance, 158, 160, 174; Second Symphony, 162; Third Violin and Piano Sonata, 163; and unity, 173, 202; "Charles Ives's Day," 210-11
Ives, George, 142, 143, 160, 173
Ives, Harmony Twichell, 149
Ives, Mary Parmelee, 142

James, William, 49-50, 53, 109, 182-83
Jesus, 19, 49, 50, 60, 63, 81, 94, 100, 103, 116, 126, 127, 135, 137, 172, 174, 177, 192, 197, 207; 'biography' of, 33, 107, 185, 199, 201; character of, 33, 200; as adamant young man, 50, 60, 172; life of, 198-201. *See also* Christ
"Jesus" as mantric charm, 172
Jews, 91, 96, 206, 207. *See also* Israel
Johnson, Marion, 133
Jonsen, Albert, 29
Jordan, Clarence, 8, 38, 112-39, 157, 171, 172, 174, 175, 176, 192, 200, 203, 210; biographical sketch, 113-25; Lord's Storehouse Plan, 117; *Cotton Patch Version*, 119, 122-24; and Fund for Humanity, 125; *Koinonia Partners*, 125; on "usership" vs. ownership, 125; central vision or image of, 126-38; images: God movement, 126; discipleship, 127-

Jordan, Clarence (*continued*)
28; *koinonia*, 128-38; God of, 131; changing theology of, 138; as 'Incarnationist,' 138. See also *Koinonia*
Jordan, Florence Kroeger, 8, 114, 117, 125
Jordan, Robert, 127-28
Jung, Carl, 193

Kazantzakis, Nikos, 199
Kelen, Emery, 42
Kierkegaard, Sören, 91, 179, 185, 196
King, Alberta Williams, 67
King, Coretta S., 66, 67, 77, 80
King, Martin Luther, Jr., 7, 38, 65-86, 89, 91, 157, 171, 172, 176, 195, 203, 210; biographical sketch, 67-68; interpreted as 'failure,' 68, 70-71; as a 'race leader,' 71-73; rumors about, 72-73; three episodes in the life of: Montgomery bus struggle, Birmingham campaign, and March on Washington, 74-77; "Letter from Birmingham Jail," 75-76; at end of his days, 77; images of, 77, 84-86, 90, 93, 106, 172; "I've Been to the Mountaintop," 77, 84-85, 106; as Moses, 77, 84-85, 172; religion as the key to, 78-80; and Black Southern religion 80-85; bibical interpretation of, 83; use of images, 84-85; and atonement, 101, 104, 106-7; on his own death, 105; vision of God of, 109
King, Martin Luther, Sr., 67
Kingdom of God, 94, 201
Kirkpatrick, John, 142, 144, 146, 152, 155, 156, 157, 165
Koinonia, 128-31, 133, 135, 173, 175. *See also* Jordan, Clarence
Koinonia Farm, 112, 118-22, 132-34, 172

Koinonia Partners, 124-25, 136-37
Kuhn, Karl Gustaf, 208

Lash, Joseph P., 42
Last Supper, 50, 94
Latria vs. dulia, 212
Lee, Dallas, 113, 114, 117, 118, 126
Legalism, 18, 28
Lehmann, Paul, 17
Lemmon, John, 22, 31
Lewis, David L., 67, 69, 70, 72, 73, 106, 117
Liberation, 84
Lie, Trygve, 43, 63
Lincoln, C. Eric, 72
Liturgy, 215
Lord's Supper, 94, 98-99, 207
Lucius, Ernst, 205
Luther, Martin, 48, 179

McClendon, J. W., Jr., 70, 87-90, 110, 195
McEntyre, Diane and John, 8, 114
Markings, (Hammarskjöld) *, (5) 51, (11) 60, (14) 47, (24) 46, (30) 105, (34) 47, (35) 103, (36) 63, (48) 47, (51) 47, (53) 102, (56) 109, (57) 55, (58) 53, (61) 52, (63) 60, (68) 50, (69) 50, 60, (73) 46, (76) 51, (81) 52, (85) 46, (86) 52, (89) 52, 53, 64, (90) 53, (91) 61, (92) 61, (101) 53, (106) 54, (110) 55, 57, 59, (115) 103, (118) 55, (121) 107, (122) 59, (123) 58, (126) 62, (151) 62, (154) 62, (159) 104, (190) 61, (205) 51, 103, (214-15) 56; discovery of, 41-42
Marshall, Denis, 160
Martyrs, 206
Marxian perfectionism, 23

*The number in parentheses is the page number in *Markings*.

Mary, Virgin, 135-36, 184, 205, 207, 214
Mass meeting, 74, 173
Maxwell, Kenneth, 42
Mays, Benjamin, 81, 82-83, 85
Metaphor(s), 84, 96, 97-98, 110, 141, 193. *See also* Images
Methodists, 74
Militarism, 172
Mill, John Stuart, 14
Miller, Richard I., 42
Miller, William R., 71
Models. *See* Saints
Moore, LeRoy, 8, 81, 82
Moral philosophy. *See* Ethic
Moral praise or blame, 30
Moses, 172
Motives, 30
Muslims, 91
Myrick, Julian, 149
Mysticism, 49, 55, 57, 82, 96, 172

Negro religion, 81-82. *See also* Religion, Black
Neo-orthodoxy, 93, 179
Newman, Francis, 49
Newman, John Henry, 184
"New morality," 14
New Testament, 33, 84-85, 172, 186, 199, 201
Niebuhr, H. Richard, 17, 29
Niebuhr, Reinhold, 14, 17, 23-28, 79
Nonviolence, 69-71, 79
Novak, Michael, 8, 110
Numinous, the, 191

Obedience, 127, 187
Old Testament, 84-85
Once-born. *See* James, William
Otto, Rudolf, 191

Parker, Horatio, 147
Pascal, Blaise, 48, 185
Pelagius, Pelagianism, 33, 180
Pincoffs, Edmund, 17, 20-22
Piper, Otto, 17
Plato, 185
Pluralism, 92, 104, 173

Plurality and unity, 173
Polycarp of Smyrna, 205-6, 209
Poor People's Campaign, 70
Prayer, 56-58, 75, 214. *See also* Saints, invocation of
Preaching, biographical, 211
Proksch, Otto, 208
Propositions, 37, 194-95, 201. *See also* Theology, propositional
Protestantism, 90, 204-5, 209
Puritans, 90, 210

Racism, 25, 70, 117, 165, 172
Rahner, Karl, 13, 184, 191, 212
Raines John C., 26-27
Ramsey, I. T., 22, 97
Ramsey, Paul, 17
Rauschenbusch, Walter, 79
Realism, Christian, 14, 23, 26-27
Reconciliation, 171-72, 174-76. *See also* Atonement
Reddick, Lawrence, 67
'Rednecks,' 79
Reformation, 207
Relics, 207
Religion, 14, 92-93, 169; as feeling, knowing, doing, 53; Black, 66, 74-75, 78, 80, 82-84; compensatory, 81, 85; American, 168-69
Religious experience, 82, 85, 90, 109, 139, 179, 180-82
Religious language, 54
Resurrection, 136-37
Richardson, Herbert W., 78
Rites, commemorative, 207
Romanticism, 181

Sacred canopy, 48
Sacrifice, 63, 102, 104
Saints, 37-38, 109, 112, 182, 185-86, 191-93, 202-3, 207-10; lives of the, 183-86, 198, 201; creative role of, 191, 'usefulness' of, 191, 210; Guardini's criteria, 186; as models, 186, 208, 213; canon of, 190,

Saints *(continued)*
207; compelling quality of, 190-92; criteria for, 190-92; communion of, 202, 212; author's view of, 204-15; evolution of the veneration of, 205-8, 212; invocation of, 205, 207, 213; prayers to, 205, 207-13; veneration of, 205, 208, 212; and worship, 205, 212-13; as God's children, 209; devotion to, 215
Saints' days, 204, 210; nontraditional, 211
Salvation, 205, 208
Sartre, Jean-Paul, 18
Schleiermacher, Friedrich, 90, 92, 178, 180-81, 190
Scholasticism, 198
Schönberg, Arnold, 151
Schonfeld, Hugh, 199
Schoof, Mark, 181
Schweitzer, Albert, 50, 60, 172
Schweizer, Eduard, 200
Scripture, language of, 57; and tradition, 193
Secularity, 109
Self, 29, 110
Self-deception, 23, 196
Service, ideal of, 59
Sheats, Ladon, 114
Shrines, 207
Silence, evangelical, 215
Similes, 98
Sin, 197, 209
Situations, ethical, 18, 21, 23
Sjöberg, Leif, 42
Smith, H. Shelton, 100, 177
Smith, James, 8, 31, 110, 195
Smylie, James H., 69, 83
Social gospel, 23, 74
Society of Brothers (Bruderhof), 132-34
Socrates, 185
Söderberg, Sten, 42
Söderblom, Nathan, 43
Son of man, 94
Songbooks, American, 157
South, 74, 172

Southern Baptist Theological
 Seminary, 114, 116, 129
Speer, Albert, 196
Spinoza, Benedict de, 19
Stark, Rodney, 18
Stevenson, W. Taylor, 189
Stolpe, Sven, 42
Story, 86; as illustration, 19-20;
 and theology, 188-89 (see also
 Theology, as story); sacred,
 189
Subjectivity, 203
Sundén, Hjalmar, 43
Swedish Lutheran, 91, 108
Sweney, John R., 160
Symbols, 193

Temptation, 23
Theodicy, 25-26
Theologian, 39, 140-41, 203
Theological interpretation, 13
Theology, 87, 107-9, 166, 168,
 170-71, 195; narrative, 7, 189;
 as story, 7 (see also Theology,
 biography as); and truth, 7,
 107; present-day, 13-14, 179;
 Christian, 34-38; definition of,
 35; ethical, 36; propositional,
 37, 178-79, 188, 198, 202; biography as, 38, 39-40, 87-111,
 171, 196-98; of character, 38;
 audience for, 40; and community, 91, 201-3; experien-
 tially based, 92, 179; and
 death, 107; biases of, 111,
 201-3; biblical, 139; of life,
 170-203; Roman Catholic, 171,
 204-5, 212, 213, 214, 215; Protestant, 171; center of, 176;
 one-sided, 192; biographic vs.
 propositional, 198; as self-
 involving, 203; Baptist, 213
Theresa of Lisieux, Saint, 183
Thielicke, Helmut, 17
Thomism, transcendental, 184
Thomson, Virgil, 147-48
Thoreau, Henry, 143, 147, 150,
 153, 155, 173, 174

Tilley Terrence, 8, 192
Tillich, Paul, 13, 40, 185, 193
Tolstoy, Leo, 50
Town meeting, New England,
 173
Transcendentalism, 149, 153,
 156, 173
Troeltsch, Ernst, 33
Truth, 7, 110
Twain, Mark, 142, 151
'Twice-born.' See James, Willi-
 am
Turner, Nat, 72, 81
Twichell, Joseph, 153, 166
Tyler, George G., 155-56

Uncarved block, 104, 168
Unitarians, 177
Unity of mankind, 80, 103, 175,
 202
Urquhart, Brian, 42, 46
Utilitarianism, 14-16

Van Dusen, Henry P., 42, 57
Vatican II, 183
Vesey, Denmark, 72
Vietnamese War, 27-28, 68, 70,
 78
Vision, 37, 84, 90, 110, 152,
 162. See also biographical
 entries, e.g., Ives, Charles
von Hügel, Friedrich, 184

Walton, Hanes, 70
Washington, Booker T., 72
Watergate scandals, 27-28
Way, the, 102
Ways of life, justification of,
 110
Williams, John A., 70, 72
Wisdom, John, 97-98
Witness, 176, 178
Wittkamper, Margaret, 114
Wittkamper, Will, 114
Whites, 25, 73, 77, 115, 117,
 119, 134, 165, 172
Worship, Christian, 210-15

Zook, Ann and Al, 114